August 7, 2004

The Greek Cities
of Magna Graecia and Sicily

Luca Cerchiai
Lorena Jannelli
Fausto Longo

THE J. PAUL GETTY MUSEUM
LOS ANGELES

First published in the United States of America in 2004 by
Getty Publications
1200 Getty Center Drive, Suite 500
Los Angeles, California 90049-1682
www.getty.edu

Christopher Hudson, *Publisher*
Mark Greenberg, *Editor in Chief*
Mollie Holtman, *Editor*
Kathleen A. Sullivan, *Copy Editor*
Pamela Heath, *Production Coordinator*
English translation provided by
Translate-A-Book, Oxford, England
Hespenheide Design, *Composition and Designer*

Library of Congress Cataloging-in-Publication Data

Cerchiai, Luca.
  [Cittá della Magna Grecia e della Sicilia. English]
  The Greek cities of Magna Graecia and Sicily / Luca Cerchiai,
Lorena Jannelli, Fausto Longo.
     p. cm.
  Includes bibliographical references.
   ISBN 0-89236-751-2
  1. Magna Graecia (Italy)—Civilization. 2. Sicily
(Italy)—Civilization—To 800. 3. Greeks—Italy, Southern—
History. 4. Greeks—Italy—Sicily—History. 5. Cities and towns,
Ancient—Italy, Southern. 6. Cities and towns, Ancient—Italy—
Sicily. I. Jannelli, Lorena, 1967– II. Longo, Fausto. III. Title.
   DG55.M3C4713 2004
   937'.701—DC22

                                            2003023715

Printed and bound by Editoriale Bortolazzi Stei s.r.l.,
San Giovanni Lupatoto (Verona), Italy

Photograph Credits

Foto Melo Minella, Palermo: 6, 22, 23, 26–27, 30–31, 163, 173, 195, 214, 215, bottom of 260–261, 270–271, 274–275, 276–277.

Foto Scala Group, Florence: 16–17, 24, 42–43, 71, 74, top of 75, 76–77, 81, 94, 95, 96, 97, 98, 99, 101, 110, 111, 145, 154, 155, 177, 181, 198, 199, 203, 225, 251.

Ministero per i Beni e le Attività Culturale, Soprintendenza Archeologica della Basilicata – Potenza (Ministry for Archaeological Artefacts and Cultural Activities, Archaeological Department of the Basilicate – Potenza): 123, 125, 126, 127, 129, 133, 141, 143.

Ministero per i Beni e le Attività Culturale, Soprintendenza Archeologica delle Province di Napoli e Caserta (Ministry for Archaeological Artefacts and Cultural Activities, Archaeological Department of the Province of Naples and Caserta): 38, 42–43, 44–45, 47, 54, 56, 57, 117.

Museo Archeologico di Gela (Gela Archaeological Museum), Gela: 225.

On the jacket: Temple of Ceres at Paestum.

On back of jacket: Limestone statue of a goddess suckling a pair of infants (*kourotrophos*), around 550 B.C., from the northern necropolis at Megara Hyblaia (The "Paolo Orsi" Regional Archaeological Museum, Syracuse).

Half-title page: One of the Riace Bronzes, 460–450 B.C., from Cape Riace (National Museum, Reggio Calabria).

Contents

Introduction

A survey of the cities of Magna Graecia and Sicily that encompasses the history and monuments of the most important centers could not begin without a general outline introducing the reader to the phenomenon of Greek colonization in Italy. This introduction aims to give an overview of the principal historical events in this area of the Mediterranean from very ancient times until the emergence of the Romans, whose powerful eruption onto the South Italian scene, beginning in the fourth century B.C., ended the independence of the Greek cities within a span of only a few decades.

Definition and Geographical Boundaries of the Expression "Magna Graecia"

Scholars have not yet agreed on the origin of the term "Magna Graecia" (*Megale Hellas* in Greek), nor are we certain of the era in which first came to be used. Its first mention seems to be by Polybios, a Greek politician and historian who lived in the second century B.C.; he ascribed the term to Pythagoras (of the sixth century B.C.) and his great philosophical school. Strabo of Amaseia, a geographer of the Augustan era (first century B.C. to first century A.D.) associated the term with the size of the territory conquered by the new arrivals from Greece. Modern scholars have their own explanations; some feel the term refers to the Greek influence in Italy, which goes back at least as early as the sixth century B.C., while others think it was the Romans who coined the phrase, comparing

this region, in a strictly geographic sense, with the Greek mainland, which in their view was restricted and mountainous.

The debate, which is more complicated than can be discussed here, has yet to reach a resolution. We are, however, reasonably certain about the boundaries of this territory—which in Roman times meant all that part of Southern Italy, except for Sicily, taken over by Greek colonization, including what was then Campania and is now the northern part of modern Campania, which includes the Greek cities of Cumae, Naples, and Dikaiarcheia (Pozzuoli). To most ancient writers, however, "Magna Graecia" meant just the Ionic coastal strip of Italy occupied by the Achaian colonies, and so one could also assume that the expression was an Achaian coinage of sometime between the sixth and fifth centuries B.C. that referred to the hegemony and influence exercised, first by Sybaris and then Kroton, over the native Oinotrian people of the area where the colonial movement began.

The term therefore seems initially to have referred only to the part of the territory occupied by the Achaian colonies; its application to a wider area, which eventually embraced the whole of Southern Italy except Sicily, came later.

The Native Population of Southern Italy

It was with the arrival of the Greeks that the native population of Southern Italy was for the first time mentioned in recorded history—albeit from a

Opposite page: statue of a young man in a tunic, known as the "Ephebe of Mozia," second quarter of the fifth century B.C., from Mozia (Whitaker Museum, Mozia-Trapani).

The Greek colonies in the
Mediterranean between
the eighth and the sixth
century B.C.

biased viewpoint, since this history was recorded by the Greeks and was, inevitably, tainted by their ideology and politics.

The available archaeological and literary evidence seems to confirm that various ethnic groups and different Italian cultures lived in the area during the period between the end of the Bronze Age (at the end of the second millennium) and the Iron Age (ninth to the eighth centuries B.C.). During this time, the native peoples were heavily influenced by a more or less active association with peoples of both the Aegeo-Balkan region and the Levantine area. These contacts were made not only in Southern Italy but also in the middle Tyrrhenian coastal strip of Etruria and Lazio, which was occupied by people of proto-Etruscan culture now known as Villanovans, who cremated their dead and placed the ashes in urns; groups of crematoria existed in Campania, Capua, and Pontecagnano, and—at least until the end of the eighth century B.C.—also in Valle di Diano, south of the Sele River.

At the time the colonies were founded, the map of the areas occupied by native peoples, insofar as we can reconstruct it from the sources, was as follows: the Opici occupied Campania; the Oinotrians, Metapontion and the Tyrrhenian shores, and later the sites of Poseidonia and Velia; the Chones, Siris and Kroton; the Sicels were settled in Lokroi and also—together with the Morgantines—eastern Sicily; and the Elymians, northwest Sicily; the Sicels were also found in central and southwest Sicily. Present-day Puglia (formerly *Apulia*), however, was occupied by people of Illyrian origin, collectively known as Iapygians; more specifically, the Dauni lived in the north of the region, the Peucetii the central part, and the Messapians the most southern part, which corresponds to present-day Salento. To the Greeks, this area was always simply "Iapygia."

The "Precolonization" Period

The Greeks who came to the western Mediterranean (Italy, Sicily, Libya, France, Spain, Corsica) in search of ideal sites on which to set up new communities were from mainland Greece, from the Aegean islands, and from the coast of Asia Minor (present-day Turkey).

Greek colonial expansion in the
Mediterranean between the
eighth and the sixth centuries B.C.

● Greek Colonies
◐ Phoenician Colonies
◆ Commercial Centers

0   100   200   300

km

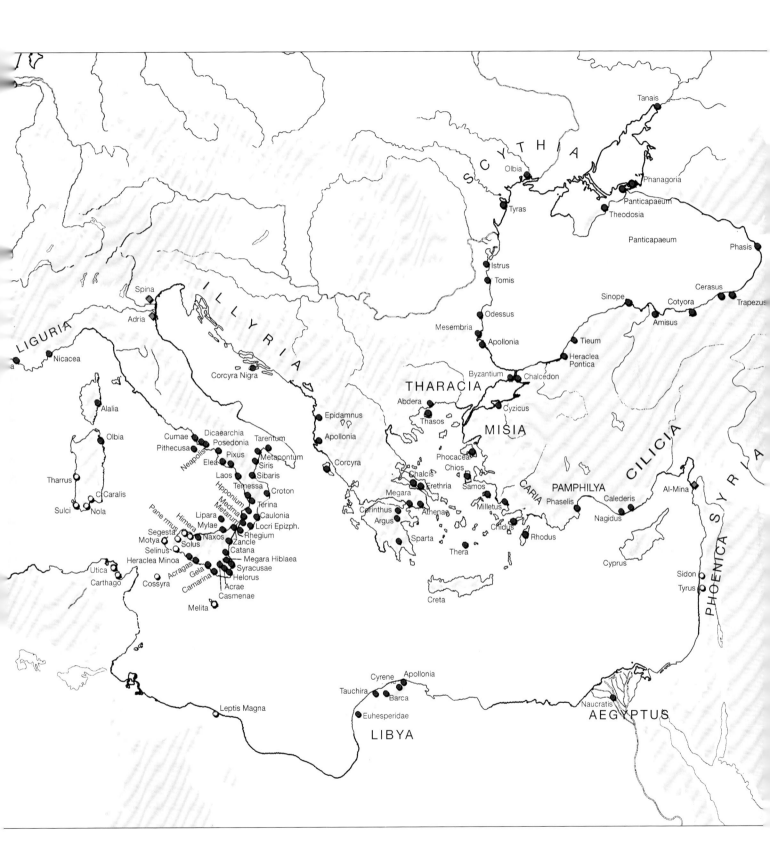

LIGURIA
Nicacea
a

Spina
Adria
ILLYRIA

Corcyra Nigra

Alalia
Olbia

Tharrus
Cl Caralis
Sulci
Nola

Cumae   Dicaearchia
Pithecusa   Posedonia
Neapolis   Pixus
             Elea   Metapontum
             Laos   Siris
Hpponium   Temessa   Sibaris
             Medma   Croton
Pane rmus   Lipara Metarum Terina
Himera   Mylae   Caulonia
Segesta   Naxos   Locri Epizph.
Motya   Solus   Rhegium
Selinus   Zancle
Heraclea Minoa   Catana
Utica   Acragas Gela   Megara Hiblaea
Carthago   Cossyra Carmarina Syracusae
                      Acrae   Helorus
                      Casmenae
             Melita

Tarentum

Epidamnus
Apollonia
Corcyra

SCYTHIA

Olbia
Tyras

Phanagoria
Panticapaeum
Theodosia

Panticapaeum

Phasis

Istrus
Tomis

Cerasus
Sinope   Cotyora
             Amisus   Trapezus

Odessus
Mesembria
Apollonia

Tieum

Heraclea
Pontica

Byzantium   Chalcedon
THARACIA

Abdera
Thasos

Cyzicus
MISIA

Phocacea
Chios

Chalcis
Erethria
Samos

CARIA   PAMPHILYA

CILICIA

Al-Mina

Megara
Corinthus
Argus   Athenae

Milletus
Chidus

Phaselis   Calederis
              Nagidus

Sparta

Thera   Rhodus

Cyprus

PHOENICA SYRIA

Sidon

Creta

Tyrus

Leptis Magna

Cyrene   Apollonia
Tauchira
          Barca
Euhesperidae

LIBYA

Naucratis

AEGYPTUS

Archaeological evidence shows that in some cases the colonists specifically chose to settle in areas previously occupied by Greeks. These earlier sojourns in the region, however, were simply for the purpose of trading, that is, of commercial endeavors undertaken by small groups of "merchants"; such activities were sporadic and impermanent and—as will be explained in detail—had no contact with subsequent settlements. References in the poems of Homer and the works of Hesiod give a picture of commerce in this period being undertaken by an aristocratic figure, not always the owner of the ship, who ranged the distant West, trading Greek goods for such materials as metals.

Some ancient settlements—such as Pithekoussai (modern Ischia) and Cumae—were deliberately chosen for their position along the route leading to mineral-rich Etruria and Sardinia. This phase of casual contacts is known as "the precolonization period," an ambiguous term indicating the time which preceded, but neither anticipated nor presaged, the subsequent "colonization," which, in any case, followed no regular pattern, either in its timing or in its underlying causes.

Both Phoenicians and Greeks involved in trading along the central and northern coasts of the Tyrrhenian Sea called at places on the Italian peninsula and Sicily. We know this from finds of pottery, but it is difficult to identify the traders from perishable goods such as textiles, which inevitably were irretrievably lost to the archaeological record, thereby taking with them any possibility of reconstructing a complete and detailed picture of all the commercial activities in the Mediterranean during this period. Euboian and Corinthian pottery has been found—though not always in context—on the coast of Salento, and particularly Otranto, and along the Ionic Calabro-Lucan arc; also on the east coast of Sicily, near the Straits of Messina, and along the coast of Campania and southern Lazio. The information such finds provide helps us to identify the routes followed by groups of Greek merchants, whose vessels traveled as far as the coast of southern Etruria. Initially, Greeks sailing out of Euboia, a long, narrow island to the east of Attica, concen-trated on the Levantine areas and, in particular, the Syrian coast, where they established commercial ports, like the one at Al Mina. It is the Euboian, Kalchedian, and especially Eretrian pottery that reveals the origins of these enterprising Greek sailors who, after the Phoenicians, were the Wrst to venture toward the distant West—to Hesperia written about by the poet Stesichoros of Himera, who lived in the seventh–sixth centuries B.C.

The presence of the Greeks in Italy and Sicily, while not a permanent one, triggered great cultural changes among the local native communities, as can be seen in the new cultural models and attitudes reflected in the pottery they produced. Imported objects began to appear in some of the communities in Calabria, Campania, and Etruria, while pottery shapes and painted decoration of a totally new design have been found alongside the traditional ones. In addition to their new pottery techniques, their social customs underwent parallel changes, transforming the way they related to the new arrivals.

While the trade and commerce that the Greeks developed in the western Mediterranean was not a direct forerunner of the subsequent colonization, it undoubtedly contributed to the spread of the geographical and ethnographical knowledge that proved so valuable on the subsequent voyages. Much of this information was passed on by the Delphic Oracle, which we know had an important influence on the colonial movement. Delphi is situated on the southern slope of Mount Parnassos, in Phokis, a region of central Greece facing the Gulf of Corinth, from which most journeys to the West began. In the eighth century B.C. it was an obligatory point of passage for the many colonists bound for the West; located here was a sanctuary dedicated to Apollo—a cult site which, at that time, had little relevance outside that region. Before the foundation of every colony, the leaders sought the advice of Apollo Archegetes (he who guides); over the years, the oracle of Apollo took on the value of a real and proper "sanctification" concerning the decisions made to settle conflicts arising between the various political factions in Greece in the Late Archaic period. This function, consolidated over

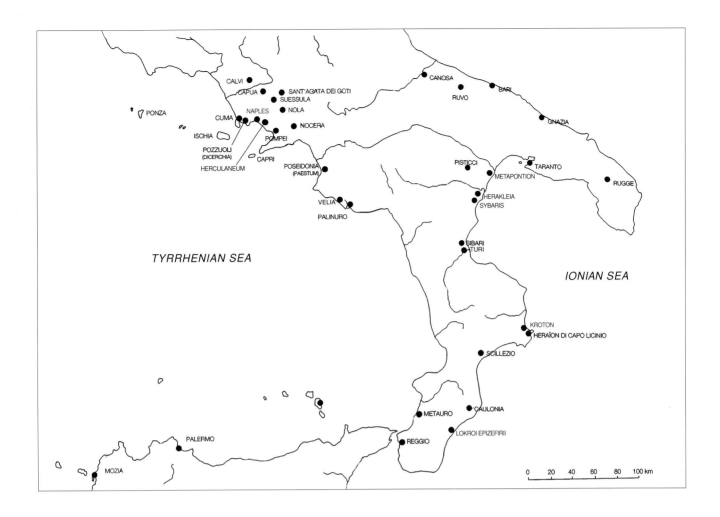

the years, meant that the sanctuary quickly assumed a great importance to the Panhellenic people, for whom it had become a fundamental point of reference.

Greek Colonization

Greek colonization, which overtook much of the western Mediterranean—above all, Southern Italy—between the eighth and sixth centuries B.C., involved the foundation of new political communities, new *poleis* formed by groups of citizens disengaged from the original community, which was known to them thereafter as the *metropolei* ("the mother city"). They brought with them the language, religious and cultural traditions, and myths and institutions inherited from the original *polis,* but were now totally independent of it—an aspect not inherent in the word *colonia,* the name normally given to these new communities. The term *colonia,* taken from the Latin *colere* (to cultivate), was, in fact, first employed by the Romans, who used it to describe groups of citizens to whom they gave land for the purpose of cultivation but who maintained ties of various kinds with Rome. Used right up to the present time, often with very different connotations, the terms "colony" and "colonization" often generate confusion. The Greeks themselves, on

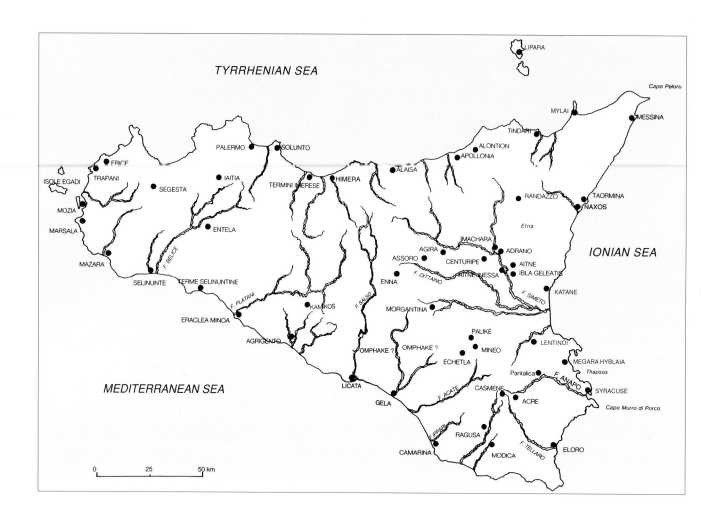

The Greek colonies in Sicily

the other hand, called these new *poleis,* created by groups of people separated from their homeland, *apoikia,* the verbal form of which, *apoikizo,* indicates the act of separation. So, while not proscribing the term "colony," now in such common use, one should nevertheless bear in mind its original meaning, and its implications when used solely in its conventional sense.

Not all members of a group whose sole aim was the establishment of a new community of citizens in a distant and barbarous country originated from a single city or a single region; often there were people from a number of cities, as happened in the cases of Pithekoussai (Ischia), which was founded by Kalchedians and Eretrians, and Cumae, con-

sisting of Kalchedians and Kymeans from Aiolia or perhaps Euboia. The leader of the emigrants was the *ekistes* (founder of the colony), usually someone from the mother city, who was accorded particular honors in the colony, such as the unique one of being buried as a hero in the *agora,* the public square where all forms of political meeting were held. The activities of the *ekistes* are described in detail in the *Odyssey,* in the passage relating to the foundation of Scherie, city of the Phaiakians (6.7–10):

> *Nausitoo, like a God, took them to the settlement at Scherie, far from the men who eat bread, enclosed the city with a wall,*

The Greek Colonies in Southern Italy and Sicily

Foundation	Chronology	*Metropoleis*	Foundation	Chronology	*Metropoleis*
Pithekoussai (Ischia)	770–760 B.C.	Kalchedon, Eretria	Himera (Imera)	648 B.C.	Zankle
Kyme (Cumae)	750 B.C.	Kalchedon, Aeolian Cumae	Kasmenai (Casmene)	643 B.C.	Syracuse
			Metapontion (Metaponto)	640–630 B.C.	Achaia Selinous
Naxos (Gardens of Naxos)	734 B.C.	Kalchedon	Selinus (Selinunte)	628 B.C.	Megara Hyblaia
Syracuse	733 B.C.	Corinth	Poseidonia (Paestum)	600 B.C.	Sybaris
Zankle (Messina)	730 B.C.	Kalchedon, Cumae	Kamarina (Camarina)	598 B.C.	Syracuse
Katane (Catania)	729 B.C.	Naxos	Akragas (Agrigento)	580 B.C.	Gela
Leontinoi (Lentini)	729 B.C.	Naxos	Lipara (Lipari)	580–576 B.C.	Knidos
Megara Hyblaia	728 B.C.	Megara Nisea	Medma (Rosarno)	575 B.C.	Lokroi Epizephyrioi
Rhegion (Reggio Calabria)	730–720 B.C.	Kalchedon	Hipponion (Vibo Valentia)	beginning 6th century B.C.	Lokroi Epizephyrioi
Sybaris (Sibari)	720–710 B.C.	Achaia			
Mylai (Milazzo)	716 B.C.	Zankle	Hyele-Elea (Velia)	535 B.C.	Phokaia (Focea)
Kroton (Crotone)	708 B.C.	Achaia	Dikaiarcheia (Dicearchia)	531 B.C.	Samos
Kaulonia (Caulonia)	end 8th century B.C.	Achaia	Skylletion (Scolacium)	5th century B.C.?	Kroton
Taras (Taranto)	706–705 B.C.	Sparta	Terina (Sant'Eufemia Vetere)	480–470 B.C.	Kroton
Siris	690–680 B.C.	Kolophon (Colophon)	Neapolis (Naples)	beginning 5th century B.C.	Cumae
Gela	688 B.C.	Rhodians and Cretans			
Lokroi Epizephyrioi (Locri)	675–650 B.C.	Lokroians	Thurii	444–443 B.C.	Panhellenic colony
Akrai (Acre)	664 B.C.	Syracuse	Herakleia (Heraklea)	433 B.C.	Athenians and Peloponnesians
Laos (near Scalea)	end 7th century B.C.	Sybaris			
Pixunte (Policastro Bussentine)	end 7th century B.C.	Sybaris			
Skydros	end 7th century B.C.	Sybaris			

built houses and a temple to the gods, and shared out the land.

Among the first acts performed by the new arrivals in a colony was the division of the available space into public areas (such as sanctuaries, *agorai*—main squares for public gatherings—and roads) and the construction of houses and allocation of land for cultivation. So, even without the presence of monumental buildings to guide them, archaeologists are still able to recreate the initial moments in the life of a new city: the planning of the political space and the *agora*, and the religious sectors and the numerous sanctuaries located either within or outside the urban area. These two sectors were the main centers where the people gathered in order to organize themselves and to create an identity for the emerging community of citizens.

Located immediately outside the urban center were the *necropoleis* ("cities of the dead," or cemeteries), the study of which has made great progress over recent years. The position of the graves, the funeral rites, and the various accoutrements employed reveal a great deal about the way a society was organized and the changes that came about in the decades that followed the foundation of a city.

Compared to the *metropoleis* of Greece itself, the organization of these new developments, created in territory untamed by previous occupation (any efforts by former native occupants were

The "Temple of Ceres"
("*Athenaion*") at Paestum

Terracotta statue of Zeus
enthroned, 530–520 B.C.,
from the urban sanctuary at
Paestum (Paestum-Salerno
National Archaeological Museum)

discounted by the Greeks), along with the new urban centers, could be planned more systematically and rigorously than had been those of the old cities. A look at the geographical position of the Greek colonial settlements reveals a number of consistent criteria, such as location close to the sea or water sources and the availability of land suitable for cultivation. Even though there were considerable differences among the individual colonial *poleis*, the territory (the *chora*) and the sea remained essential factors in the formation of a new community. Though the size and nature of the territory may have differed greatly, it remained nevertheless an important characteristic for the *apoikia* (the colonists) inasmuch as it guaranteed the self-sufficiency and, by the same token, the independence of the city.

Apoikia, it is said, implies the act of separation, but what motivated groups of citizens to leave their homeland and found a new and completely independent city? In the past scholars have cited such reasons as demographic crisis, the lack of viable land caused by famine, climate change, or overcrowding, as could occur in some of the mountainous and infertile regions of the Balkans. Others considered that colonization was prompted by the search for new commercial outlets and came almost as a natural consequence of those contacts made during the "precolonization" period. While in some cases the colonial movement may have been influenced by these factors, it would be quite wrong to see them as the prime motivation. Current research tends to distance itself from overgeneralizations of this kind and concentrates instead on closer examination of individual, and often widely differing, cases.

The motivations were, in fact, as manifold as the political communities were numerous; it is worth remembering that Greece, in its Archaic and Classic periods, was not an integrated state, but a collection of cities (*poleis*) and ethnic (*ethne*) entities with different political and institutional structures, cultural and mythological traditions, and dialects, but all existing within the framework of the same cultural mold. So it is at the heart of the geopolitical and social history of each city, or

ethnic group, that one must seek the reasons for the colonization phenomenon.

In many cases (Taranto or Lokroi, for example) a study of the myths of foundation helps to reveal the social and political background of a *polis* making ready for the colonial experience. For instance, the expulsion of a group of citizens from their own community, with a categorical ban on a return to the homeland, often stemmed from some serious political and social crisis, known to the Greeks as *stasis*. Such situations could obviously occur only in an organized community (one where the political structure was already clearly established, or in the process of being so) within which social categories were essentially defined by the ownership of land—the essential qualification for the acquisition of political rights. Often, and after only a few generations, this same situation occurred again in the new cities, since the direct heirs of the first founders inevitably got the best parcels of land in the urban center and, as a result, property and institutional offices became concentrated in their hands. Examples of this can be seen in the *Gamoroi* (the Landowners) of Syracuse, the *Pacheis* (the Prosperous Ones) of Megara Hyblaia, or the *Hippeis* (the Knights) of Leontinoi. The crises this situation inevitably produced resulted in new groups of *apoikiai* setting up new settlements, generally known by yet another ambiguous term—sub or under colonies—almost as if to accentuate, as forcefully as possible, a dependency that did not, in fact, exist.

There were many reasons for the foundation of settlements: the one at Siris was founded by exiles from Kolophon, who were obliged to abandon their own city to escape the dominion of the Lydians; Velia was founded by the inhabitants of Phokaia who were fleeing from the Persians of Ciro; Dikaiarcheia (Pozzuoli) was founded by people of Samos forced out by the tyranny of Polykrates. Opportunities of a political nature were behind the foundation of Thurii and of Herakleia in the fifth century B.C. Completely different, however, was the process of "refounding," which consisted of a radical change in the social and political order and included the redistribution of land. The causes of this "refounding" may have derived from internal

The Ludovisi Throne, detail of the Birth of Venus, 460–450 B.C., from Lokri. Discovered at the Villa Ludovisi in Rome in 1887 (National Museum, Rome)

problems in the city itself, but more often such a refounding came in the wake of the conquest and violent destruction of the city and the consequent takeover by new inhabitants. This happened in a number of Siciliote cities, such as Kamarina, a *polis* "refounded" twice following the destruction of the city, first by Hippokrates of Gela in 492–491 B.C. and then by Gelon of Syracuse in 461 B.C.

Alongside the *apoikiai*—cities with their own founders, political institutions, and, in particular, their own territory—were other, quite different, types of settlements. These were the *epineia*, essentially commercial ports of call, like those set up by Cumae along the Phlegraean coast, or military centers, permanently maintained to control the territory, like Eloro, Acre, and Kasmenai, founded by Syracuse at the end of the eighth and the first half of the seventh century B.C.

The permanent presence of new communities speeded up the processes of cultural change already dealt with in the section on so-called pre-colonization; these processes affected not only the native population but also the colonizers themselves. In the new lands the Greeks met, and sometimes clashed with, people who already had a developed political, social, and cultural structure. The superior organization of the new arrivals generally guaranteed victory for the Greeks on both political and military levels in their confrontations with the native races, with whom they were nevertheless obliged to associate to some degree, with a resulting transference of intellectual ideas. The use of slave labor, mixed marriages, and the employment of mercenaries are only some aspects of this social mobility, which gave rise to a new and specifically local culture about which it is difficult to generalize—unlike the cultural aspects of the various Greek communities established along the Italian coast.

Political Institutions and Monuments

Data relating to the political institutions of the cities of Magna Graecia and Sicily are quite scarce, but in general these differed little from those of the rest of the Hellenic world, although there were variations. In any case, it is not possible to

reconstruct the sociopolitical framework of individual *apoikiai* because of the fragmented nature of the documentary evidence.

Occasionally new discoveries cast light on certain aspects, but only partially, as happened at Kamarina, for example, where the discovery of a large number of epigraphic records made it possible to understand of the civic organization of the *polis* at the beginning of the fifth century B.C. With regard to the city's institutions, we can say that there is clear evidence that they included an assembly (*ekklesia*) and the citizens' city council (*boule*). Through literary and epigraphic sources we know about the existence of a series of magistracies such as the *prytaneis* (ruling members of the *boule*), the *strategos*, and the "*demiurges.*" Few details are known, however, about the workings of these citizen offices.

We know the name of a lawmaker, Karonda of Katane, whose activities can be placed between the seventh and the sixth centuries B.C., and we know that at Lokroi the first written laws were promulgated by Zaleuco in the middle of the seventh century B.C. We have little information about such institutions as the *bouleuterion* (meeting place of the *boule*), the *ekklesiasterion,* and the *prytaneion,* in which burned the sacred flame of the city community.

No *bouleuterion* has been found in Magna Graecia, but in Sicily there are several: at Agrigento, Morgantina, Acre, Taormina (the ancient *Tauromenion*), Solunto, and Monte Iato. The type of architecture used in these buildings was characteristically a closed rectangular structure inside which was the *cavea*, usually covered, with semicircular or U-shaped rectilinear tiers of seating for the participants. The *ekklesiasterion*, as we already said, was the meeting place of the assembly, the *ekklesia,* which welcomed all those having full rights of citizenship. The one in Athens had decision-making and executive powers and functioned as the electoral body for the elective magistracy, but we do not know what precise function it served in the various Siciliote and Italiote cities (Italiote is the name given to the Greeks who had settled in Italy).

Initially the assemblies were held inside the *agora* in suitable areas furnished with wooden stands (*ikriai*) set around an area called the orchestra. These structures, as was later the case for the theater, served a number of purposes (cultural, political, or competitive). In western Greece, three circular, tiered structures have been identified as *ekklesiasteria:* one each at Metapontion, Poseidonia, and Agrigento. The earliest of these monuments is the one at Metapontion, where a wooden phase was found that dates from the end of the seventh century B.C.

The *prytaneion* constitutes the religious heart and the symbol of the city, in that it is the site of the sacred flame, the communal hearth (generally linked to the homonymous deity Hestia). The *prytaneis,* or senior members of the *boule,* who served one year in office, received foreign delegations and particularly favored guests. The remains of two buildings at Megala Hyblaia and Morgantina have each been identified as a *prytanikon,* but not everyone is agreed on this.

Among the various types of architecture of a public nature, we should also mention the *stoa*s, colonnaded buildings that served a number of functions, including political ones. Originally shelters for the faithful in large sanctuaries, they soon became used also in public places of a secular character. The earliest *stoa* (end of the seventh century B.C.) used for this purpose that we know of is that of the *agora* at Megara Hyblaia. In later eras this type of architecture was increasingly employed, precisely because of its usefulness as both an enclosure and a boundary to open spaces.

An area of particular importance for a new city was the *heroon* (a building or place dedicated to heroes) of the *ekistes,* situated in the public square. There are few buildings that can be identified as *heroa* with any certainty in the colonial world, other than the one at Poseidonia, and possibly one at Megara Hyblaia, and also one at Cirene, the city in North Africa, founded by the inhabitants of Thera, whose leader was Batto. The lyric poet Pindar, who lived from the end of the sixth into the fifth century B.C., wrote in his *Odes:*

Temple known as "Temple of the Concordia," in the valley of the temples at Agrigento

Aphrodite Landolina, first half of the second century B.C. Marble copy found in Syracuse (National Archaeological Museum, Syracuse)

Opposite page: columns of the temple at Segesta

there on the poop of the Agora (Batto)
dead, lies alone.

He was happy among men, and after,
As a hero (was) honored by the people.

Excavations carried out in the *agora* at Cirene have made it possible to identify the tomb of the *ekistes*, right where the poet indicates. It consists of an earth tumulus with a base made up of a ring of stones, the center of which was filled with charred bones, ashes, and earth. In the second half of fifth century, because of works to enlarge the *agora*, the tumulus was rebuilt a short distance away, this time containing a cenotaph—an empty, box-shaped tomb with a flat cover. In the fourth century B.C., following a new reorganization of the square, the tumulus was dismantled and the tomb, under a new cover with a pitched roof, was enclosed in a wall which took the place of the tumulus.

The *Apoikiai* of Magna Graecia and Sicily

The earliest Greek settlement in the West was attributed to the Euboians, and in particular the inhabitants of Kalchedon and Eretria who founded the settlement at Pithekoussai around the middle of the eighth century B.C. The colony's inhabited area consisted of small groups of houses spread all over the island, in accordance with a way of life and form of settlement organization that was typical of the Late Archaic period—a time when the cities and their politico-territorial structure in mainland Greece, too, were still seeking a definitive form.

The situation at Cumae, founded a little later by Euboians—in this case Kalchedians and Kymeans, who gave their name to the city—was much different. The first foundation on the mainland was by no means peaceful: the siege the Greeks mounted against the settlement of the Opici—the native people already occupying the area destined to become the Greek city—ended violently. The improvement in the organizational quality of the new settlement, compared with that of Pithekoussai, was clear to see. The new community already had all the characteristics of an Archaic city, with its *ekistes*, its territory, its institutions, and its urban structure that was typical of a *polis* of the Late Archaic period.

Within a few decades there seems to have been a change in the political and institutional structures governing the organization of a community, the result of a transformation triggered in mainland Greece which, when given a final boost by the *apoikiai*, saw the development, over the centuries, of a new political, institutional, and urban order that affected the whole of the Greek world. The foundation of Cumae, with its new way of organizing its territory, provoked a crisis with Pithekoussai at the start of the seventh century B.C. During this period, Cumae had underscored its control over the surrounding area by creating small ports (*epineia*). Similar ports are found today at Pozzuoli, where the Samnites founded Dikaiarcheia, in 531 B.C.; at Misceno, further south; and at Partenope in the Pizzofalcone area—the site which, following the foundation of Naples at the beginning of the fifth century B.C., became Paleapolis ("the old city") to the new community.

Again around 730 B.C., other Kalchedian colonists founded Zankle (Messina) and, shortly after that, Rhegion (Reggio Calabria) close to the strait at an important passage to the Tyrrhenian. Also dating from this time is Naxos (the Gardens of Naxos), which shortly afterward contributed to the foundation of Leontinoi (Lentini) and Katane (Catania), built on the fertile plain surrounding Mount Etna.

A little further south, around 733 B.C., the Corinthians arrived and founded Syracuse, followed a few years later by the Megareans, who founded Megara Hyblaia in the Gulf of Augusta.

In the last decades of the eighth century B.C., other groups moved from Achaia, a region on the north coast of the Peloponnese that was occupied by a number of villages, some of which subsequently developed into urban centers. These nuclear settlements—Helike, Aeghion, Rhypai, Bura, Ege—provided some of the founders: the *ekistes* of Sybaris came from Helike, that of Kroton, from Rhypai, and Ege supplied the *ekistes* of Kaulonia.

The Achaian colonization was limited to the strip of Ionic coast occupied by the Oinotrian people, while further south, the Lokroians, after annihilating the native population, founded Lokroi Epizephyrioi at the start of the seventh century. Two years before, Taranto had been founded in Iapygian territory by the Spartans, or rather, according to historians Antiochos and Ephoros, by illegitimate Spartans under the leadership of Phalanthos, who arrived directly from Amyklai, the ancient sacred center of the Lakonian city. More or less contemporary with Lokroi was Siris (now Policoro in the Matera province), founded by Kolophon, a city in Asia Minor.

The foundation of these two cities, and of Gela, established by Cretans and Rhodians in 688 B.C., ended the first period of colonial activity, which had lasted less than a century. The second wave of colonization was inaugurated by the *apoikiai* in Southern Italy and Sicily themselves. In 683 B.C., Syracuse founded Acre, while around 650 B.C. the people of Zankle together with exiles from Syracuse settled at Himera. In the middle of the seventh century B.C., Megara Hyblaia founded Selinunte, while the Lokroians founded three cities on the Tyrrhenian coast: Medma (Rosarno), Hipponion (Vibo Valentia), and Metauros (Gioia Tauro).

Around 630 B.C., the Sybarites called for a contingent of settlers from the motherland to help found Metapontion; at the end of the seventh century B.C., they themselves founded the city of Poseidonia on the Tyrrhenian coast, a few miles from the river Sele. At about the same time as Poseidonia came Kamarina, founded by Syracusan *apoikia*, and shortly after, Agrigento (580 B.C.), a Geloan city.

In 540 B.C., people of Phokaia fleeing the Persians founded Velia, which was situated, to quote the geographer Strabo, "200 stadiums (about 23.6 miles [38 km]) to the south of Poseidonia"— a city that played a significant part in the choice of the site. The foundation of Velia followed that of other cities from Phokaia: Marseilles, the ancient Massiglia, on the south coast of France; Aleria (Alalia) on Corsica (565 B.C.); and Ampurias in Catalonia, formerly Emporion.

In 531 B.C. came Dikaiarcheia ("where justice reigns"), subsequently renamed Puteoli (Pozzuoli) by the Romans, founded by political exiles from Samos, which was governed at that time by the tyrant Polykrates.

The cities of Terina, Naples, and Kroton, founded in the area of Sant'Eufemia Vetere, were only begun at the start of the fifth century B.C.

The Panhellenic foundation of Thurii dates from 444–443 B.C. The city, established near the ruins of Sybaris, counted the historian Herodotos of Halicarnassos among its new citizens. Ten years after the clash between the new city and Taranto came the foundation of Herakleia, built on the contested territory of the people of Siris.

Brief Historical Survey

The historical events involving the Greek cities of Italy and Sicily have been handed down by a number of authors, in particular two great historians of the fifth century B.C., Herodotos and Thucydides, whose main works have come to us intact. The principal historian of the West Greek world was, however, Antiochos of Syracuse, who lived in the second half of the fifth century B.C. Unfortunately, only fragments of his work survive. Also useful are references in Ephoros, native of Aiolian Kyme, who in the middle of the fifth century B.C. wrote a universal history of Greece. In the fourth century B.C., such historians as Philistos of Syracuse, Licos of Reggio, and Timaios of Tauromenion were also actively recording events, but little of their work remains. Much later, in the first century B.C., were the historians Diodoros of Syracuse and Dionysios of Halicarnassos, authors respectively of a universal history and of *Roman Antiquities*, and the geographer Strabo of Amaseia, whose description of Italy contains historical references of great interest amidst the geographical data.

Finally, a certain amount of information can be found in the works of the historians of the Imperial period, including the Latin Livy, Pliny, Velleius, Patercolus, and Justinian and the Greek Polyenos, Pausanias, Athenaios, and, from the sixth century B.C., Stephanos of Byzantium, to mention the most important ones.

Opposite page: Metope with Perseus slaying Medusa, 530 B.C., from Temple C at Selinunte (Regional Archaeological Museum, Palermo)

Pages 26–27: Temple E at Selinunte

Bronze tablet recording a loan made to the city by the sanctuary of Zeus at Lokroi, 350–250 B.C., from Lokroi (National Museum, Reggio Calabria)

In the Archaic period, the history of the Italiote and Siciliote cities was marked by violent events that resulted in the more or less total destruction of several cities. Essentially, strong territorial rivalries were at the root of these violent clashes, such as those in the second quarter of the sixth century B.C. that brought about the capitulation of Siris. The city, according to Justinian, a historian who lived in the third and second centuries B.C., was completely razed by the Sybarites and the Metapontians, and by the leader Kroton, who wanted to take control of Siris. For similar reasons, a few years later Kroton sent a large army against Lokroi. This encounter took place near to the Sagra River, where a small army from Lokroi and Rhegion managed to beat Kroton and save the city from probable destruction.

The defeat of Kroton does not appear to have had any consequence for the control of the territory, but from the point of view of political policy it did provoke a serious backlash. It was at this time that the philosopher Pythagoras, fleeing from Samos, came to Kroton to found a new school. Established around a religious and philosophical movement, this soon developed into a political ideology that had the same influence on the government of Kroton as it had on other cities where the Pythagorian doctrine was spread.

At the end of the sixth century B.C., ongoing problems over control of the territory between Kroton and the Sybarites provoked the clash which brought about the total destruction of Sybaris, which had been one of the most powerful cities in Magna Graecia. The sudden disappearance of the city initiated a series of reorganizational processes within the territory which not only affected the Greek cities (Kroton, Metapontion, and Poseidonia) but also the native population in the interior who had come under the control of the Achaian city. For many years the Sybarite refugees tried, on more than one occasion, to rebuild their city, and finally succeeded, though only partially, in the middle of the fifth century B.C. with the help of Athens.

In 484 B.C. Megara Hyblaia was razed to the ground, destroyed by the army of Gelon of Syracuse. Some of the inhabitants were sold as slaves and the rest integrated into Syracuse. Between the fourth and fifth centuries B.C., some individual figures like Gelon of Syracuse dominated the history of the colonies in southern Italy; the phenomenon of tyranny was particularly strong in the cities of Sicily. Around 600 B.C. Panezio became tyrant of Leontinoi and between 570 and 554 B.C. declared himself tyrant of Agrigento. In 505 B.C. Kleander became tyrant of Gela, followed in 498 B.C. by Hippokrates, who instigated a hegemonic policy toward eastern Sicily.

Two years after the death of Hippokrates, in 491 B.C., Gelon, member of the noble family of the Denominides, became tyrant, placing him on a brilliant political path that, within the space of a few years, brought him control of most of Sicily. The conquest of Syracuse constituted the first stage of this enterprise. Having transferred his command to his new city, Gelon formed an alliance with Theron, tyrant of Agrigento from 488 B.C. In order to reinforce his power, Gelon did not hesitate to transfer to Syracuse, en masse, those social groups from other cities who guaranteed him support. The culminating moment of the tyrant's hegemonic policy came with his victory in the Battle of Himera, at the side of Theron of Agrigento against the Carthaginian army called to the aid of the tyrants Therillos of Himera and Anassilaos of Rhegion. The victory was considered

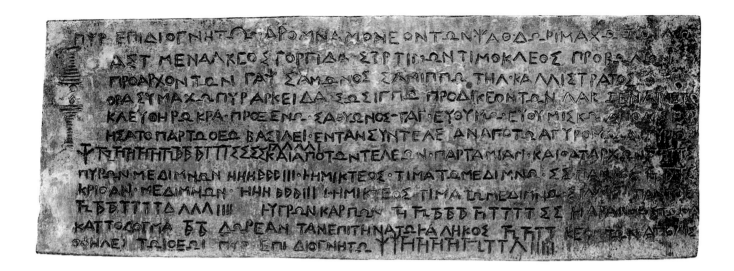

the equal of the famous Battle of Salamis, won by the Greeks against the Persians and recorded in Herodotus.

Even the death of Gelon in 478 B.C. did not change the political attitude of the city, by then led by the tyrant Hieron, who remained in power until his death around 467–466 B.C. The new tyrant consolidated the power of Syracuse, turning his interests increasingly to Magna Graecia. In 474 B.C., in the waters off Cumae, the Syracusan fleet, sent to support the Cumaeans, defeated the Etruscans, putting an end to their interventions on the coast of Campania. As early as 524 B.C. the Etruscans had tried, unsuccessfully, to assail Cumae, home of Aristodamos, who at the end of the century made himself tyrant of the city—a role of short duration. The battle of 474 B.C. clearly demonstrated that, in the initial decades of the fifth century B.C., Cumae was not up to the task of controlling its territory unaided against the Etruscan menace; it was obliged to seek help from powerful Syracuse, which, after the victory, established a garrison on the island of Pithekoussai.

The fifth century B.C. saw the end of many tyrannies, in particular that of the Dinomenides of Syracuse, the Emminidi of Agrigento, and that of Anassilaos of Rhegion, whose fall created new difficulties in the city, now obliged to confront the advance of native armies who in the past had supported the tyrant. There was also Ducezio, who, at the head of an army of Sicels, succeeded in forming a confederation of Sicel cities, including Inessa and Morgantina, which sent armies to menace Agrigento. Defeated in the Battle of Nomai, he was forced by the Syracusans to go into exile in Corinth. A few years later he returned to Sicily, with the consent of the Corinthians and perhaps also of the Syracusans, to found the city of Kalacte near the strait, but he died before completing this undertaking.

In the course of the fifth century B.C. powerful Athens appeared on the Western political scene. The city showed particular interest in the area that was once Sybaris, the area of Rhegion, and three other Kalchedian cities in Sicily, as well as the Gulf of Naples. In this same period Athens received a request from Sybarite refugees to refound their old city, a refoundation that was undertaken as a Panhellenic venture that also saw the birth of Thurii, the colony where Herodotos finished writing his *History*.

The new *apoikia*, who had immediately targeted the territory of Siris, caused a clash with neighboring Taranto; the situation appeared momentarily resolved in 433 B.C. with the foundation of Herakleia in the destroyed area of Siris. The

Bronze tablet recording a loan made to the city by the sanctuary of Zeus at Lokroi, for the contribution to the king, 350–250 B.C., from Lokroi (National Museum, Reggio Calabria)

Pages 30–31: The theater at Segesta

subsequent events in the new city, with disagreements—sometimes violent ones—between the Peloponnesian and the Athenian citizens, constituted a Western mirror image of the increasingly sharp clashes between the Athenians and the Spartans, encounters that gave rise soon afterward to the Peloponnesian Wars.

The first military intervention by the Athenians in Sicily was brought about by the war between Syracuse and Leontinoi, supported by other Kalchedian cities. The second and decisive incident came to a head after a request for help received from Segesta, threatened by Selinunte and Syracuse. The Athenian expedition in Sicily, undertaken between 415 and 413 B.C., ended in a terrible defeat for Athens, which also had a disastrous effect on the progress of the Second Peloponnesian War. For Syracuse, on the other hand, the victory consolidated its position in the confrontations not only with the Greek cities in Sicily but also with those of Magna Graecia, to which it then turned its attention.

In the meantime, under slow but steady pressure from groups of Osco-Samnite peoples who went to occupy the historic sites of the Opici and the Oinotrians, the attitude of the native population was also changing. It was a process that had already started in sixth century B.C. and which can be said to have ended, at least partially, only in 356 B.C. with the secession of the Brettii from the Lucanians. It is clear that the definition of new ethnic groups was not only due to the advance of people coming from Sannio, but was also the result of a dynamic process of change in the indigenous element resulting from its long period of contact with the Greek colonial environment and that of Etruscanized Campania.

A politico-cultural leap by this indigenous world in ferment was also caused by the mercenary armies in which many of them served. The use of Lucanian mercenaries by Poseidonia seems to be confirmed today by archaeological evidence, thanks to the discovery of a necropolis used by the military at the gates of the city, where the funeral rites were conducted in the same manner by contemporary Campanian and Lucanian groups. Later on, mercenaries, predominantly Campanian, who called themselves Mamertines, from *Mamers,*

Oscan name for the god of war, were recruited by Agathokles, tyrant of Syracuse, whose attitude was responsible for the start of the First Punic War and the consequent invasion of Sicily by Rome.

The same Campanians were responsible for the capitulation of Cumae in 421 B.C.; three years previously the same thing had happened to Capua. By welcoming the social representatives of the Campanian élite, who in several cases were given political office, Naples avoided becoming involved in military conflict. It was probably also in order to face threats from these indigenous groups, whose political, social, and military structures increasingly resembled those of the Greeks, that some of the Achaian cities (Kroton, Kaulonia, and Sybaris, on the river Traeis, formed by refugees from Thurii) decided to form a confederation, the League of the Achaian Cities.

Syracuse, too—thanks to the politics of Dionysios I, who became tyrant following events that came to a head after the war with Athens—had its sights increasingly focused on Italy. To this end the tyrant was not too proud to enter into an alliance with the Lucanians, who had arrived to threaten Thurii. This play of alliances between Greek cities and the native population, and the ever-increasing involvement of cities from the Greek mainland, gives the most useful insight into the events in the Greek colonial world between the fourth and the third centuries B.C. Two cities, Taranto and Syracuse, both of which were strong on an economic level, managed to direct the politics of the West during these years. The two cities often found themselves on the same side in conflicts like that with the Sicilian expedition by Athens, which was at that time supported by the Messapian prince, Artas.

It was precisely against the Messapians that Taranto had to fight debilitating battles in the course of its history, and between 473 and 467 B.C. it suffered a serious defeat that was recorded in ancient sources as the greatest slaughter ever suffered by Greeks. This disaster, involving the flower of Tarantan aristocracy, probably eased the passage of the city to a democratic regime. In the second half of the fourth century B.C., Taranto managed to seize the reins of the League of Achaian

10. Silver drachm with cock on obverse and incused square on reverse, before 482 B.C., from Himera mint (Service for Cultural and Environmental Artifacts, Numismatic Dept., Syracuse)

11. Silver tetradrachm of Agathokles with head of Kore/Persephone on obverse and Nike crowning a trophy on reverse, 310–304 B.C., from Syracuse (The "Paolo Orsi" Regional Archaeological Museum, Syracuse)

12. Gold stater with veiled head of Hera on obverse and horseman on reverse, 340–334 B.C., from Taranto (National Archaeological Museum, Taranto)

1
2
3
4
5
6
7
8
9
10
11
12

Lekythos in the Gnathian
style with female figure
seated on a *diphros* holding
a mirror in her right hand,
around 340 B.C., from tomb 1
in the Lupoli quarter, Taranto
(National Archaeological Museum,
Taranto)

Cities, by then transformed into the Italiote League, and to transfer its seat to Herakleia. These were the years when the figure Archytas, follower of Pythagoras, and *strategos* (general) for seven consecutive years, dominated Taranto and maintained close ties with both Dionysios I and his son, Dionysios II, who succeeded him as commander of Syracuse during this period.

Meanwhile, in the name of the freedom of the Greek cities in the West against the threat from the native barbarians, help was sought ever more frequently from the motherland. From Corinth came Timoleon, who not only managed to save Syracuse from the Carthaginians but whose strategic ability contributed to the downfall of the Sicilian cities and brought them under the control of Syracuse. Taranto, too, was obliged to ask the help of Sparta in its war against the Messapians and the Lucanians, who nevertheless managed to conquer Herakleia after they had killed the Spartan king Archydamos III in 338 B.C. The seat of the Italiote League was liberated later, thanks to the intervention of the king of Epiros, Alexander the Molossan (uncle of Alexander the Great), called to Italy again by Taranto.

The series of successes by Alexander against the Messapians, Lucanians, and the Brettii caused hostility on the part of Taranto. After liberating Paestum also for a short time, Alexander was assassinated by a Lucanian exile at Pandosia, near Cosentia, in 331 B.C. A few decades later (304–302 B.C.), Kleonymos, son of the Spartan king Kleomenes II, arrived in Italy from Sparta, but he too was obliged to return home because of Taranto's hostility.

At Syracuse, after the death of Timoleon, a new political personality, Agathokles, emerged and had himself nominated *strategos* with full executive powers. The new tyrant dominated the Sicilian political scene at the end of the fourth century B.C. Agathokles' dream was the unification of

Sicily under the command of Syracuse. With this objective in mind, he attacked the Carthaginians, taking the war to Africa. In 306–305 B.C. he assumed the title of king, comparing his command to that of the Hellenistic princes who, in those same years, struggled among themselves for the kingdoms born of the dismantling of the empire of Alexander the Great.

On the South Italian scene the Roman army began a slow expansion toward the south, starting in Campania and Apulia, then the rest of Southern Italy, and finally Sicily. The Italian adventure of Pyrrhos, called to Taranto to fight the Romans, constitutes the epilogue to the history of the cities of Magna Graecia. Pyrrhos won some great victories initially, but they were not to last. His undertakings ended with the defeat of Maleventum against the Romans in the spring of 275 B.C., a rout which forced Pyrrhos to leave Italy and abandon the cities of Magna Graecia to their fate. In 272 B.C. Taranto, the last Italiote city still free, surrendered to the Roman consul Lucius Papirius. The Siciliote cities held on to their independence a little longer, controlled, for the most part, by Syracuse, where Hieron II, after Pyrrhos left the island, proclaimed himself king in 264 B.C.

The outbreak of the Second Punic War between the Romans and the Carthaginians, following a request for help on the part of mercenaries garrisoned at Messina, signaled the powerful invasion of Sicily by the Romans. At the end of the war, which came after a naval victory off the Egadi islands, in 241 B.C., Rome made the whole island into a province, with the exception of her ally, the Syracuse of Hieron II, who was given control of various cities. Hieron's shrewd politics kept the city independent and autonomous until his death in 215 B.C., after which the city, allied with Carthage, was besieged and destroyed in 212 B.C.

With Syracuse, the last bastion of Greece in the West crumbled.

The Gulf of Naples

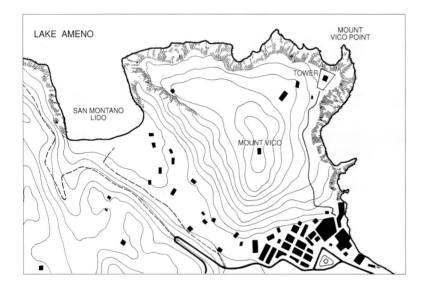

should be remembered that Archaic Greek geography was based on the experiences of sailors and merchants who ventured into unknown waters; at that time Campania represented the western frontier of the world, beyond which lay the mythical ocean, the river that encircled the earth and divided it from Hades. These early attempts at geographical orientation were based on Odysseus' return from Troy; some of the crucial locations in this epic voyage can be identified on the coasts of Lazio and Campania. The kingdom of Circe was near the promontory of Circeo and the site of the Sirens close to the Sorrento peninsula; the access to Hades corresponded to the Lake of Averno in the Cumae area.

The ancient historians did not consider Pithekoussai to be a true colony; it did not, for instance, bear the name of any of its founders, unlike Cumae, which was established only a generation later on the Phlegraean coast. Pithekoussai seems to have been established by groups who, like the early American pioneers, went West to seek their fortune. They imbued it with the character of an "open city" that concentrated its energies largely on the production of craft goods and trading, and attracted an influx of people of all kinds: first the Phoenicians, merchants and pirates par excellence, then Etruscans and Italians from Lazio, Campania, and Apulia. The ancient sources record that the island was renowned both for "the fertility of its soil and its production of gold artifacts" and, of

Plan of Pithekoussai

Opposite page: view of the Phlegraean coast and the island of Ischia

ISCHIA / PITHEKOUSSAI

History

The first permanent Greek settlement in the West was established on the island of Ischia, in the Gulf of Naples, around the middle of the eighth century B.C. The colonists came from the cities of Kalchedon and Eretria, in Euboia, and called the island Pithekoussai, or Island of Monkeys. Why this name? Probably because of the marginal character of this far outpost, in wild country that evoked the distant lands where monkeys roam. It

The "shipwreck" krater (two-handled drinking vessel), with a drawing of a detail, 725–700 B.C., from the necropolis on Ischia (Villa Arbusto Archaeological Museum, Lake Ameno, Naples)

course, for ceramics. They also record that it was periodically devastated by volcanic eruptions and earthquakes. One of these natural disasters destroyed the first settlement, which was already weakened by internal disorder. Archaeological evidence puts this event at the start of the seventh century B.C., probably around the time of the foundation of Cumae, the consolidation of whose territory undermined Pithekoussai's role in the area and forced it to reorganize.

Pithekoussai remained within Cumae's orbit until the end of the fifth century B.C. After the great naval battle of 474 B.C., in which the allied fleets of Cumae and Syracuse defeated the Etruscans, the island was garrisoned for a few years by the Syracusans, but they too were also obliged to flee following an earthquake. The island then became quite definitively a part of the territory of Naples and a base from which it controlled navigation in the Gulf of Naples. The settlement, however, continued to produce its traditional crafts, making use of the excellent clay quarries the island provided.

The Organization of the Territory and of the Inhabited Areas

The available archaeological evidence relates primarily to the earliest phase of the settlement, from its foundation around the middle of the eighth century B.C. to the middle of the sixth century B.C. Immediately on their arrival, the Greeks dispersed over the whole island, building a series of villages which were given over to the cultivation either of essential food crops or more valuable products, such as oil and wine for trading. The main center of this system of settlements was located near Lake Ameno and, like other Greek cities of the eighth century B.C., it was not concentrated in a single large entity but split into small groups.

The most important "quarter" of the settlement was situated on the highest part of Mount Vico overlooking the sea and the natural port to the east and, to the west, the necropolis, located in the valley of San Montano.

Archaeological material found on Mount Vico covers the whole span of life on the island down until the first century B.C. Fine ironwork was produced on its slopes, at least in the Archaic period, using the basic raw materials that were available

locally, and analysis has shown that traders carried some of these items as far as the island of Elba. In the eighth century B.C. the Greeks lived side by side with the Phoenicians, as is shown by finds of pots inscribed in that language. It is likely that this association enjoyed some form of divine protection; the discovery of a small model of a temple dating from the eighth century B.C. shows that a sanctuary must

The Goblet of Nestor, with a drawing of its inscription, 725–700 B.C., from tomb 168 of the Ischia necropolis (Villa Arbusto Archaeological Museum, Lake Ameno, Naples)

have existed during that early period. The discovery of architectural terracottas used for roof decoration, dating from the first half of the sixth century B.C. and the end of the fifth century B.C., also confirms that there were sacred buildings on the acropolis at that later time.

The port quarter developed at the foot of Mount Vico, and this too was put under the protection of a sanctuary located on a height in the Pastola district, on the hill slopes of Mezzavia. This sacred area was where the extraordinary complex of the "Stipe dei cavalli" (stipe: a collection of votive offerings found in sacred areas—in this case, horses) was brought to light; this collection is now exhibited in the Villa Arbusto Archaeological Museum at Lake Ameno. The dedication of these stipe was occasioned by the accidental uncovering, at the start of the sixth century B.C., of some eighth-century B.C. tombs; tradition required that the dead who had been disturbed be placated by a ritual which invested them with hero status. For this purpose a funeral pyre was built and banqueting vessels, scent containers, and a large vase, decorated with a border of weeping figures to represent mourners were laid upon it. Added to these were offerings of terracotta statuettes representing a hermaphrodite, carts pulled by mules, and model ships.

The cult was traced to the goddess Hera. The powerful queen of the gods enjoyed particular favor in Euboia, the region of Greece where most of the early colonists of Pithekoussai originated, and the success of all their expeditions was entrusted to her. Hera was in fact the goddess who protected navigators and at the same time safeguarded the independence of the houses and the stability of the family; her goodwill assured the favorable outcome of sea voyages and the successful development of a new settlement in foreign territory. The votive offerings placed in the "stipe dei cavalli" are an illustration of this multiple role. The presence of the model ships referred to the deity's typical role as protector of sailors; at the same time the offering of mules represented the wedding procession and, thereby, the importance of marriage in ensuring the group's survival by providing legitimate descendants.

The harbor quarter was where the potters plied their trade, probably not far from the clay quarries for which Pithekoussai was famous in ancient times. Kilns from the Hellenistic period can be seen today at an exhibition site set up below the Church of Saint Restituta.

A third quarter of the "city" was built on the Mezzavia hill, which bordered the southern edge of the flat port area and continued up to the acropolis on Mount Vico. A site has been excavated—and left on view—in the Mazzola area that was inhab-ited from eighth to the beginning of seventh centuries B.C., at which time it was destroyed by a landslide. Craftsmen skilled in metalwork were employed at Mezzavia. Traces of slag have been found in workshops where iron was forged, but also produced were ornaments in bronze and precious metals. One interesting discovery was a bronze pin, which had been discarded because of a fault in the molding. It is of a type well known all over the Italian world and was probably invented by craftsmen of Pithekoussai. Another discovery—of a small piece of lead weighing 8.79 g—is connected with the work done in precious metals: a lead weight originating from the homeland of the colonists, it appears to have been used in the precise work done by goldsmiths.

The discovery of the precision weight seems, from an archaeological point of view, effectively to confirm the information passed down by the ancient historical tradition of Pithekoussai, which, as mentioned above, was renowned for its "gold materials" (chryseia), meaning the gold artifacts made by expert craftsmen and widely exported to Campania and central Italy.

The Necropoleis

At the foot of Mount Vico, in the bay of San Montano, extensive excavation has been carried out in the necropoleis that were in use throughout the life of the settlement. During the eighth century B.C. there were two distinct types of funeral rite: the adults were cremated and the ashes deposited under small tumuli of stones; children, and people of subordinate rank, were buried in graves. The graves contained groups of bodies, probably family groups.

The burial goods give an extraordinary insight into the richness of the interwoven relationships in the community, but also of its many different components. They include ceramics imported from Greece—table services, vast scent bottles, large containers for the transport of wine and oil—and ornaments, many of them made from precious metals, such as seals and amulets from Phoenicia, Syria, and Egypt. Most worthy of note among them is a goblet imported from Rhodes, found in tomb number 168 and dating from around 730 B.C. It bears one of the earliest preserved Greek inscriptions: "I am the goblet of Nestor, fine to drink from, but whoever drinks from this goblet will instantly be seized by desire for the well-crowned Aphrodite." This is a parody of the goblet written about in the *Iliad* and inscribed with the name of the celebrated hero Nestor. Homer's version was a beautiful bronze vase with decorations inlaid in gold, so heavy that one person could hardly lift it when it was full. It was used not for wine but for an energy-giving beverage that served as a restorative for battle-weary heroes. This quote creates a delightful analogy— seen against the background of the free and easy atmosphere of the symposium—between the hero in the *Iliad*, who was the venerable and wise counselor of King Agamemnon, and the man who drank from the goblet of Pithekoussai and dedicated himself, not to feats of valor, but to lustful desire aroused by the goddess Aphrodite.

Another extraordinary item is a krater—a two-handled pot used in the symposium to serve a mixture of wine and water. The vessel, made at Pithekoussai and dating from the same era as the goblet, is decorated with a shipwreck scene. Beneath an overturned ship bob the corpses of sailors being eaten by fish—a terrible death for Greeks, who felt themselves under an obligation to honor the dead with funeral rites and who were troubled by thoughts of the presence of unsettled souls on earth; this scene also reflects the dangerous lives led by the courageous navigators who ventured abroad on the far seas.

The House at Punta Chiarito

We have already mentioned the agricultural villages that came into being very early on in the history of the island. One of these settlements has recently been explored on the promontory of Punta Chiarito, in the Forio d'Ischia district, immediately to the west of the Sant'Angelo peninsula. The excavation has uncovered remains of some houses dating from the second half of the eighth century B.C., built on an oval, semicircular, or polygonal floor plan, with walls of stone chips and pebbles, and a palisade to support a roof made of vegetable matter. The houses had already been abandoned when they were buried by ash from a volcanic eruption at the start of the seventh century B.C. The abandonment of the "artisans' quarter," in the Mezzavia area, was probably prompted by the same catastrophe, which, according to the ancient historians, was responsible for the departure of the entire population of the island.

The settlement at Punta Chiarito was reoccupied at the start of the sixth century B.C., and the old dwellings restored, but once again the new occupation was short-lived. It was, in fact, swept away by a torrent of mud before the middle of that century. Three houses from this phase were brought to light; the complete excavation of one oval-shaped structure has produced a rich cache, sealed inside a layer of mud and preserved in the condition it was in at the time the mudslide struck. The materials are exhibited in the National Museum at Naples together with a life-size reconstruction of the interior of the house.

The house, measuring 7×4 m, was partitioned into two areas, a kitchen with a hearth and an ample storeroom; it may also have had a second floor built on a wooden platform. The roof was tiled. In the room with the hearth were a loom, arms for defense and for hunting, tools for cutting wood, and fishing tackle. The storeroom contained big jars of provisions, amphoras, both locally made and imported Greek and Etruscan ones, for storing water, wine, and oil, and a service of tableware, also imported from Greece, including a krater, a large vessel used for liquids at the symposium.

Also recovered from the storeroom was a little hoard of small lumps of bronze, used as metal weights for a system of exchange that did not yet make use of coins. Outside the house were deer's antlers that had been worked into handles for tools or components for decorative ornaments.

CUMAE

History

According to ancient historical tradition, Cumae was the first of the Greek colonies established on the Italian mainland. Archaeological evidence also confirms the great antiquity of the settlement, which probably dates from no later than 730–720 B.C. The city was founded by two distinct

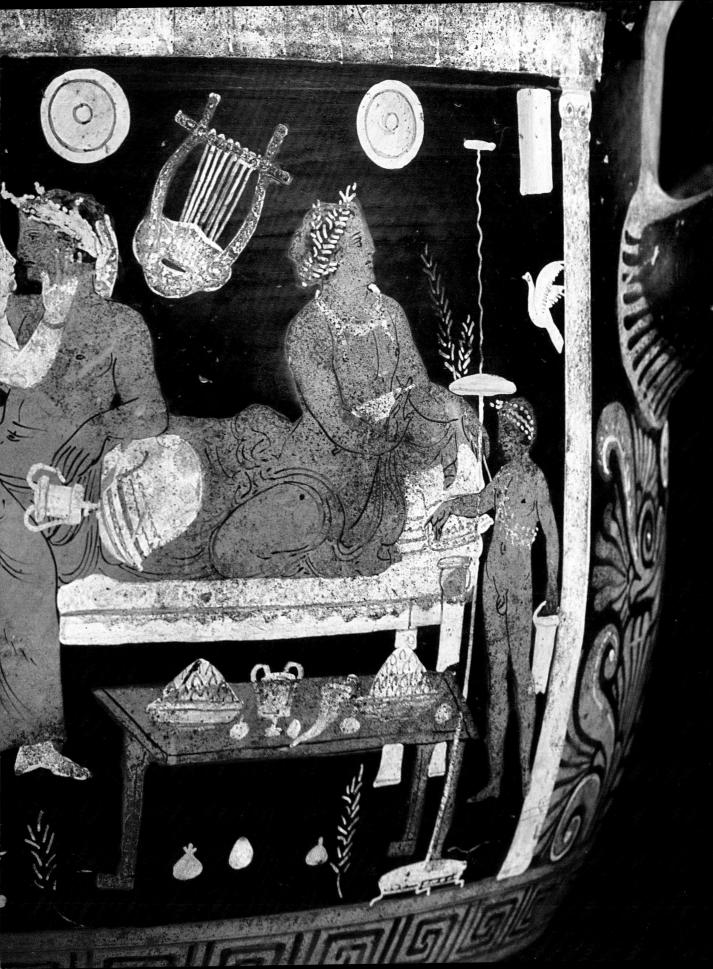

groups of colonizers working together: those who had already settled on Pithekoussai, originally from Kalchedon, and those coming from Kyme, a city situated on the northwest coast of the Anatolian peninsula, for which the new settlement was named. As leaders of the colonial expedition each group furnished an *ekistes* (founder of the colony), the first being Megastene, and the second Hippokles.

Situated in a formidable strategic position, at an obligatory point of passage for ships traveling the route that joined the upper and lower Tyrrhenian Sea, from its earliest beginnings Cumae played a leading role in developing trade and cultural relations between the Greek world and Lazio and Etruria. The colony also made similar strides with the indigenous centers in Campania. In 524 B.C., according to the historian Dionysios of Halicarnassos, Cumae repulsed an attack launched by a coalition of "Etruscans, Umbrians, and Dauni and many other barbarians." The historian adds that the invading army was motivated by greed, aroused by the city's prosperity. In the course of the battle, which took place at the gates of Cumae, Aristodamos first came to public notice. Twenty years later, having once again vanquished the Etruscans at Ariccia, in Lazio, he proclaimed himself tyrant and ruled for twenty years before being overthrown and killed.

In 474 B.C. the Etruscans moved once more against the Greek settlement. The encounter on this occasion took place at sea, in the waters offshore from the Phlegraean city, which, with the help of the Syracuse fleet, won a decisive victory. In the course of the fifth century B.C., Cumae saw its own role in the lower Tyrrhenian diminished by emerging powers such as Syracuse and neighboring Naples.

In 421 B.C. the city was conquered by the native Campanians who, as ancient traditional history emphasizes, retained "the customs and laws of the Greeks." During the First Samnite War and the Latin War of 343–338 B.C., Cumae proved itself a faithful ally to Rome and was rewarded in 334 B.C. by the right—albeit only partial—of citizenship. The city remained faithful to Rome even during the difficult periods of the war against Hannibal.

The City and Its Territory

Cumae was built at the northern limit of the Phlegraean Fields, on the coastline facing the islands of Procida and Ischia, sheltered to the south by Cape Miseno. Rising from the coastal plain was the limestone spur of Mount Cumae, which was occupied during the Iron Age (the ninth to the eighth centuries B.C.) by an indigenous village and subsequently became the acropolis of the Greek city at the foundation of the colony. The acropolis now faces a beach, but in ancient times it rose sheer above the sea; it was prolonged by a low spur, stretching out to the south and overlooking a small bay, now silted up, which was one of the city's ports.

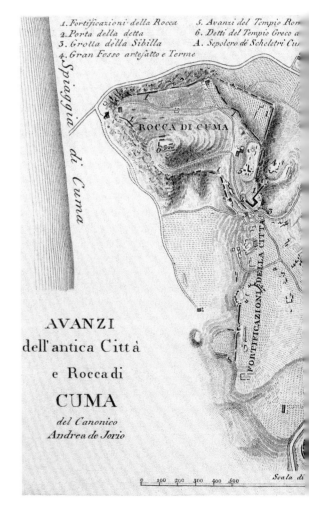

Another port was already in use when the Greeks arrived and was probably situated to the north, in the coastal lagoon of Lago di Licola—drained in 1922—which must originally have had access to the sea, thus offering a safe haven to shipping.

The inhabited area occupied a hollow of level ground lying between the acropolis and Mount Grillo to the east. At least during the sixth century B.C. this was defended by a boundary wall enclosing an area of 272 acres (110 hectares). The necropolis developed north of the inhabited area, extending for about 1.9 miles (3 km) along the old road that bordered the Lago di Licola as far as the northern limit of the city. The city was not very large; it covered an area of approximately 4 square miles (6 square km) from Lake Fusaro in the south to, as was stated above, the plain of Licola in the north, where a natural boundary was formed by an area of swamp bordering the much larger territory of the powerful Etruscan city of Capua.

An imposing wall built of limestone blocks, dating from the transitional period between the sixth and fifth centuries B.C., was found in this area. It is thought to be the remains of the imposing ditch, constructed for the dual purpose of drainage and defense with which, according to the ancient historians, the tyrant Aristodamos surrounded the entire territory of Cumae.

The city has a thousand years of history, which lasted until medieval times, when only the area around the acropolis was still inhabited. In this long series of events, the plan of the Greek colony has undergone many profound changes, but fortunately it is still possible to trace the basic elements.

The Acropolis

The formidable position of the acropolis, which dominates the coast and the plain, made it the defensive pivot of the fortification works and, at the same time, the religious fulcrum of the city. It consisted of two terraces and a lower spur to the south surrounding the small bay that formed the port. The principal sanctuaries were built on these elevated positions, from which they overlooked the dwellings and their land.

The system of fortifications of the acropolis was linked to the long gallery of the so-called Cavern of the Sybil, an impressive tunnel excavated in the limestone along the terrace that faces the entrance to the port. Considered at first to have been the site from which the Sybil of Cumae issued her prophesies, this imposing and immensely fascinating structure is now thought to have been a passageway to the upper defenses of the acropolis. Its present appearance is the result of successive transformations; in the original phase, dating from the fourth to the third centuries B.C., it must have consisted solely of the upper, trapezoidal part—a straight passage with no internal connections. In the Roman era the paved area was lowered and, as it was no longer required for defensive purposes, the gallery

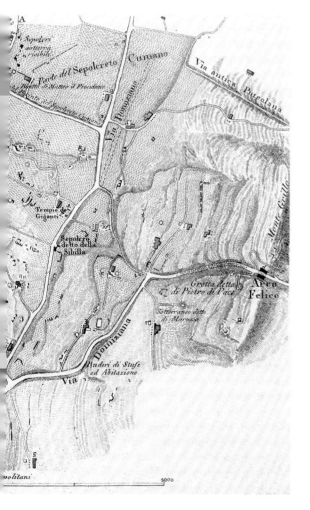

Daedalic statuette in terracotta, middle of the seventh century B.C., from Cumae (National Archaeological Museum, Naples)

Jewelry from Cumae
From the top:
Pair of gold fibulas in the form of leeches, fourth century B.C., from a collection of grave goods (Stevens Collection, National Archaeological Museum, Naples)

Electrum fibula in the form of dragon, end of eighth–beginning of seventh century B.C., from a grave from Fondo Maiorano (Stevens Collection, National Archaeological Museum, Naples)

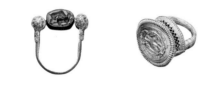

Gold ring with engraved sardonyx scarab, fourth century B.C., from a collection of grave goods (Stevens Collection, National Archaeological Museum, Naples)

Gold ring with setting formed of two thin disks, fourth century B.C., from a collection of grave goods (Stevens Collection, National Archaeological Museum, Naples)

Imported Greek cups, first half of the eighth century B.C., from tomb 3 in the necropolis of Cumae (National Archaeological Museum, Naples)

became a covered walkway, blending with the spectacular system of terraces which, from the sea, gave the acropolis a monumental appearance.

From the "Cavern of the Sibyl" the Via Sacra (the sacred way), constructed during the reign of the emperor Augustus, gives access to the acropolis. The road ended in an imposing gate giving onto a flight of steps leading up to the terrace of the Temple of Apollo. It is possible to discern phases in this gate dating from late antiquity and the medieval period, when a monumental square tower (the "Byzantine Tower") was built, but in some parts it is evident that these incorporated an older fortification built of limestone blocks. One can see some of the remains of these older fortifications from the slope that leads up to the Temple of Apollo. Today the temple is reached by walking up this slope, as it probably was before the monumental additions of the Augustan period.

The terrace, site of an ancient indigenous village that was destroyed when the colony was founded, was leveled and flattened during the second half of the sixth century B.C., when the sanctuary began to take on monumental dimensions. Terracing work dating from the Archaic period is discernible both from the east side, facing the "low city" and Mount Grillo, and along the north side opposite the Temple of Apollo, where several strata of the wall have survived.

In both these sectors the most ancient walls were rebuilt during the Hellenistic period by the construction of new outer layer of masonry and a filling of limestone chippings. The temple stood on the southeast corner of the terrace; a dedication from the Roman era confirms its dedication to Apollo, the god who, according to an ancient tradition, gave guidance to the colonists in the foundation of a city. Only the foundations from the Archaic period, oriented north–south, remain. The sacred building itself was probably a peripteral temple—it had a *cella* surrounded by a colonnade. In the Augustan era the temple underwent radical reconstruction, which included changing its orientation so that the steps at the entrance faced the edge of the terrace to the east. The *cella* faced onto an entrance porch decorated with Ionic columns, made of stone or bricks coated in stucco. In the

Black-figured *lekanis* cover depicting the slaughter of Astyanax, son of Hektor, by Neoptolemos during the taking of Troy, C Painter, 580–570 B.C., from Cumae (National Archaeological Museum, Naples)

The "Cave of the Sibyl" at Cumae (Naples)

built the labyrinth at Knossos. To escape from Minos, Daidalos flew to Cumae from Crete and decorated the doors of the temple with striking episodes from the saga of the Minotaur: the love between Pasiphae and the bull; the construction of the Labyrinth; and Theseus and Ariadne's thread. The only episode that the mythical craftsman did not have the courage to represent was the tragic flight of his son, Ikaros.

In the *Aeneid*, the Cave of the Sibyl is close to the Temple of Apollo; Aeneas visited the Sibyl to find out his destiny. Virgil describes her as a priestess who, possessed by Apollo, appeared in a trance-like state and produced obscure responses, writing her predictions on leaves and then letting them blow away in the wind, which jumbled up the sequence and therefore their meaning.

The figure of the Cumaean Sibyl had a particular importance in Roman religion. Historical tradition attributes to her the so-called Sibylline Books, a collection of oracles and ritual rules consulted in cases of particular emergency. According to legend, when the books were new, an old woman offered to sell them to King Tarquin the Proud. When the king said the price was too high and refused to pay it, the old woman twice burned three of the books—six in all—then returned to offer the remaining three to the king at the same price as before. Tarquin, finally convinced, bought them without bargaining.

The "Greek Cistern" dates from the Archaic period. It is big rectangular room, trapezoidal in section, with walls built of blocks, which must originally have risen up out of the ancient Campanian plain. It was probably the site of a monumental fountain associated with Apollo's medical powers. To one side of this "Greek Cistern" is a portico from the Hellenistic period through which one can catch a glimpse of the foundations. Anatomical votive offerings were found nearby, and could well confirm that a cult of healing waters existed. Finally, at the northern extremity of the terrace, one can see the remains of a temple from the Republican era, whose foundations were partially built over the aforementioned substructure from the Archaic period.

course of the same reconstruction work the monumental staircase was also built, cutting though the older fortifications.

Augustan propaganda was at the root of this redesign; the emperor put the cult of Apollo to new purpose, seeing in the god his own tutelary deity, the divine archer who routed the Egyptian fleet of Anthony and Cleopatra at Azio. Under the influence of this propaganda the temple at Cumae assumed a particular significance; Virgil, in the *Aeneid*, maintains that it was constructed by Daidalos, the mythical sculptor and craftsman who

The fascia of the building had two columns set into the anta walls, which project beyond those of the *cella*.

The Sacred Way linked the terrace of the Temple of Apollo with the upper terrace of the acropolis, on which stood the so-called Temple of Jove, though this attribution has not been confirmed. From the terrace where the temple stood, which is now reached by way of a tangle of scrub oak, there is a magnificent view over the whole extent of the ancient city. Of the first monumental phase of this temple, probably dating from the end of the sixth century B.C., there remain only the foundations built in blocks of limestone, reused at the time of the radical transformation of the temple in the first Imperial age. In this phase, the sacred building contained a *cella* that was divided in three along its length and enclosed by a perimeter wall of lattice-work pierced only by three narrow access doors on the short east side. It is assumed that the older sacred building also had a continuous enclosure around it, to conceal the space reserved for celebration of the cult. If this theory is correct, the "Temple of Jove" could have been connected with cult and mystery rites.

In the course of the fifth century A.D., the sacred building was transformed into a Paleochristian basilica, and numerous burial chambers found in the foundations of the Archaic temple date from this era. No later than the eighth century A.D. it became a Catholic cathedral dedicated to Saint Maximus.

A third sanctuary from the Archaic period was found on the southern prolongation of the acropolis in the locality of Fondo Valentino. In this area, excavations carried out in the 1800s uncovered the foundations of a sacred building which may be connected with findings of architectural terracottas, ceramics, and female statuettes from the Archaic period. The temple can be attributed to the goddess Hera, whose name is mentioned in some inscriptions on pottery from the sixth century B.C. Hera was the other great goddess in the pantheon of Cumae, venerated by the Greek colonizers not as the wife of Zeus but—as was the case in Pithekoussai—in her Archaic role as the female

deity who protected sailors and safeguarded the community's independence, defense, and reproduction. A historical tradition, certainly older than that already mentioned of Apollo, connects her directly with the founding of the city, at the time when the first colonists arrived from Pithekoussai and expelled the indigenous inhabitants living on the rock of the acropolis.

The position of the sanctuary in Fondo Valentino admirably illustrates the goddess' complex attributes. The temple stood just outside the city walls on the terrace that overlooks the entrance to the port—a location not unlike that of the sanctuary on Pithekoussai, probably also dedicated to Hera. The goddess oversaw the defense of the entrance to the city and at the same time guaranteed the effective protection of the navigators.

The role of Hera at Cumae is recorded in an extraordinary epigraphic document dating from the seventh century B.C., whose findspot is unknown. It is a small bronze disk bearing the inscription: "Hera will not permit a return to consult the oracle." The object was probably taken out accidentally on the occasion of a consultation with the oracle; it was the prerogative of the goddess, repository of all divine knowledge, to give or refuse an answer.

The Lower City

In the urban area at the foot of the acropolis, only one section of the Roman Forum has been extensively excavated. Linked to the fortifications that ring the acropolis and follow the ridge of its southern spur, the city walls ran toward the east and then along a line retraced in the north by the Strada Vicinale (local road) to Cumae, and in the south by the old Arco Felice road. In all probability the wall carried on up and along the crest of Mount Grillo. The building of the wall seems to date from the middle of the sixth century B.C., and shows numerous phases of construction. The phase that made the most impact monumentally dates from the time of the tyrant Aristodamos, at the end of the sixth century B.C. It consisted of two parallel lines of masonry built of limestone blocks, laid on edge,

Page 50: ruins of the "Temple of Jove" on the acropolis at Cumae (Naples). In the foreground, the baptismal font installed when the temple became a Paleochristian basilica

Page 51: ruins of the Temple of Apollo on the acropolis at Cumae (Naples)

in a position which supported a rampart. Of the old city's road network, the phase from the Roman era can be seen, with its basalt-surfaced streets, perhaps laid at the time when Roman citizenship was granted to the city in 334 B.C. Research is currently being undertaken to see whether it is possible to uncover a road system from the Greek era.

In A.D. 95 the Via Domiziana was built to improve communications between Rome and the important port of Pozzuoli. The road entered Cumae through the northern wall, crossed the Forum, and exited by a channel sliced though Mount Grillo. To secure this opening, the "Arco Felice" was inserted; an imposing piece of sophisticated engineering, it made a monumental entrance to the city and also served as a viaduct linking the two sides of Mount Grillo. Beneath it one can still see a wide, basalt-surfaced stretch of the Via Domiziana.

The Forum of the Roman city was built on the eastern slope of the acropolis; it was bounded to the west by the Capitolium and to the east by a Templars' building from the end of the first century A.D., incorporated into the "Masseria del Gigante" (Giant's Farmhouse). On the two remaining sides were monumental porticoes. The Forum's construction, like the road plan, dates from the urban reorganization undertaken in the wake of the granting of the right of citizenship. The area was, however, already occupied by buildings of a monumental nature from the fifth to the fourth centuries B.C., traces of which have come to light in recent excavations.

The construction of the Capitolium also dates from the final decades of the fourth century B.C., which links it with the planning of the Forum area. From the original phase of the temple, we find preserved the imposing podium built from limestone blocks, which faced the Forum square to the east. On the opposite, western façade there used to be an inscription on the pavement, engraved in Oscan, commemorating the dedication of the pavement by the Heii family, but this has been lost. The sacred building had a long, narrow *cella* with a room to the rear surrounded by a *peristasis* with tufa (a rock formed of volcanic ash fused by heat) columns.

The "Arco Felice" at Cumae
(Naples)

Silver didrachm with a woman's head on obverse and a shell with barley on reverse, 420–380 B.C., from Cumae
(National Archaeological Museum, Naples)

Funerary scene with matron and handmaiden, fourth century B.C., from the necropolis at Cumae (National Archaeological Museum, Naples)

PARTENOPE AND NAPLES

History

The history of Naples has its origins in the settlement at Partenope. The site took its name from the siren Partenope ("of the voice of virgins"), encountered by Odysseus in Homer's *Odyssey*. As was already mentioned in the section on Ischia, the stages in the voyage of Odysseus were drawn from the experiences passed on by Euboian mariners in the western Tyrrhenian Sea and were an archetypal representation of their perilous colonial adventures. The site of the Sirens is now believed to have been on the Sorrento peninsula, a peninsula difficult to round by sea because of the winds which blow in every direction, creating conditions in which it is easy to imagine one hears the insidious song that caused the ships to founder on the rocks. But Odysseus was too clever to fall into the trap, and, according to a mythical tradition that grew up out of Homer's epic tale, the three Sirens were so overcome that they threw themselves into the sea and drowned.

According to the myth, the body of Partenope, carried by the current, ended up on the beach at Naples; the siren was buried and the cult that developed around her tomb became a cornerstone of a new settlement. A more widely held historical version attributes the founding of Partenope to Cumaeans but, alongside this, an alternative theory links it to mariners from Rhodes who had landed there in the remote past. Assuming that this myth refers to the earlier, precolonial trading contacts, then it is most likely that the settlement was indeed founded by Cumaeans, as this would fit perfectly into the Phlegraean city's policy of expansion, which saw the creation, as far back as the end of the eighth century B.C., of satellite settlements at other key points in the Gulf of Naples, such as Pozzuoli and Miseno.

On the basis of archaeological data Partenope, founded in the first half of the seventh century B.C., was still flourishing at the start of the fifth century B.C., the time of the foundation of Neapolis (the

Recent excavations have uncovered the remains of some architectural decorations. Particularly splendid is a Doric-type frieze in tufa with metopes decorated with painted figures; the tiled roof was embellished with antefixes bearing winged female figures.

The temple underwent radical reconstruction in the first half of the first century B.C. and at the end of the next one. At that time it contained three colossal statues of Jove, Juno, and Minerva, now housed in the Archaeological Museum of Naples. The statue of Jove is carved entirely from marble, whereas those of Juno and Minerva are acroliths, with marble heads and extremities only, while the bodies were sculpted in a different material.

"New City"). From then on, the earlier settlement continued to coexist beside the more recent one, assuming the role of Paleapolis (the "Old City"). Historical tradition offers neither a date nor any account of the circumstances surrounding the foundation of Naples. It was, however, settled by Cumaeans, in fulfillment of a prophesy predicting the reestablishment of the cult of Partenope. The historian Strabo records that the tomb of the siren was still visible in his day.

According to the most recent archaeological evidence, the city was founded at the beginning of the fifth century B.C. Because of the excellent resource represented by its port, Naples quickly acquired a central importance among the cities of Campania, usurping Cumae's control of maritime traffic in the Gulf. In particular, it became the communication link preferred by Athens, which, according to historical tradition, figured largely in the foundation efforts of the city. The visit of the Athenian admiral Diotimos to Naples, probably in the second half of the fifth century B.C., was emblematic of the importance of the relationship between the two cities. Historical tradition records how Diotimos, in response to a demand by an oracle, instituted a contest of torch-light races in Partenope's honor.

At the end of the fifth century B.C., unlike Cumae, Naples was not overrun by the indigenous armies of Campania because it had been able to integrate the

Plan of Naples:
1. Greek walls
2. Square of Pietrasanta: parts of houses from the Hellenistic period
3. *Odeion*
4. Theater
5. San Paulo Maggiore: temple of the Dioskouroi
6. San Lorenzo Maggiore: structures from the Forum
e Necropolis of the Hellenistic period
g Necropolis of the Classical period
I Piazza Bellini
II Sant'Aniello a Caponapoli
III, IV, V Via Foria
VI Hellenistic *hypogeum* from Cristallini
VII Castelcapuano

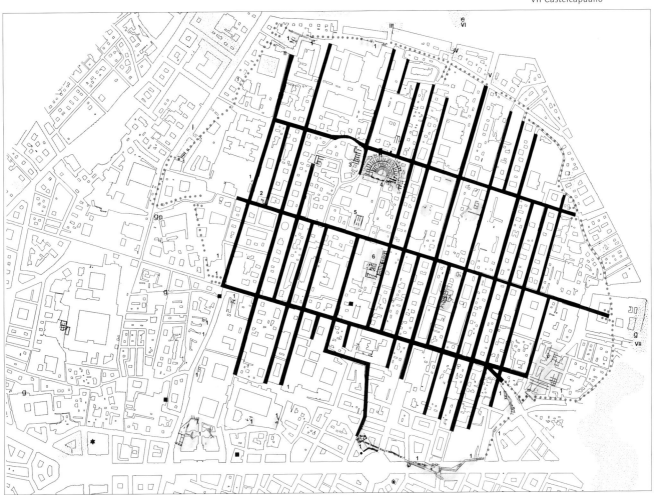

Red-figured Attic *pelike* (distinctively shaped amphora) depicting Helen emerging from the egg, between her brothers, the Dioskouroi Castor and Pollux; to the sides are Leda and Tindareos. Opposite page: side B of vase, depicting Dionysos between two maenads. Attributed to the "Painter of Nice," end of fifth century B.C., from Via San Tommaso d'Aquino at Naples (National Archaeological Museum, Naples)

Greek wall in Piazza Cavour, Naples

Roman Imperial era, when Naples became an ideal resort for recreation and rest.

The Old City: Partenope

Ancient Partenope was built on the hill slopes of Pizzofalcone, extending over the neighboring island of Megaride, which has long been joined to the mainland and is now the site of the Castel dell'Ovo. To understand the siting of the settlement one must envisage a very different landscape from that existing now: a promontory, stretching out to the sea, which extended into a deep creek and was equipped with a port situated, in all probability, within the area of what is now the Municipal Square.

The most consistent archaeological traces of Partenope were found in the remains of a necropolis that came to light at the foot of the Pizzofalcone hill and included items from two distinct periods. The earlier period spanned the last half of the seventh and the first half of the sixth century B.C. and confirms the antiquity of the settlement as it was handed down by historical tradition. The more recent one dates from the fourth century B.C., when Partenope became Paleapolis.

The New City: Naples

The Ancient Landscape and the Fortifications   The Greek city occupied a broad quadrilateral space of about 173 acres (70 hectares), which included the present Via Foria, Via Constantinopoli, the Corso Umberto, and the Via Carbonara. It covered a plain that was originally surrounded and protected on three sides by gorges, sloping down in a series of terraces toward the sea in the south. On this incline the inhabited platform ended in an escarpment cut transversely by natural riverbeds which gave access from the beach to the old city. The most recognizable of these today is that of the Via Mezzocannone.

The inhabited plain was fortified by a powerful wall which followed the uneven contour of the land, making full use of its defensive potential. There are several phases of construction evident in this fortification, though its original course remained unaltered. The earliest phase, dating from the founding of the city, was built of large

native element into its citizenship, even nominating some of them to the post of magistrate.

At the start of the Second Samnite War (327–324 B.C.) both the Romans and their adversaries (a coalition of Samnites from the Campanian city of Nola and others from Taranto) sought an alliance with Naples. In 327 B.C., during a dramatic meeting of the citizens, the Neapolitans chose to ally themselves with the enemies of Rome and received reinforcements from the Samnite and Nolan armies, which were garrisoned at the old settlement of Partenope—by then known as Paleapolis. The Romans besieged the city, placing their army between Naples and Paleapolis and, after a year of suffering the discomforts of war, the city's aristocracy decided to go over to the Roman side and delivered the city by stealth, putting the Samnites and the Nolans to flight. In that way Naples succeeded in obtaining favorable conditions for peace within the new framework of an alliance with Rome, which in turn was assured of a formidable naval base for commerce and military operations.

In exchange the city retained its autonomy, thus safeguarding its institutions, the use of its language, and its identity as a Greek city—a refined cultural image that continued to stand out in the limestone blocks set on edge, and was a single structure in some places and in others a double line of masonry reinforced internally and filled with rock chips.

In the second half of the fourth century B.C., perhaps during the second of the Samnite Wars, the old wall was reinforced by a new one built of limestone blocks placed in front of the earlier one, which then became the rear section of a double wall. Typical of this phase of construction were the so-called quarry marks: letters from the Greek alphabet cut into the blocks at the time they were extracted to facilitate counting and control. A later phase of restoration and reconstruction of the walls dates from the end of the third century B.C., the time of the wars with Hannibal (218–201 B.C.).

The city walls were furnished with towers, either square or circular. Traces of the fortifications are still visible in quite a few places in the historic center. The best ones can be found around Piazza Cavour, behind the school, and in Piazza Bellini. The former, which are a splendid sight, make up a part of the sector of the wall that lined the northern face of hill where the dwellings were situated, dominating the natural gorge squeezed today into the Via Foria. The wall, constructed with the orthostate blocks, dates from the fourth century B.C.; it was 9 m high with stepped foundations to counteract the slope of the land. It abutted an earlier wall slightly further back. The sequential link between the walls built in the fifth century B.C. and those built in the fourth century B.C. is clearly visible in a part in the Piazza Bellini, in which one can see both the older fortification with its double wall of blocks set on edge, and the more recent one with the orthostate blocks.

The Urban Settlement The urban part of the Greek city is still perfectly recognizable in the existing road network of the historic center, with its regular warp and weft of streets that cross at right angles, following the traces of the ancient ones. It was divided by three main thoroughfares running east/west (*plateiai*), following respectively, from north to south, the route of Via Anticaglia and Via Pisanelli, that of Via dei Tribunali and that of Via San Biagio dei Libri.

These main thoroughfares, of which the one corresponding to Via dei Tribunali was perhaps 14 m wide, were intersected by perpendicular minor streets (*stenopoi*) 3 m wide forming long, narrow blocks which, at least in the middle strip of the city, were 185 m long and 35 m wide. At the center of the urban web a broad, free area was set aside, six blocks long and two deep. Because in Roman times this area was occupied by the Forum, it is more than possible that in the past it was used as the public area (*agora*) of the Greek city. In the Imperial era the space used for the Forum was divided into two sectors, serving different purposes, to the north and south of the *plateia* that is now Via dei Tribunali: the northern one was reserved for religious functions and political gatherings and the one to the south for commercial activities. The first one contained the Temple of Dioskouroi and, to the north, along the *plateia* of Via Anticaglia, the two theaters, one of which was covered (the *odeion*), while the other, larger one, was open. The only remains of the temple are the foundations and a few columns incorporated into the façade of the Church of San Paulo Maggiore. Inside one of the buildings one can still see the tiers of seating and the foundations of the large theater.

The southern sector of the Forum was occupied by the extraordinary monumental complex that came to light beneath the basilica and the convent of San Lorenzo Maggiore. This complex, now open to the public, was divided into two terraces by a elaborate system of foundations that gave a dramatic monumental appearance to the slope of the hill. On the upper floor was the Macello (the building that housed the market), while the foundations of the *tholos* (the circular central body) have been preserved in the church cloisters. On the lower floor, the substructure contained a series of *tabernae* facing onto a *stenopos* and an arcade on the southern façade. The complex from the Roman era, which extended older terracing work, probably dated from the fifth to the end of the fourth century B.C. Of this, elements remain of its retaining wall made up of limestone blocks, reused in later parts of the wall or located beneath their foundations.

Silver diadrachm with a woman's head on obverse and an anthropomorphic bull on reverse, 450–430 B.C., from Naples (National Archaeological Museum, Naples)

The Acropolis The acropolis was located in the area of the Church of Sant'Agniello a Caponapoli, on the northwest summit of the inhabited plateau. It was here that the city's principal sanctuary was located. Its later enlargement required some changes to a part of the urban grid.

In the absence of monumental remains, a cult area came to light beneath the convent of San Gaudioso with the discovery of one or more deposits of votive offerings that contained busts and terracotta statuettes of women related to the cult of Demeter and her daughter Kore, deities connected with death but also with reproduction and female fertility. The bulk of this votive evidence was from the second half of the fourth century B.C., but some statuettes found in excavations in an adjacent part are proof of an older use of the sacred complex. These date from the fifth century B.C. and even, in one case, actually from the last quarter of the sixth century B.C., leaving open the possibility that the sanctuary existed at the time of old Partenope.

The Necropoleis The *necropoleis* extended, as always, beyond the city walls. The principal burial ground, in use since the first days of the settlement, was located in the area of Castel Capuano, on the east side of the city. Its uninterrupted use continued from the fifth century B.C. to the end of the Roman era. On the northeast slopes, along the gorge of Via Foria and Via Carbonara in the Sanità quarter, however, numerous tombs from the Hellenistic period have been uncovered, dating from the fourth to the middle of the third centuries B.C. This find centers on large funeral *hypogea* (burial chambers carved from the rock) dug out of the seam of limestone, some of them furnished with imposing façades, that were located in showy positions along the access roads to the city.

Particularly deserving of mention among these are a group of four *hypogea* in Via Cristallini in the quarter of the Virgins. One of them stands out for its richly embellished architectural partitions and its painted decorations. Access to these *hypogea* was through the imposing façade decorated with half-columns and perhaps crowned by a tympanum (triangular area forming front of a pediment). The vestibule, with cover and pitched roof and, to the rear, a double bench at the center of which was a sculpted table for offerings. The funeral chamber opened on a lower level and was accessed via a stairway.

The walls were lined with plaster columns with elegant capitals decorated with a little Medusa head; between them ran painted decorations of branches, banners, and laurel wreaths framing sarcophagi made in the form of funeral couches with decorated feet and mattresses and cushions carved out of the stone. Finally, on either side of the entrance door were paintings of candelabra and bronze vases. The most impressive element of the whole decorative spectacle was the large head of Medusa carved on a disk, decorated with leaves and snakes, which crowned the vaulted arch of the far wall. The representation of the monster whose gaze, according to the myth, turned everything she looked upon to stone, evokes the infernal passage of death, the voyage of no return beyond the Doors of Hades.

Poseidonia/Paestum

Above: plan of Paestum
indicating the principal
functional areas

On opposite page: the
"Temple of Ceres" (*Athenaion*)

History

Poseidonia was founded by Achaian colonists from Sybaris with the help of a contingent from Doris; history does not record the names of the founders or the date of its foundation, but, calculated from the archaeological evidence available, this can be set around 600 B.C.

According to a brief reference by Strabo, before the actual colony was founded, a preliminary "fortified outpost" (*teichos*) was set up beside the sea; according to one theory, this was located more to the south, on the Agropolis promontory, where historical tradition places the sanctuary of Poseidon, the god who gave his name to Poseidonia.

In the course of the sixth century B.C. the city took on a preeminent role in the southern Tyrrhenian area. Its influence in dealing with the native people of Lucania (Oinotria) made it possible for exiles from Phocaea to found Velia (Elea) around 540 B.C., and a little later they helped the Sybarite refugees to found Laos after they had been obliged to abandon their city following its violent destruction in 510 B.C., thus creating a new Sybaris near the river Laos (the present-day Lao). Poseidonia appeared in many respects to take on the entire political and commercial legacy of the ancient mother city—something that is clearly indicated by coins minted in the first half of the fifth century B.C., which were of a weight and design similar to the Sybarite coinage.

At the end of the fifth century B.C. the city was conquered by the indigenous Lucanians; this event does not appear in the historical record, but is indicated by the important changes in funeral rites and in the type and contents of the tombs that can be seen to have taken place in the *necropoleis* around this time. It was probably the Lucanians who changed the name of the city from Poseidonia to Paestum. Their "conquest" should not be seen as a military defeat of a Greek city by "barbarians," but rather as the result of a process of integration and political recognition of the

indigenous element in the Greek structure. Above all, this is confirmed by the fact that everything within the city—the monuments and public spaces and the religious and political institutions set up by the Greek colonists—continued during the time of the Lucanians as before.

Between 334 and 331 B.C., the city was occupied by, or perhaps even welcomed, Alexander the Molossan, king of Epyros, called to Taranto to lead the Italiote League against the Lucanians, the Brettii, and the Samnites. In the third century B.C., after the war against Pyrrhos, Paestum came under the control of Rome, which, in 273 B.C., made it a colony, with rights under Latin law. The city went on to become one of the naval allies of Rome, to whom it continued to give considerable support during the difficult years of the Second Punic War (218–201 B.C.).

The establishment of the Roman colony caused a major reorganization of the inhabited area. The most obvious sign of this was the position of the Forum, which occupied an area smaller than that of the *agora* of the Greek city and encroached on the north face of the southern sanctuary.

The Organization of the City

The city was built on the left bank of the river Sele, at the center of a fertile coastal plain, which the settlers intended primarily to exploit for agricultural purposes. The inhabited area developed on a limestone platform, slightly elevated above the plain. To the west was a lagoon connected to the sea that offered good port facilities; this has now disappeared. A second lagoon opened out about 1.9 miles (3 km) to the south, near the mouth of the river Solofrone, in the Linora area, and it was there that the maritime quarter of the city was situated, connected by a road leading to Agropolis. Along this road, a short distance from Poseidonia, excavations revealed the necropolis near Tempa del Prete, which included the famous "Tomb of the Diver," now on display in the Archaeological Museum of Paestum.

The urban development covered an area of about 439 acres (120 hectares) and was surrounded by an imposing, and still well preserved, perimeter wall almost 3 miles (5 km) long. This

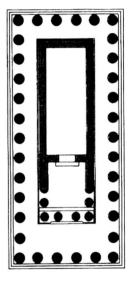

Plan of the Temple of Neptune
(Temple of Apollo [?])

On opposite page: the Temple
of Neptune and, to the right,
the Basilica (*Heraion*)

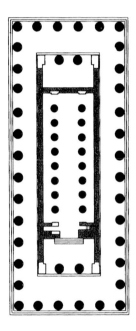

was made up of two lines of masonry connected internally by straps, filled with earth and stones. Originally it was at least 7 m high, surrounded by a ditch and protected by 28 round or square towers or, in one case, pentagonal. Three of the four access gates—the Siren Gate on the east side, the Justice Gate to the south, and the Marine Gate to the west—have been preserved almost intact, while the last one, the Golden Gate to the north, was badly damaged during the building of the modern road, which today still crosses the area of the old city. The present state of the wall is the result of successive additions which, in some sections at least, included doubling the size of the earlier phase. While the reinforcements could possibly have been connected to the withdrawal of the Latin colony, the construction seems to go back to the Lucanian phase of the city, at the end of the fourth century B.C.

In its essential arrangement, however, the plan of the urban center, where the residential area was divided by a wide central strip destined for public functions, dates from the time of the foundation of the city. This central strip was divided into three areas and extended over approximately 0.6 of a mile (1 km) from north to south, and more than 330 yards (300 m) from east to west. The middle part was the vast square (*agora*) where the major political activities took place; the sectors to the north and south, where the great stone temples are still to be found, contained the sanctuaries.

In the northern sanctuary was the Temple of Athena (the so-called Temple of Ceres); the southern one contained the temple dedicated to Hera, known as the Basilica and the so-called Temple of Poseidon, probably dedicated to Apollo. The three temples have a common orientation that differs from that of the streets and blocks. This seems to indicate a desire to differentiate the space reserved for the gods from that used by men, a policy also applied in the ancient temple buildings at Metapontion.

The two sanctuaries developed in the earliest days of the colony at the beginning of the fourth century B.C.; the street network, while planned at the time of the foundation of the city was, however, only constructed at a later stage, in the last quarter

of the sixth century B.C. It was arranged on two main arteries (*plateiai*) that crossed the city at right angles from one of the gates in the wall to another. The road that ran north–south from the Golden Gate to the Justice Gate was 10 m wide; the one running east–west from the Siren Gate to the Marine Gate was 20 m wide. Two more *plateiai* ran parallel to the east–west road, to the north and the south at a distance of 330 yards (300 m). These three east–west roads were intersected at right angles by minor streets (*stenopoi*), 5 m wide, thereby forming long, narrow blocks 35 × 273 m in size.

The north–south *plateiai* separated the residential sector from the public area. The central east–west artery and the parallel one to the north, separated the area of the *agora* from the two parts used for the sanctuaries. The modern road, which crosses the archaeological area, has interrupted the continuous expanse of the *agora*, which extended beyond it, behind the present Archaeological Museum. Thanks to recent excavations, it has been possible to verify that there was a sacred area on the southeast border of the main square, indicated by the presence of votive pits that were in use from at least the fifth century and until the second and first centuries B.C.

The Urban Sanctuaries

The Northern Sanctuary The northern sanctuary was situated on the highest point of the city, in a prominent position compared to the adjacent *agora*. It was dedicated to Athena from at least the time that the great stone temple (the so-called Temple of Ceres) was built at the end of the sixth century B.C. It is not impossible, however, that the goddess was venerated right from the first phase of development of the sanctuary, dating from the start of the sixth century B.C. In addition to Athena, Aphrodite, Dionysos, and Demeter were probably also represented in the sacred area. The cult of Athena continued during the Roman period, when she was worshiped under the Latin name of Minerva, who was associated with of Jupiter.

The oldest monument in the sanctuary was a small temple built at the beginning of the sixth century B.C., of which the foundations are still

Below: plan of the Basilica

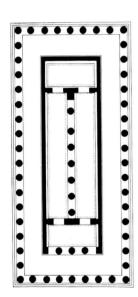

visible to the southeast of the main temple. To the east it is possible to see an ancient treasury (*thesauros*) and a series of porticoes.

The Temple of Athena constituted the monumental center of the sanctuary. It faced east toward the great altar where the cult was celebrated. The temple itself, 14.5 × 32.9 m in size, was surrounded by a continuous Doric colonnade (*peristasis*)—six columns on the short and thirteen on the long sides. The very deep *cella* was approached via an entrance porch (*pronaos*) of which each of the anta walls ended in a half-column. The façade was embellished with six Ionic columns, four set in the façade and two behind it, parallel to the anta walls. At the sides of the door between the *cella* and the porch were two shafts for ladders that gave access to the roof for maintenance work.

The *peristasis*, the porch with its colonnade, and the *cella* were built on different levels, rising progressively and connected by steps; this accentuated the monumental aspect of the building and, in particular, emphasized the importance of the *cella*, which housed the cult statue. The decoration of the façade and the temple elevation was particularly fine, especially in its use of two kinds of stone. Along the architrave ran a frieze of metopes and triglyphs framed in cornices (*cymatia*) decorated with ovolos, leaves, and wave motifs. The protruding parts of the pitched roof (*geisa*) supported by the lower façade, visible from below, were decorated with coffers that framed rosettes and stars. Above that were the eaves (*cyma*) with lion-head spouts alternating with palmettes on the long sides or just palmettes on front edges of the roof over the façade.

The Southern Sanctuary The activities of the city's most important cults were celebrated in the southern sanctuary, especially that of Hera, the goddess who guaranteed the fertility of both women and the soil and, at the same time, guided and defended the colony. Some votive inscriptions indicate that other deities were also present, in a complex system of cults that continued to flourish even during the Roman era. Worthy of note among these are Apollo, to whom was probably dedicated the "Temple of Poseidon," and

Zeus, venerated in an Archaic inscription with the attribute Xenios (the "hospitable"). A magnificent terracotta cult statue from 530–520 B.C. now exhibited in the Archaeological Museum is probably also a representation of the god. The married couple Zeus and Hera are depicted in later terracottas, bearing testimony to the importance of the marriage rite as the focal point of legitimate reproduction in the community. Use of the sacred area was not restricted to the Greeks; also found here were the remains of terracotta roofs decorated in a style indicating that they were gifts dedicated to the centers by "Etruscanized" Campanians.

The southern sanctuary, too, had its beginnings in the first half of the sixth century B.C. Among the earliest items uncovered was a series of stone stelai—perhaps connected, as at Metapontion, to the cult of Apollo—that was found in the southern section of the sanctuary where the altars and temples were built. On one of these is inscribed the name of the centaur Chiron, expert in the medical arts and tutor of Achilles; another had been reverently preserved in a small box made from stone slabs. An altar from the same period came to light northwest of the Temple of Hera (the so-called Basilica), as did the remains of a roof in terracotta tiles from an older sacred building.

The first stone temple was the Doric one dedicated to Hera, begun shortly after the middle of the sixth century B.C. but only finished around 520–510 B.C., after two changes to the original plans for the *cella*. Measuring 24.5 × 54.3 m, it had a *peristasis* of nine by eighteen columns and was made up of a deep *cella*, a closed room to the rear (*adyton*), which probably contained the cult statue, and an entrance porch (*pronaos*) with three columns between the antas.

The *cella* was divided into two parts by a central line of six columns, and linked to both the *pronaos* and the *adyton* by two pairs of entrances that allowed people to circulate in the interior when participation in the cult warranted. The capitals were decorated in fine relief. At the bases they bear a decoration of leaves, in some cases with a sculpted ring of palmettes and lotus flowers or rosettes above it.

The architrave of the *peristasis* supported a frieze of metopes and triglyphs, framed in two cornices sculpted in a different stone and decorated with ovolos and leaves. The edge of the roof was sumptuously decorated with polychrome terracottas. This was made up of a box facing, an upper fascia with fake lion-head spouts on the long sides, a kind of paterae on the short, sloping sides which served as eaves (*cyma*), and antefixes in the form of palmettes and lotus flowers securing the last row of tiles on the roof.

The second stone building was the "Temple of Poseidon," probably dedicated, as mentioned before, to Apollo. The temple, measuring 24.3 × 59.9 m, dates from a little before the middle of the fifth century B.C. Built in the now canonical Doric order, it had a *peristasis* of six by fourteen columns which surrounded the *cella* with a room open to the rear (*opisthodomos*) and a front porch (*pronaos*) with two columns between the antas.

The *cella* was divided into three rows by two lines of seven columns each, which supported a second sequence of smaller columns; the upper floor was reached by two stairways, of which the two shafts can be seen on either side of the door into the *cella*. The elevation had a continuous frieze of metopes and triglyphs, surmounted by the protruding cornice of the roof (*geison*).

East of the two temples were the altars. Of the two in front of the "Temple of Poseidon," the one nearest to the sacred building dates from the Roman era. Behind it, only traces remain of a larger altar from the fifth century B.C. Along the northern side of the sanctuary were other sacred buildings, not all of them positively identifiable. Under the *macellum,* or market, from the Roman period one can glimpse the foundations of a temple from the end of the sixth century B.C. which, unlike the larger temples, was aligned with the road and extended to the west beneath the so-called Curia. Immediately to the east was a large sacred complex dedicated to the cult of Asklepios, the healer god and son of Apollo. The phase now visible is from the fourth century B.C., and consists of an enclosure with a courtyard with porticoes, a waiting area for the faithful, and a wide recessed platform where the cult was practiced. Near the sacred enclosure there should have been a shrine to Aphrodite, indicated by inscriptions to the goddess found on vases.

To the south of the temple situated beneath the "Curia" and the *macellum* stood the "Amphiprostyle Temple," built during the transition from the fourth to the third century B.C. over an older cult structure. The building, of which only the foundations remain, was oriented in the same way as the major temples, and was 30 m long and 8 m wide. It faced the east and was divided into four areas: two frontal spaces with a façade with four columns; an entrance porch; and a deep *cella*, paved with stone slabs, in the center of which there was probably a sacred well. According to a recent theory, the temple could have been dedicated to Herakles. In the final part of the fourth century B.C., or at the start of the following century, the sanctuary was enclosed by a massive wall built of blocks (*temenos*), easily recognizable along the western side, while its northern boundary was marked by a portico that bordered the main east–west *plateiai*.

The *Agora*

The *agora* was made up of an enormous square which extended over an area of 330 × 300 m. For a long time it remained simply an open space set aside for meetings and the citizens' political activities. It was divided into two sectors, though it is unlikely that this division occurred before the second half of the fourth century B.C. The area to the north was the site—as will be seen—of important public monuments and retained its original politico-sacred function; that to the south was reserved more for the commercial activities of the marketplace. The Latin colony's Forum was later situated here, and even extended over part of the southern sanctuary.

In the northern sector of the *agora* are two monuments that are emblematic of the city's political image: the assembly building (*ekklesiasterion*) and a shrine to a heroic cult (the so-called "Hypogeal Shrine"). Both monuments were built in the Greek period of the city and, after continuing to be used during the Lucanian period, were buried at the time of the Roman conquest—an act

Hydria (water vessel) in bronze, 520–510 B.C., from the "Hypogeal Shrine" at Poseidonia (National Archaeological Museum, Paestum-Salerno)

performed by the new colonists to signal the definitive rupture with the political structure of the past. The assembly building, circular in shape, was constructed in 480–470 B.C. Steps carved out of the rock which led to the two entrances are still visible. Other buildings were probably added to it, set on an embankment enclosed by a perimeter wall, also circular. Inside this building archaeologists found a votive stele dating from the end of the fourth or the beginning of the third century B.C. which bears a dedication to Zeus written in the Oscan dialect of the Lucanians. The stele was probably surmounted by a statuette of the god, donated by one of the city magistrates, and evidently implies that the circular building and the political activities

carried on there came under the auspices of the principal celestial deity.

The *ekklesiasterion* was surrounded by a large enclosed space which also contained other buildings; one, a quadrangular shrine situated immediately to the north of the assembly building, was probably erected at the end of the fourth century B.C. Another small temple, about 20 m to the west, may have been dedicated to Zeus. Built of reused materials, it dates from the fourth century B.C.; the *cella,* paved with stone slabs, still remains, but whether there was a *pronaos* with antas is uncertain.

The "Hypogeal Shrine," built around 520 B.C., was further to the west. It consisted of a great tomb

divided into compartments, partially carved out of the rock, with walls made of stone blocks. It was roofed with stone slabs, with a second, pitched roof placed over the top of the first and tiled. The monument was probably covered by an earth mound. In reality the tomb was a cenotaph and contained no body. However, it did contain an exceptional find, now exhibited in the Archaeological Museum: on a table in the center were five iron swords and along the walls were eight large bronze vases, intended for the storage of wine and honey. Beside these was a black-figured Attic amphora depicting the arrival of Herakles on Olympos. What explanation can one give for this exceptional monument? The presence of a tomb within the dwelling area is a complete anomaly; the dead were strictly segregated from the living and the *necropoleis*— with a few exceptions, such as at Taranto—were placed outside the city walls. Only people of exceptionally high rank were buried within the city. The "Hypogeal Shrine" was therefore the likely seat of a heroic cult (*heroon*), placed in the heart of the square at the center of the ancient city's political area. In this way, Poseidonia venerated the mythical hero, founder of the colony.

With the arrival of the Romans the cult was suspended. The Latin colonization was like a refoundation of the city and the old hero was no longer required. The shrine was encircled with a wall of rectangular stone blocks and covered with earth.

On page 74: metope with dancers, 500 B.C., from the Temple of Hera at the mouth of the river Sele (National Archaeological Museum, Paestum-Salerno)

The Territory

From the moment of its foundation, control of the city's vast territory was ensured by a ring of sanctuaries that marked its boundaries and put the colony's new lands under divine protection. To the north, about 5.5 miles (9 km) from the city, a famous sanctuary dedicated to Hera was built near the bank of the river Sele, a natural boundary beyond which lay the territory of the Etruscans, who occupied an important permanent settlement at Pontecagno. The sanctuary of Poseidon was undoubtedly situated on the southern slopes opposite this, on the Agropolis promontory, where traces of a sacred building from the Archaic period have indeed been found.

In the interior, where the coastal plain gave way to hills, ancient tradition places a sanctuary, still to be discovered, dedicated to Artemis, the virgin goddess of the wild countryside. Other cult places formed a kind of "sacred belt" around the city and separated the area reserved as living space from the *necropoleis.*

At a greater distance, little country sanctuaries were created on the edges of the cultivated areas, near springs, or beside roads. These protected the city's agricultural areas and at the same time served to associate the peasant population with a cult dedicated not to Hera but to Demeter, the goddess who gave the first grain to humankind.

The rich and fertile land around Poseidonia does not seem to have played a great part in the first centuries of the life of the colony, as it was particularly suited to cereal production, a form of cultivation that did not require farmers to live permanently outside the city. A drastic change in this situation in the middle of the fourth century B.C. is indicated by the discovery of number of small burial grounds, evidence of an increase in family-type farms occupying the agrarian area, though this movement seems to have exhausted itself in the course of a generation. The part of the countryside that was permanently occupied was centered either on the plain or on the line of hills around the city, and concentrated on the development of specialized crops, such as olives and vines, whose cultivation needed a workforce that was constantly in attendance.

The Sanctuary of Hera at the Mouth of the River Sele

According to ancient tradition, the sanctuary was founded by Jason, leader of the Argonauts, in thanks for the protection afforded to the heroes' expedition on their voyage aboard the Argo. It was venerated under the name of "Argive."

The saga of the Argonauts offered a mythical parallel to the adventures of the colonists and lent them legitimacy, together with the right to conquer unknown lands. The sanctuary was built in an area of swamp close to the river, in the kind of wild country that best represented the power of the goddess. Its foundation dates from the beginning of the sixth century B.C., the same as that of the city. The earliest evidence of the cult is an ash altar, enclosed in the first half of the sixth century B.C. by a wall and incorporated into one of the altars of the great temple buildings at the end of the sixth century B.C. Two monumental porticoes situated to the northeast of the altar date from the first half of the century; the first housed what was possibly a banqueting room (*hestiatorian*), connected with public ceremonies held at the sanctuary.

Dating from around 570–560 B.C. is a series of exceptional sculpted metopes which, at the time they were found, were assumed to be connected with a building (the so-called *Thesauros*) that, as will be seen, was in fact built during the transitional period between the fourth and the third century B.C. Thanks to a recent discovery, these can now be attributed to a sacred building of which only traces of the foundations remain beneath the aforementioned temple from the Archaic period. According to one theory about its original form, the older temple had a colonnade (*peristasis*) of six columns on the short side, twelve on the long, and a *cella*, measuring 7.58 by 21.50 to 22 m, with a small porch (*pronaos*) preceded by four columns.

The metopes were sculpted in a style evoking the Ionic order of eastern Greece, using two different techniques: one group is characterized by very strong relief which makes the figures stand out boldly; in the other the molding is much less pronounced and the contours of the figures, which were probably finished in color, assume a much greater importance. Their decoration has been

Above: lion-head spout, 500 B.C., from the Temple of Hera at the mouth of the river Sele (National Archaeological Museum, Paestum-Salerno)

Below: archaic metope with Herakles slaying the giant Halcyoneus, 560–550 B.C., from the Temple of Hera at the mouth of the river Sele (National Archaeological Museum, Paestum-Salerno)

Painted side from the Tomb of the Diver, depicting lovers, 480–470 B.C., from the Tempa del Prete necropolis (National Archaeological Museum, Paestum-Salerno)

drawn from a rich mythological repertoire: the labors of Herakles play an important role, as do images of such heroes as Achilles, Ajax, and Odysseus, and pictures of the episodes from the adventures of Orestes and the saga of the Argonauts, who were connected—as we have seen—with the foundation of the sanctuary itself.

The building of the great temple at the center of the sacred area dates from the sixth century B.C. The temple, measuring about 18.60 × 39 m, has survived only to the level of its foundations. Built in the Doric order, it faced east and had a *cella* with an entrance porch (*pronaos*) and a

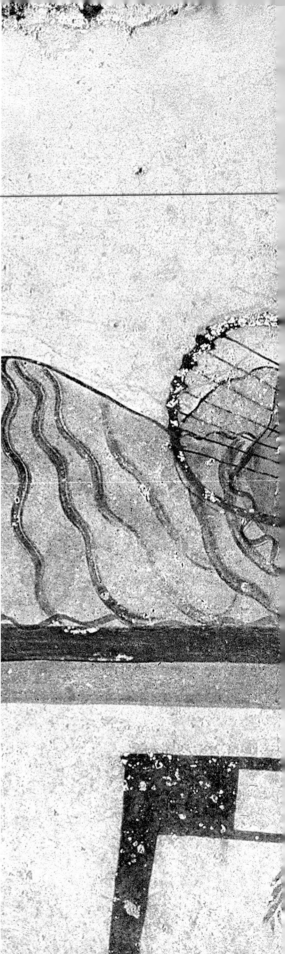

On pages 78–79: cover slab from the Tomb of the Diver, 480–470 B.C., from the Tempa del Prete necropolis (National Archaeological Museum, Paestum-Salerno)

closed room to the rear (*adyton*), surrounded by a *peristasis* of eight by seventeen columns. Two stepped towers were placed at the entrance to the *cella;* the anta walls of the *pronaos* ended in half-columns, with two Ionic columns set between them. Particular emphasis was applied to the façade, broadening the width of the ambulatory between the *pronaos* and the colonnade of the *peristasis.* As for the elevation: the architrave was surmounted by a frieze of metopes and triglyphs, framed by two limestone cornices decorated with a double garland of leaves (*cymatia*). The metopes were tastefully decorated in the Ionic order with sculpted couples of female dancers following the lead of a single companion—a theme employed also in friezes found in Sybaris

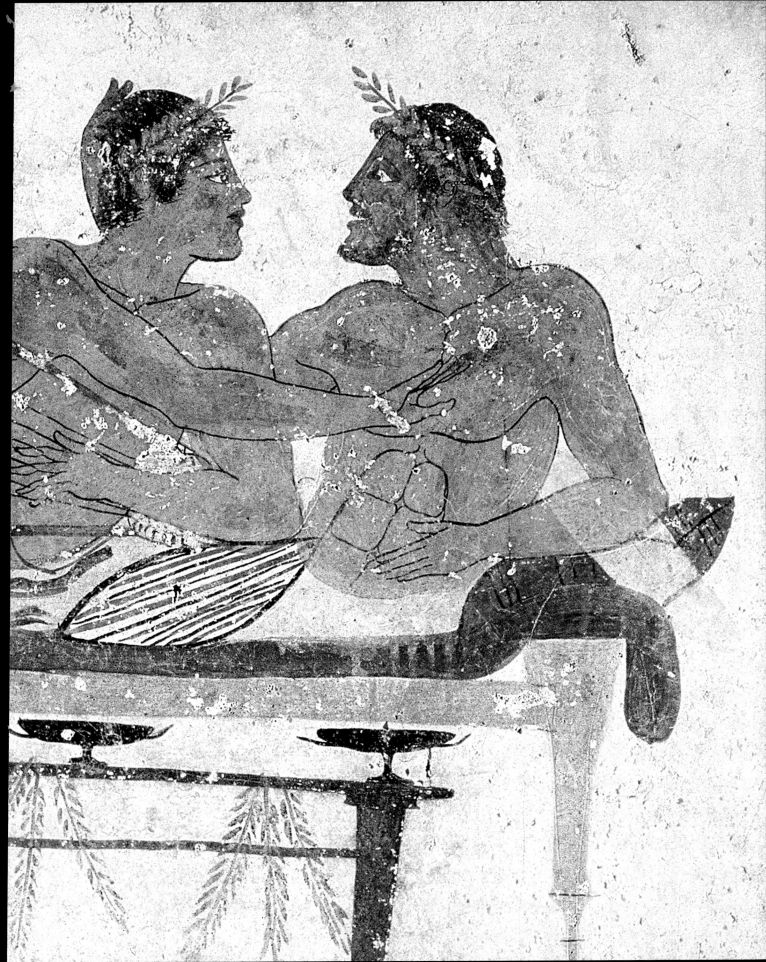

and Rhegion. The roof was furnished with eaves with lion-head spouts, also in limestone.

To the east of the temple two altars of different sizes have been found; the smaller one—enclosed, as mentioned previously—was the ancient ash altar. Seriously damaged at the end of the fifth century B.C., the sanctuary was extensively rebuilt in the Lucanian era. At the beginning of the fourth century B.C., apart from the restoration of the temple, two structures were built over the top of the one from the Archaic period, using reclaimed materials, with porticoes set at right angles to each other. Libation ceremonies took place in one, while the other seems to have taken over the function of the real banqueting hall from the older portico.

To the north of the main temple, and with the same orientation, was the so-called *Thesauros,* to which the older series of metopes were originally thought to have belonged. This misconception came about because, during excavation of the building, numerous architectural items from the Archaic period were recovered, but recent excavations have placed the temple's date at the transition from the fourth to the third century B.C.

The *Thesauros,* measuring 12.60 × 9.05 m, was built on a bed of sand dug out to create a small canal for the drainage of the surface water. It took the form of a simple rectangle, with an east-facing façade, probably with antas. The precise information now available about the time it was built suggests that the architectural elements from the Archaic period, found close by, probably came originally from other buildings and were reused to decorate its elevation.

The construction of one last important monument, in use in the sanctuary during the Lucanian era, dates from the beginning of the fourth century B.C. It was destroyed at the time of the foundation of the Roman colony. This building was built on a square plan, 12 × 12 m, about 80 m to the east of a temple, of which the foundations—a stone plinth worked in folded elements—have been preserved. Its small entrance faced south and it was probably covered by a roof with a pitch of one in four.

Found in its interior was a marble statue of Hera; the goddess was represented seated on a throne, wearing a tall, cylindrical headdress (*polos*) while her hands, which rested on her lap, held a cup for libation and a pomegranate.

The iconography of Hera derives from that of the statue sculpted by the famous sculptor Polykleitos for the sanctuary of the goddess in the Greek city of Argos. This was consciously exploited by the Lucanians in an attempt to create for themselves a prestigious origin similar to that of the Greeks, under the protection of Argive Hera. The same iconographic type was repeated in thousands of statuettes in terracotta produced locally, dedicated simultaneously in all the sanctuaries of the city, and diffused even more widely around the plain of the river Sele.

The square building stood on the site of an earlier collection of votives that had accumulated between the end of the sixth and the end of the fifth centuries B.C., and has yielded, in its turn, an immense deposit of votive items dating from as late as the early decades of the third century B.C. So it was probably not by chance that it was built on the site of the older cult site, whose function it appears, in some way, to have inherited.

The votive material was most probably contemporary with the life of the monumental building. Apart from statuettes of females, jewelry, containers for cosmetics, and jars for storing or preparing food, it included numerous loomweights and also a large number of coins. It was a vast, cohesive collection, all related to the feminine world, which exalted the role of women as pivotal to the household; an expression of beauty but, at the same time, repository and custodian of the wealth and patrimony of the family.

The plan of the square building also seems to confirm this cultural picture. In fact its architecture evokes that of the domestic scene and, in particular, that part of the house used as a storeroom (*pyrgos*). With this in mind, it has been suggested that the loomweights that were recovered were perhaps connected with the ancient ritual of weaving sacred vestments in honor of Hera.

Velia

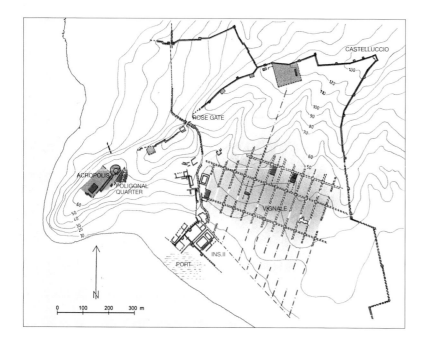

attempt to establish themselves near the colony at Alania (Aleria) in Corsica, which failed only a few years later after a violent naval battle against the allied fleets of the Etruscans and the Carthaginians, the Phocaean exiles headed for the coast of Southern Italy. Having first taken refuge at Rhegion (Reggio Calabria), they succeeded in founding a new city in a bay south of the Gulf of Poseidonia. They called the city Hyele, taken from the word for a spring, which subsequently became Elea. The name Velia, given to the city by the Romans, also derives from the same root, Hyele.

Historical tradition reveals that the indigenous Oinotrian population conceded the land for the foundation of Velia to the Greeks, and that neighboring Poseidonia made no objection. Because only a limited amount of agricultural land was available to them, the founders made use of their traditional skills as courageous sailors and enterprising merchants, and the city lived for the most part on the resources available by sea; Velia took on an essential and lasting role in controlling the trade that was developing along the Tyrrhenian coast toward Cumae, Rome, and Etruria, and still farther north to Marseilles, a city also founded by Phokaian colonists.

But Velia was not just a city of merchants; it produced some great intellectuals, such as the philosophers Parmenides and Zeno. Zeno founded the "Eleatic School" and was at the same time deeply committed to political activities.

Urban plan of Velia

On opposite page: the "Rose Gate" (Porta Rosa). In fore-ground: the Archaic gate

History

Velia (Elea) was founded around 540 B.C. by refugees from Phocaea, a Greek city located on the coast of Asia Minor. At the time of the Persian conquest of Phocaea, around 545 B.C., the inhabitants fled en masse. Some of them undertook the long sea voyage to the western Tyrrhenian, a journey described by the historian Herodotos. After an

Marble head of Parmenides,
first century B.C., from Velia
(Depository of the Superintendency,
Ascea Marina-Salerno)

Parmenides, born in the second half of the sixth century B.C., produced legislation which long governed the city; Zeno, during the fifth century B.C., fought against the installation of a tyrannical government. A portrait of Parmenides, together with commemorative ones of three people responsible for founding the school of medicine, was discovered in a large public complex dating to the Augustan age that was possibly dedicated to the Imperial cult.

Because of the strength of its constitution, according to the historian Strabo, Velia, with a smaller population and fewer resources, victoriously resisted a joint attack by the Poseidonians and the Lucanians, probably during the second half of the fifth century B.C. In order to strengthen its defenses against the Lucanians and Dionysios I, tyrant of Syracuse, at the start of the fourth century B.C., the city joined the Italiote League, sending its fleet to assist in military actions. After the fall of Taranto in 272 B.C., it became one of Rome's naval allies.

The Urban Area, Port, and Fortifications
The city was established on the coast of Cilento, about 18.6 miles (30 km) south of Poseidonia, not far from modern Ascea. The living area occupied a rocky height and the slopes to its rear. In ancient times the area on which the city was built looked very different from the way it does now. The acropolis consisted of a protected promontory within the gulf, overlooking two small, shallow bays to the north and south, which provided natural harbors; these have long since been filled in. One was fed by the river Alento and the river Palistro, and the other by the small river Santa Barbara.

It is possible that the old port was located in the southern bay, which was in a very favorable position, well sheltered from the winds, at the foot of the acropolis. Southeast of this an artificial basin was constructed, possibly in the fifth century B.C., to counter the effects of progressive silting up of the bay. Its location was discovered via geophysical prospecting.

From the Archaic period onward the city was protected by a wide perimeter wall that followed the natural contours of the land, enclosing an area of about 100 hectares. Within this space, the urban area was divided into three distinct quarters separated by large open spaces: the acropolis and the two quarters of the "low city" that corresponded to the two small inhabited areas of the coastal plain. The principal thoroughfare of the city was built to link these two quarters to a deep valley that led up to the eastern ridge of the hill of the acropolis; only the quarter south of the acropolis has been systematically investigated. In the earliest phase of their construction, the walls were built of mud brick set on a foundation socle of polygonal masonry—that is, built from rough-hewn polygonal stones rather than rectangular ones, according to a technique much used in eastern Greece, original home of the colonists.

In the course of the first half of the fifth century B.C., the wall took on monumental proportions with the addition of towers and new stretches built on a foundation of square blocks, which extended the older walls into the residential area, separating the three quarters of the acropolis and the "low city." Major reconstruction work on the walls, in accordance with the most up-to-date ideas about defense, also took place at the end of the fourth century B.C., with extensive restoration and the construction of more new towers. The walls, rebuilt following the same route as the older ones, were laid with fired bricks, or blocks of sandstone alternating with blocks of limestone set in a checkerboard pattern, built on a socle of square stone blocks.

On the southeastern slope of the acropolis was an extension of the fortifications, with walls built of square blocks with rusticated decoration and round towers, which encircled the oldest area of the port, by then filled in and occupied by houses. The South Marine Gate, flanked by a robust square tower and reached by a ramp that descended toward the beach, dates from this time. The road that linked the southern quarter to the one in the north started from that point, then ran on through the valley on the eastern side of the hill of the acropolis. Paved with limestone blocks and flanked by ditches and embankments faced

with sand, the road led to a saddle protected by a gate built of square blocks, perhaps dating from the Archaic period. At a later date the entrance was given a more imposing aspect by the construction of the extraordinary "Rose Gate," one of the most notable monuments in Velia. It consists of an arch built from sandstone blocks, surmounted by a second small arch, possibly intended to join the two sides of the entrance. On the southwestern side, the escarpment of this entrance was reinforced by imposing terracing constructed of cement work laid with square blocks. The gate, which probably dates from the first half of the third century B.C., was found by investigators to have been blocked with a wall built of courses of stone blocks and both fired and unfired bricks. This wall, removed in the course of the excavations, has recently been recognized as something added after the vault and the lateral reinforcing walls had been built; together with other details about its construction, this leads us to the conclusion that the gate was never completely finished.

The Acropolis and the Sanctuary

Any attempt at reading the architectural plan of the acropolis is badly hampered by the presence of a Norman-Angevin castle built between the eleventh and thirteenth centuries A.D., which greatly altered the original topography of the hill.

The earliest inhabited area, that of the first generation of colonists, was on the acropolis. Of the Archaic settlement there remains primarily a sector along the southeast slope of the hill; its upper area, situated on the terrace of the acropolis, was destroyed around 480 B.C. by the construction of the city's principal sanctuary.

The quarter along the slopes of the acropolis was built on three terraces with the same orientation as a road, about 3.5 m wide, which ran up to the top of the hill. Smaller streets connected to this larger one, some of which passed through the narrow spaces between the houses; these streets followed the natural slopes of the hill and also served to drain away the water. A large canal for the collection of water, lined with polygonal tiles, ran

Silver didrachm with the head of Athena on obverse and a lion with Nike in flight on reverse, fourth to third century B.C., (National Archaeological Museum, Naples)

along a natural hollow on the eastern boundary of the area that has been explored. Because they were built on a slope, the houses had to withstand the uneven force of gravity. For this reason the outside walls, which also served as retaining walls, were built of stone polygonal work while the remaining ones were built of mud brick on a stone foundation. The houses were small and rectangular in shape, generally consisting of two rooms with beaten-earth floors, sometimes with a well and a courtyard. They probably had tiled roofs.

A different type of dwelling was found on the terrace overlooking the acropolis, used later as the sanctuary to Poseidon Asphaleios. Originally the type consisted of a quadrangular room reached by way of a small portico, and it was later augmented by two more rooms and a courtyard. On the upper terrace, in the southwest sector of the plateau facing the sea, the acropolis also included a sacred area. Connected with this in some way are a splendid wall in polygonal work, perhaps part of the terracing, that was discovered at the front of the west façade of the temple from the Classic period, and the remains of bronze containers and vase inscriptions from the start of the fifth century B.C. dedicated to Hera and Athena—both goddesses concerned with marine matters and the protection of navigation.

Around 480 B.C. the arrangement on the acropolis underwent radical change. The dwellings were dismantled so that the entire sector could be taken over for public use with the building of a monumental sanctuary. The hill was then "monumentalized": an imposing retaining wall, built from big parallelepiped blocks, lined the upper terrace and formed the enclosure for the sanctuary on the heights, while lower down in the valley a later terrace wall of square stone blocks has obliterated the old living area.

On the summit of the plateau was a temple, probably dedicated to Pallas (of the city) Athena, of which the part dating from the fourth century B.C. has been preserved. The imposing tower of the medieval castle was built over it, destroying the walls. All that remain are the massive foundations and a corner of the *cella* with a small opening (*opisthodomos*) in the rear wall. The foundations of the temple have overlain an older layer of foundations made from blocks which perhaps belonged to an earlier phase in the construction of the sacred building.

At the northeast corner of the terracing surrounding the sanctuary was the theater, partly carved out of the rocky slope of the hill and partly built on an artificially constructed platform. Today only the phase from the Imperial Roman era in the second and third centuries A.D. is visible. However, this covers two earlier phases, dating from the first half of the fifth century B.C. and the end of the fourth century B.C., of which there remain the ruins of the outside walls, and also the steps from the more recent of the two phases. The construction of the theater, together with the erection of the temple building, was part of the original plan to "monumentalize" the acropolis. Apart from the production of plays, the theater was probably also used to house citizens' political assemblies.

In the course of the fourth century B.C. other monumental buildings were added to the acropolis. Dating from this period was a road which, by way of a ramp, ran through the ancient terracing and round the steps of the theater, to connect with the monumental entrance, now visible beneath the foundations of the chapel belonging to the medieval castle. On the upper terrace was a portico bordering the shorter side of the temple, rebuilt to its original size, while on the lower terrace, a long, covered building dating from the end of the century, which may have been an offertory, abutted the wall surrounding the sanctuary. On the ridge of the acropolis, to the northeast, were other natural terraces along which ran the northern wall that formed part of the fortifications of the ancient city.

As far back as the fifth century B.C. other sanctuaries were built on these terraces, as if to extend the sacred protection all around the city. The one nearest to the acropolis, already occupied in the Archaic period, was dedicated to Poseidon. The sacred area was made up of a square with gates on three sides, in which inscriptions on stone stelai from the first half of the fourth century B.C., add *Asphaleios* to the name of the god. The literal meaning of the word is "who offers security" and invokes the connection of Poseidon to everything concerned with navigation. On a second terrace, situated above the "Rose Gate," a courtyard paved with bricks has come to light, containing a portico and a little temple with a porch with antas in its center. Finally, in the north, was the larger enclosure dedicated to Zeus, built on artificially leveled ground, also made up of a paved square with a great altar from the fifth century B.C. A series of stone stelai from the same period identify the deities venerated and specify their particular competence: Zeus, as the protector of navigators, was given the attributes Orios (protector of the winds or patron of good seasons), Pompaios (he who guides), and Olympios Kairos, the deity who personifies good times, the joyous moment—in ancient tradition the youngest of the sons of Zeus.

Worth noting, finally, is the recent theory that a big public complex from the Hellenistic period, built on another terrace now established as supporting the main square (*agora*) of the Greek city, was a sanctuary dedicated to Apollo's son Asklepios, the healing god. The monumental complex was situated in the central strip of the old city, corresponding to the long valley up which the road climbs toward the "Rose Gate." On the lower terrace of this complex one can see a circular space surrounded by walls, with doors on three sides, bounded at the front by a fountain.

The Southern Quarter of the Low City

The quarter situated on the hill of the acropolis has been the site of many excavations, which have produced evidence of the way the ancient dwelling area was organized, from the moment of foundation to the end of the Roman era. The traces of the earliest urbanization date from the beginning of the fifth century B.C. A survey carried out to a greater depth in the so-called *Roman Block II*—the great public building already mentioned that was possibly connected with the Imperial cult—found the remains of houses built on stone plinths, with

walls of mud brick, tiled pitched roofs, and beaten-earth floors. The archaic quarter, sheltered from the sea and at the lower end of the slope of the hill, was destroyed by a terrible flood around the middle of the fifth century B.C. Shortly afterward, the site was reused for a new settlement comprising narrow blocks, 37.5 m long. The blocks were formed by three main streets (*plateiai*) running east–west crossed at right angles by minor streets (*stenopoi*) which climbed the slope in a northeasterly direction, stopping probably only when the rise became too steep. The network of blocks was bounded in the south by a *plateia*, running parallel to the line of the city wall, which intersected the other streets transversely.

The houses occupied quasi-rectangular lots that were subdivided by minor streets, 2 m wide, parallel to the others. In the examples that have come to light, the polygonal brickwork technique was still used. At the end of the fourth century B.C.,

blocks were laid out in the free space between the main southern artery and the city wall; these were larger than the earlier ones, and set at right angles to the wall and the road. The houses within them were built around a central courtyard (*peristyle*) and a well, some of them embellished with mosaic paving and fine furnishings.

Dating from the first decade of the third century B.C. was an extraordinary bath building built immediately below the presumed sanctuary to Asklepios and fed by an eternal spring. The complex, one of the oldest in Magna Graecia, contained a dressing room paved with hexagonal terracotta tiles, a large area intended for collective bathing, and an area containing oval terracotta individual baths. The large room for collective bathing was paved with mosaics set in a mortar made from tiles and amphora, crushed and mixed with lime, and had a square in the center with geometric motifs and a lateral frieze of dolphins. The baths were heated by means of a furnace that sent hot air through interlinked chambers beneath the floor, which was supported by pilasters made from crushed bricks.

The Territory

Ancient history emphasizes the small size of the Velia territory, laying heavy stress on the city's maritime activities. In fact, Velia had access to a land area that, while undoubtedly limited, was not without resources. The coastal plains of the Alento (smaller in antiquity than today) and the hilly spurs that surrounded them were well stocked with wood, which was indispensable in the building of ships, and were ideal for specialized agriculture and the raising of livestock.

While there are some traces of occupation during the Archaic period, the land appears to have been more fully exploited from the fourth century B.C. onward. A defensive system of small forts was developed along the "frontier" provided by the hills at the same time the land along the edges of the plain was covered in small, permanently occupied farms. An important settlement has been excavated at Moio della Civitella, 9.3 miles (15 km) northeast of Velia at the pass leading to the Calore Valley. Occupied as early as the end of the sixth century B.C., the settlement was fortified at the start of the fourth century B.C. An imposing wall of square stone blocks, still in an excellent state of preservation, encircles a dwelling area (arranged on terraces) built during the third century B.C.

Lokroi Epizephyrioi

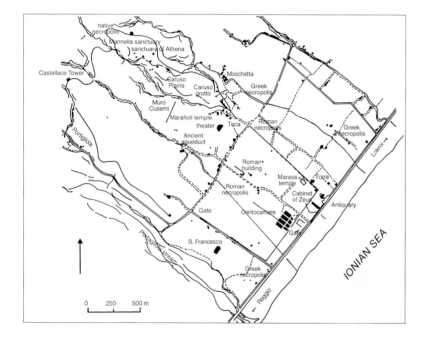

Plan of Lokroi Epizephyrioi

On opposite page: base and columns of the Ionic temple in the Marasa quarter, Lokroi (Reggio Calabria)

History

The city was founded by colonists who came from the region of Lokris in central Greece. The colonial contingent was probably made up of people either from western Lokris, or Punizia, situated beside the Euboian Sea, or from eastern or Ozolian Lokris, facing the Gulf of Corinth.

According to Strabo, the colonists, under the leadership of Evante, the *ekistes* (founder of the colony), first installed themselves at Cape Zephyrios (now Cape Bruzzano), with the consent of the indigenous population, the Sicels. The event occurred in the same period in which Archytas of Corinth was traveling to Sicily and for that reason—as will be seen—the foundation was also contemporary with that of Kroton. Only four or five years later, the Lokroians expelled the indigenous people, having tricked them with a faked truce, and transferred to their permanent site near to the Esopis hill, about 12 miles (20 km) north of Cape Zephyrios. Traditional history sets the date the city was founded in 679–678 B.C. or 673–672 B.C., but archaeological evidence puts it earlier, at the end of the eighth century B.C.

According to historical tradition passed down by Aristotle, the colonists were slaves who ran away with women from the most noble Lokrian families, with whom they had come into contact during the absence of the husbands, who were away in Sparta fighting in the Messenian War. This tradition, which caused lively debates among the ancient people, demonstrates the importance the government of the colony attached to the narrow aristocratic elite of the "One Hundred Houses" from which the Lokrian women came and also the emphasis placed on the female as the most important element in the continuity of the noble families.

Top picture: large circular
kiln built of mud bricks, at
Centocamere, Lokroi (Reggio
Calabria)

Lower picture: in foreground:
the wall of the *cella* of the
proto-Archaic temple, end of
the seventh to the beginning
of the sixth century B.C.;
farther back: three slabs from
the mouth of the sacred pit
placed in the center of the
naos of the Ionic temple,
480–470 B.C., in the
sanctuary in the Marasa
quarter, Lokroi (Reggio Calabria)

Right: the theater at Lokroi

From the end of the seventh century B.C.
onward, the city extended its domain onto the
Tyrrhenian side of the peninsula, into the fertile
plain of Gioia Tauro, where the colonies of Medma
(now Rosarno, near the Mesima River) and
Hipponion (now Vibo Valentia) were founded, and
subsequently occupied the site of Metauro (present-day Gioia Tauro), already established by the
Kalchedian Zankle (Messina). In the first half of the
fifth century B.C., the Lokroian influence pushed
farther north, occupying the site of Temesa, already
under the control of Sybaris and Kroton.

A great victory was won by the city, aided by
Rhegion, around the middle of the sixth century
B.C. against the more powerful people of Kroton,
in a battle close to the Sagra River, at the edge of the
Greek city of Kaulonia. Tradition emphasizes the
miraculous nature of the victory, obtained against
overwhelming forces, thanks to the intervention of
the Dioskouroi, who lined up in battle on the side
of the Lokroians.

The agreement with Rhegion broke off in
477 B.C. when the latter, under the leadership of the
tyrant Anassilaos, attacked Lokroi but was held
back by the intervention of the tyrant of Syracuse,
Hieron. From this time onward, a solid alliance
with the Sicilian city existed, which lasted right
through the fifth and fourth centuries B.C. In the
last thirty years of the fifth century B.C., Lokroi several times supported Syracuse against Athens and
Rhegion, providing a solid support base for the
Spartans and Syracusans during the Athenian
expedition to Sicily in 415–413 B.C. The alliance
with the Sicilian city was consolidated at the start
of the fourth century B.C., when Dionysios I, tyrant
of Syracuse, married a noble Lokroian woman and
became a part of the city's aristocracy.

Lokroi became the linchpin in the policy of
expansion exercised by Dionysios in Southern
Italy, at the expense of Kroton and the Italiote
League led by that city. Lokroi found him a potent
ally against the Italic Lucanian people. Probably
around 356 B.C., in view of old alliances and the fact
that he was descended from a Lokroian woman, the
city welcomed Dionysios II (Dionysios' son) after
he fled from Syracuse. However, he behaved in a
despotic and oppressive manner toward his hosts

and was expelled in 346 B.C. One of the consequences of the revolt against Dionysios II was the replacement of the former oligarchic regime by a moderate democracy. The introduction of a monetary system in the city, very late by comparison with other cities of Magna Graecia, may also have been connected with this.

From the middle of the fourth century B.C. onward, Lokroi had to face threats from the Brettii, who, according to ancient tradition, were an offshoot of the Lucanians. In order to defend itself against this menace, in 282 B.C. the city welcomed a Roman garrison, and then immediately afterward put themselves in the hands of Pyrrhos, king of Epyros; in 276 B.C. this sovereign pillaged the treasure of one of the principal sanctuaries of the city, which was dedicated to Kore/Persephone.

With the defeat of Pyrrhos, the colony became part of the naval alliance of Rome. During the Second Punic War, Lokroi went over to Hannibal and was conquered by Scipio in 205 B.C. The city was put under the control of Quaestor Pleminio, who committed some terrible atrocities including, yet again, the pillaging of the treasure of Persephone. His behavior was subsequently punished by the Roman senate and the Lokroians were reunited with all that had been stolen from them.

The Territory and the Urban Settlement

The city covered the area that is now occupied by the districts of Locri and Portigliola, on the Ionian Sea side of the province of Reggio Calabria. It was not far from the line of the beach, which in ancient times must have been further inland from where it is today.

According to tradition, its territory consisted of the area between the Sagra and the Halex rivers which, respectively, marked the northern boundary with the Greek city of Kaulonia, and with that of Rhegion to the south. The Sagra most probably corresponds to the modern river Turbulo, and the Halex is the Galati, the mouth of which is near Cape Spartivento. The inhabited area occupied a strip of coastal plain and a hilly zone beyond it culminating in the low hills of Castellace, Abbadessa, and Mannella, separated by valleys that cut through them longitudinally. Judging from the oldest materials found in the necropolis and around the area of the sanctuary, the colony was founded at the end of the eighth century B.C. in an area formerly settled by native peoples. A site from the Iron Age was found inside the urban area. Immediately to the north, regular groups of cave tombs found on the upland plain of Ianchina indicate that there was a settlement there in the eighth century B.C. At the time of the foundation of Lokroi, the native population, overshadowed by the Greek city, abandoned this settlement and moved further inland.

The ancient city occupied an area of 568 acres (230 hectares) surrounded by an imposing wall which, at least during the Hellenistic period, extended from the sea to the high ground toward the interior. Outside this wall were the *necropoleis*, of which the most notable was the one to the southeast at a site called Lucifero.

Two phases of the construction of the walls are apparent, the earlier one contemporary with the planning of the urban layout, toward the middle of the sixth century B.C., when the wall enclosed only the area of the low city. Extensive stretches from the

The Ludovisi Throne, in marble: left, female playing flute; center, the birth of Venus; right, cloaked woman burning grains of incense, 460–450 B.C., from Lokroi, found at the Villa Ludovisi in Rome in 1887 (National Museum, Rome)

Archaic period have come to light in the southern sector, near Centocamere, and to the east in the region of Parapezza and Marsala, where outer layers of masonry laid with sandstone and limestone blocks were added.

In both these sectors the gates are recognizable. On the southern side of the wall, facing toward the sea, there was a monumental entrance dating from the end of the sixth century B.C., consisting of a *propylon* with antas and a central column, set on solid block paving. On the east side the access was a simple opening with the jambs of the gate set at an angle to the wall. At Centocamere, the walls made a sharp bend to the east to avoid the "U-shaped *Stoa*," an older monument belonging, as will be seen, to a sanctuary of Aphrodite, situated immediately outside the urban area. This building was so close to the wall that the wall's defensive value is doubtful. At least on the southern side, the wall seems to have been built purely to mark the limit of the urban area and to assert its cultural and political influence over the surrounding strip developed around the landing area of the port. In the fourth century B.C., the ancient part of the wall served as a wing against which were placed the two porticoes, built on either side of the imposing *propylon*.

The city wall was rebuilt between the fourth and third centuries B.C., reusing the older structure, which was reinforced and perhaps heightened with mud brick. A typical example of this type of reconstruction was found in the stretch of wall at Centocamere, where the most recently constructed part incorporated the earlier one, deviating in its course so that it went in a straight line over the by-then demolished "U-shaped *Stoa*." At the eastern corner of the same stretch are two structures built of stone blocks, running at right angles to the wall, which in all probability were the jetties of a harbor basin.

The Hellenistic fortification was protected by square, elliptical, and circular towers, set at angles to the wall or beside the gates. Perhaps it was only during this phase that a defensive system was set up in the highest part of the city, with walls that followed the crests of the hills and protected the valleys below, blocking or channeling the flow of the river with imposing barriers. On the summit of the hills at Castellace and Mannella, big square towers dominated the surrounding countryside, giving wide-range control over the territory. Plans for the urban settlement, specifically the low city, were drawn up around the middle of the sixth century B.C., while the hilly sector was occupied only sporadically, with large areas left wild.

The "Dromo," a modern road following the coast which divides the "low city" from the hill zone and ends on the west side at one of the city gates, must have been built along the route of an ancient artery. In the Centocamere area, archaeologists have excavated an extensive area of the residential sector, built on a road (*plateia*) 14 m wide which ran in an east–west direction toward the port in the Parapezza area. Long, narrow blocks, separated by minor roads meeting the *plateia* at right angles (*stenopoi*), which varied from 4 to 4.5 m in width, faced onto the north side of this road.

The strip of valley between the *plateia* and the city wall was only built up during the course of the fourth century B.C., with blocks of varying sizes and roads that were not at right angles to the main artery. Extensive excavations in the Centocamere

quarter have produced valuable data about the use to which this sector in the old city was put, and also about the style of the houses, with their cobbled foundations and mudbrick walls. Naturally, the discoveries were largely from the most recent phase of the inhabited area, from the end of the fourth to the end of the third century B.C. Until the middle

eter, and still has the upper floor of mud brick that was used for firing, the perforated grid on which the items were placed, and the chamber below ground, where the fire burned. The kilns, often in groups, were placed inside the houses, and the presence of wells, little drainage channels, and other equipment needed for working and cleaning

of the third century B.C. the quarter was given over to artisans, as evidenced by the numerous kilns for the production of vases, bricks and architectural fittings, and figured terracottas. A large example of one of these kilns can be seen in the residential area near the city walls, south of the *plateia*. It is circular in shape, almost 4 m in diam-

the clay make it possible to identify the space occupied by the workshop.

Both inside and outside the city walls, the streets were lined with small shops and their storerooms, made up of lots with an open space in front and a small room to the rear. In the second half of the third century B.C. the southern quarter

was converted to a different purpose; the kilns were dismantled and the internal area of the blocks was divided into lots varying from 120 to 250 square meters. Houses were now built around a large central open courtyard and, in addition to the residential part, which by this time generally included two stories, also had rooms destined for stabling and storage or, perhaps in the grander houses, accommodation for slaves.

The Sanctuaries

The sanctuaries were situated along the perimeter of the city walls, both inside and outside, forming a "sacred belt" for the protection of the city.

The Urban Sanctuaries and the Theater In the southeast sector of the walls, near the port in the Parapezza quarter, there was an important sanctuary in the area of Marasa that was probably dedicated to Aphrodite. Numerous phases of its construction can be seen today, although because of depredations in the nineteenth century they are in a precarious state of preservation. The temple had a different orientation from that of the urban center—a ritual characteristic already noted at Poseidonia and at Metapontion.

The older installation, dating from the end of the seventh or the start of the sixth century B.C., was a building measuring 22 × 8 m, made up of a long, narrow *cella* and a small entrance porch (*pronaos*). The *cella* was probably divided internally into two halves by a central line of columns. All that is preserved of this building is part of the foundations around the perimeter of the *cella* and *pronaos,* built from sandstone blocks. The walls were built from mud brick, and the entablature and columns were wood. The interior of the *cella* was lined with terracotta slabs painted with geometric motifs. A similar terracotta lining also protected the roof, which had eaves (*cyma*) decorated with a braid motif.

At the southern corner of the temple there are three bases for offerings. Another two similar foundations, perhaps pertaining to altars, are visible nearer the front, close to the great altar of the temple from the fifth century B.C. In the third quarter

of the sixth century B.C., the temple was again rebuilt in mud brick and wood, with limestone blocks used for its foundations. The interior of the partially modified *cella* had a line of square blocks that served as bases for the columns and an open room to the rear (*opisthodomos*), which probably had a façade of four columns. There must also have been a similar façade on the opposite side, giving access to the *pronaos*. Around the *cella* was a colonnade (*peristasis*) of about 17 × 35 m, of which only part of the perimeter foundations remain. The *peristasis* possibly had six columns on the short sides and fourteen on the long sides. The roof was covered with polychrome terracotta tiles similar to those common in Sicily.

Around 480 to 470 B.C., the ancient temple was demolished and reconstructed with a different orientation, using a type of limestone that is not found locally and was probably imported from Syracuse. The new building, of which the rear part of the foundation on three levels has survived, was 19 × 45 m in size and built in the Ionic order. It contained a *cella* with *pronaos* and *opisthodomos* with two columns between the antas and two flights of service stairs giving access to the roof set between the *cella* and the *pronaos*. The temple was encircled by a *peristasis* of six by seventeen columns with fluted bases and capitals with volutes decorated with motifs of interwoven leaves. One of the columns has been mounted on a modern block at the southwest corner of the *peristasis*. The architrave was surmounted by a cornice with a toothed pattern between friezes of ovolos; the eaves (*cyma*) were decorated with lion-head spouts and were replaced in the course of the fourth and third centuries B.C. Some splendid eave slabs, with carved lion-heads, could have been part of the temple decorations; they were reused in the foundations of the "House of Lions," a cult building located outside the walls, which will be discussed below. Around 420 B.C. a splendid carved group, now in the Archaeological Museum at Reggio Calabria, was placed on the façade of the temple. It consists of a female figure similar to Aphrodite coming out of the sea near the Dioskouroi, mounted on horses supported by tritons.

An important element of the cult, useful in the identification of the deity venerated in the temple, was a structure connected to rituals of a chthonic type at the center of the *cella*. This consisted of a well lined with slabs of limestone (*bothros*) which, after the superimposition of various monumental phases, ended near the corner of the *cella* of the earliest temple.

According to a recent hypothesis, the parapet of this structure consisted of one of the most notable masterpieces of the art of Magna Graecia: the "Ludovisi Throne," now kept in the National Museum in Rome. It is a marble carving, dated between 460 and 450 B.C., showing three panels sculpted in intricate bas-relief. On the main panel is a representation of the birth of Aphrodite, who is emerging either from the sea or from the depths of the earth, between two nymphs who are holding a veil over the lower part of her body; on the side panels are a naked hetaira playing a flute, and a cloaked woman engaged in burning grains of incense.

In the space in front of the temple a very large altar was placed beside the earlier ones. Finally, in the course of the fifth century B.C., a portico was built against the wall for the purpose of welcoming the cult participants.

Climbing back up to the city along the southern slopes of the walls, one comes across a temple dedicated to Zeus, near Casa Marafioti. The building stood in an elevated position, on a height enclosed by imposing terracing, which dominated the lower part of the city. It was probably founded in the third quarter of the sixth century B.C. Still recognizable at the start of the nineteenth century but now completely devastated by looting, the temple was of the Doric order, with a *cella* perhaps having a chamber at its rear and surrounded by a *peristasis*. The roof was rebuilt in the fifth century B.C., with a lining of slabs decorated with repetitive linked motifs and eaves (*cyma*) embellished by lion-heads and palmettes and lotus motifs, with triangular holes to drain the water. Also part of this reconstruction was a terracotta acroterion, now in the Museum at Reggio Calabria, showing a dioskouros on horseback supported by a sphinx. The attribution of the

temple to Zeus was confirmed by the discovery in the area immediately below the theater of a dedication from the Hellenistic period which applies to him the attribute of "Savior" (*soter*)—an epithet appropriate to the god's abilities.

Perhaps the thirty-nine inscribed bronze tablets—an exceptional discovery found inside a stone box about 100 m downhill from the temple—were also linked to the same sanctuary at Casa Marafioti. The tablets are from between the end of the fourth and the first half of the third century B.C., and form part of the archives of a sanctuary to Zeus Olympios. In them are noted the loans made to the city, for example, for the "construction of towers"—an event connected to the rebuilding of the city walls, which is dated by archaeologists to the same period as the tablets. In the inscriptions mention is made of the magistracy of the city and of a "king" (*basileos*)—a title given to a supreme magistrate or, possibly, a commander such as Pyrrhos or Agathokles of Syracuse. On the southeastern slopes of the sanctuary at Casa Marafioti was a theater, possibly built in the second half of the fourth century B.C., with many changes made in the Roman era. Of this there remain the tiers of the seating (*cavea*) subdivided into seven sectors, which were carved out of the side of the hill, the semicircular orchestra, and the foundations of the stage. Behind this monument, a short distance away, were some houses lining the long *stenopoi* that are the extension of those retraced in the Centocamere quarter.

Last of all is a sanctuary to Athena, situated lower down on the southern slopes of the Mannella hill, behind the walls to the east. The foundations of a little sacred building and statuettes of the goddess, dating from the end of the sixth century B.C., belong to this sanctuary.

The Suburban Sanctuaries   In the Centocamere area, immediately outside the south wall, a second important sanctuary of Aphrodite, linked with the port quarter, existed from the High Archaic period onward. Forming part of this was the so-called U-shaped *Stoa*, a large, colonnaded building arranged along three sides of a vast rectangular space 55 by 66 m and opening toward the sea. We have already mentioned the fact that this construction caused the city walls of the first half of the sixth century B.C. to deviate from their normal course; the wall made a sharp angle around the place the monument occupied.

Of this complex, only the foundations of cobbles and reused limestone blocks remain today. The walls were built of mud brick and wood. The building was made up of a central colonnaded main section and two perpendicular arms, divided into small, rectangular rooms opening onto porticoes around the central square. In the original project, built between the end of the seventh and the beginning of the sixth century B.C., the wings contained six rooms, but around the middle of the sixth century B.C. they were extended in order to provide five more. It is probable that this was a banqueting hall used in the course of ritual ceremonies; it has been estimated that the rooms could each have contained nine couches placed against the walls. The remains of the meals and of their associated ritual goods were buried in the central square, in more than 350 pits dating from the middle of the sixth to the middle of the fourth century B.C. Apart from ceramics used at table and in the kitchen, and an abundance of animal bones, the shafts contained terracotta statuettes, predominantly of male personages such as Dionysos draped on a bench with a lyre or a goblet in his hand.

The discovery of two vases with dedications to Aphrodite played a decisive role in the identification of the cult. The presence of the goddess gave rise to the supposition that the "U-shaped *Stoa*" could have been connected to the ritual of sacred prostitution, typical of her cult in the eastern world. The complex was demolished around the middle of the fourth century B.C., when another colonnaded structure was built above the main part of the building; that too was destroyed when the city walls were rebuilt.

The sanctuary of Aphrodite extended toward the east, where a small sacred building was discovered that dates from the beginning of the fifth century B.C. It was built of stone blocks, and divided into a vestibule and three rooms, with an internal altar. Its connection to the goddess was confirmed by a dedication to Aphrodite in stone from the end of the fifth century B.C. Built over this shrine, toward the middle of the fourth century B.C., was the "House of Lions," named for the previously mentioned eave slabs with lion-head decoration from the second half of the fifth century B.C., which were reused in the construction of its foundations. The complex covered an area of about 400 square meters, laid out with a large courtyard and a colonnaded portico decorated with polychrome stucco, with rooms on two floors facing onto it. It has recently been suggested that the building was a sanctuary of Adonis, the beautiful and tragically short-lived youth beloved of Aphrodite.

At the beginning of the eastern arm of the city walls, immediately to the north of Parapezza, excavations uncovered a sanctuary dedicated to Demeter, which was in use from the second half of the sixth century B.C. until the third century B.C. Its attribution to the goddess was confirmed not only by the votive material and the cult equipment found but also by a mutilated inscription which included the attribution of *Themosphoros*. The *themosphoros* was, in fact, the typical feast of Demeter, linked to the sowing season and the purification of women both as wives and mothers. The sanctuary was bounded by a wall which must have enclosed buildings of an impermanent nature. An abundance of votive offerings refer to the cult, among them miniature ceramic artifacts, notably cups and receptacles for water (*hydriai*), female statuettes, and the remains of sacrifices and ritual meals. Particular mention should be made of a pit, lined and covered with tiles, from which issued four tubes, made from different materials, linked to libation and the consequent need to disperse liquids below ground.

The most famous sanctuary at Lokroi, in constant use from the seventh to the third centuries B.C. was, however, connected with Kore/Persephone, daughter of Demeter. This was the site of an important treasure, sacked more than once in the tortured history of the city. The sanctuary was built in wild countryside near the north wall of the city, on the southwest slope of the Mannella hill, on a terrace stretching out into the valley running between the

height and the Abbadessa hill. In the second half of the fifth century B.C., the area of the sanctuary was subjected to an extensive rebuilding program. The terrace was extended using imposing terracing work that also functioned as an embankment against the torrent that descended deep into the valley. A kind of aedicula made from limestone blocks was erected around a square pit, also lined with blocks. This housed a massive accumulation of votives, which illustrate the variety and richness of the dedications at the sanctuary. Among them are objects of importance to Greece and also to the Etruscan world: items of armor, like helmets and swords; great bronze vases with decoration in relief; and figures made in various materials. Among the items produced locally—naturally more abundant—are the votive terracottas, heads and statuettes of women, all connected with the cult of the goddess. But the most typical offering at the sanctuary consisted of terracotta plaques (*pinakes*) showing scenes from the cult of Persephone; dating from the first half of the fifth century B.C., they typify the work done by the craftsmen of Magna Graecia. The goddess was celebrated first in her virgin state (*Kore*), then reaching adulthood, and then acceding to the privileged status of a married woman. Thus represented on these plaques are scenes relating to her girlhood, her abduction by Hades—metaphor for the act of matrimony—and her appearance on the throne beside her husband and accompanied by other deities.

Finally, also worthy of note is the important rustic sanctuary at Grotta Caruso, situated in the high part of the city near to the northeast arm of the wall. The cult, originating at the start of the sixth century B.C., sanctified a grotto from which issued a spring, captured in a basin made in the Hellenistic period. Characteristic of this later phase is the dedication of models of grottos, nymphs, and fountains, as well as offerings of tablets picturing three nymphs side by side. Such deities are also associated with a river god, Eutymos, who had the body of a bull and the face of a man. He was the Lokroian victor at the Olympic Games, deified in his lifetime, of whom ancient tradition records a victory over a demon that was terrorizing the city of Temesa.

Kroton

General plan of Kroton

On opposite page: base and column in the sanctuary of Hera Lakinia at Cape Colonna, Kroton

History

Kroton was founded by colonists who originated in Achaia, a region in the Greek Peloponnese. According to historical sources, the leader of the expedition was Myskellos of Rhypai, who was assigned the site of the colony by the Delphic Oracle. Arriving in Southern Italy to explore the area he had been allocated, Myskellos saw the territory that the Sybarites had barely finished founding and, feeling that it was superior to what

he had been assigned, returned to consult the oracle again to ask to be allowed to change. The oracle categorically refused and told him to be content with what he had been offered. Myskellos then left on his final journey to Kroton, accompanied on his expedition by Archytas of Corinth, who was on his way to Sicily to found Syracuse. According to another story, the final destination of both Myskellos and Archytas' expeditions derived from a joint consultation with the oracle, who asked them whether they desired health or riches more. Myskellos chose health and was allocated Kroton while Archytas, who chose riches, got Syracuse. This stress laid on the healthy climate enjoyed by Kroton reminds us of the famous exploits of its athletes, victorious in all the most important athletic contests in ancient Greece.

Around 570 B.C. Kroton, together with Sybaris and Metapontion, formed the coalition that destroyed the city of Siris. A short while later they moved against Lokroi, which had opposed that undertaking; this time they suffered a ruinous defeat near the river Sagra (the modern Turbolo). The river lay far to the south of Kroton, on the border between Lokroi and the Greek city of Kaulonia, near Punta Stilo in the district of Monasterace Marina. Even though historical tradition regards this center as an Achaian colony, with its own *ekistes* (founder), the location of the battle seems to indicate that it was nevertheless subordinate to the hegemonic center, Kroton.

Thrown into crisis after the Battle of the Sagra, the morale of the colonists was raised by the arrival from Samos, in 530 B.C., of the philosopher Pythagoras, who, in a campaign against the existing culture of luxury and laxity, reformed the city's customs and set up a school centered on himself which attracted the members of the new ruling class, selected from among the city's narrow aristocracy.

At the end of the century, Kroton marched against the Sybarites in a war engendered by Kroton's refusal to repatriate five hundred Sybarite aristocrats who had taken refuge there from Teli, the Sybarite tyrant. In 510 B.C. the Kroton army overthrew the Sybarite forces near the river Traeis (the modern Trionto) and, after a brief siege, conquered and destroyed the city. Tradition mentions how, in the final, decisive encounter, the Krotoniate forces were led into battle by the famous athlete Milo—many times victor in all the Panhellenic games—disguised as Herakles.

The victory over the Sybarites signaled a period of massive expansion for Kroton, which extended its influence over the Sybarite territory and, for the whole of the first half of the fifth century B.C., opposed all attempts to rebuild that city, right up to 444–443 B.C., at which time Thurii intervened. In that same period, Kroton extended its territory toward the Tyrrhenian coast, ousting the Sybarites from their control of Temesa and founding the city of Terina immediately to the south on the plain of Lamezia (now Sant'Eufemia Vetere). According to ancient tradition, Terina was the starting point for a road that takes the shortest route across Calabria from the Tyrrhenian to the Ionian sea. At the other end of it was Scillezio, in the Gulf of Squillace, to the north of Kaulonia—also controlled by Kroton.

The management of the land of the Sybarites, with its enormous productive potential, had a destabilizing effect on the internal balance of the colony. While the Pythagorean aristocracy was pressing to be reinstated into the Sybarite nobility, which had lined up against Teli, the democratic faction, led by a noble called Kylon, wanted them dispersed among the citizens of Kroton. The crisis, occurring toward the end of the sixth century B.C., prompted Pythagoras to flee to Metapontion and saw the start of a period of violent discord which provoked a brief attempt at tyranny and ended,

around the middle of the fifth century B.C., with the massacre of the Pythagorean faction, whose holdings were burned down.

Around 430 B.C., as a defense against the native peoples of the interior, Kroton organized a league which included Kaulonia, together with a community of Sybarites who had been excluded from the foundation of Thurii and had settled near the river Traeis. At the start of the fourth century B.C., this league, founded near the sanctuary of Zeus Homarios, became the Italiote League, with a greatly extended membership of Magna Graecian cities, all sworn to defend the alliance against the Italic Lucanians and the tyrant of Syracuse, Dionysios I. Kroton assumed the leadership of the alliance, which now met near the city's main sanctuary to Hera, on the Lacinio promontory (the modern Cape Colonna, named after a lone surviving column). The second decade of the fourth century B.C. saw the decisive battle between Kroton and Dionysios I, who, most probably in the year 378 B.C., stormed the city and went on to occupy it for the next twelve years. On this occasion, the sanctuary of Hera Lakinia was sacked by the tyrant and a great deal of its treasure was removed.

The control of the league was then assumed by Taras (modern Taranto), which moved the seat near Herakleia. This was the beginning of the decline of Kroton, which, in the course of the fourth century B.C., came under pressure from another of the Italic peoples, the Brettii. In 296 B.C. the city was taken and sacked by Agathokles, another tyrant of Syracuse who, years before, had aided Kroton in its struggle against the Brettii. A few years later (between 280 and 270 B.C.), the city became heavily involved in a war between Pyrrhos and the Romans, which left it seriously depopulated.

During the Second Punic War in 215 B.C., a very weakened Kroton was conquered by the Brettii, who were allied with the Carthaginians. The inhabitants abandoned the city and went to Lokroi. In 204 B.C. Hannibal transferred the inhabitants of Thurii to Kroton, which constituted the last Italian outpost of the Carthaginian general, who dedicated a stele bearing a description of his exploits in the sanctuary to Hera Lakinia. In 194 B.C. the city was declared a Roman colony.

The Layout of the City

Kroton was built around a wide creek at the mouth of the river Esaro, which may have served as the harbor for the ancient city. The settlement developed along both banks of the river, occupying an enormous area that was protected by a fortified perimeter wall about 8 miles (13 km) in length. The necropolis—of which only the southern margin has been extensively investigated—was encircled by a perimeter wall and was located outside the city walls. The urban area was dominated by what is now Castle Hill—the acropolis of the colony—situated immediately to the south of the delta area. Recently, remains from the Greek colonial phase of the wall, together with material dating from the seventh to the third centuries B.C., have been discovered beneath buildings constructed in the medieval era.

Even though the modern city has been built on top of the ancient inhabited area, archaeological excavations have been able to recreate the various strata and the layout of the Greek city. The earliest evidence is offered by ceramics from the last two decades of the eighth century B.C. found in the inhabited sectors. These probably date to the time of the initial street plan, which divided the area into distinct nuclei, separated by large open spaces. The settlement was urbanized, at the end of the seventh century B.C., with the establishment of three distinct quarters: one to the north, which seems to have been bounded by a deep natural depression, and two south of the river. Their orientation was governed by the existing contours of the land, which converged on the strip of lowland carved out by the river. The streets, about 5 m wide, used the natural slope to drain away the surface water.

Around the middle of the fourth century B.C. the urban settlement underwent major reconstruction and blocks were built that measured 35 × 70 m and were separated by roads 5 m wide. Within these blocks, individual houses occupied plots 23 × 17 m in size. In addition, specific areas were set aside for the production of such things as metal goods and pottery.

An important public area, perhaps relating to the *agora,* has been investigated in the area of the stadium. One of the items that came to light in the course of excavations was a small temple built of stone blocks, with Doric stone columns and eaves decorated with terracotta lion-heads, dating from sometime in the fourth century B.C. Nearby was an imposing building from the second half of the same century, with a courtyard surrounded by a portico that had wooden columns.

Only a few stretches of the fortified city walls have been found. They were made up of two parallel lines of masonry built from square stone blocks, with a filling (*emplekton*) of earth and stones between them. They appear to have been constructed in a number of stages over the period between the middle of the fifth century to the end of the fourth century B.C.

An important sanctuary was found in the inhabited sector north of the Esauro River, just outside the walls in the Vigna Nuova area, on a small hill above the Papaniciaro, a little watercourse that joins the Esauro further down the valley. This cult centered around a sacred building of which several phases of construction dating from the first half of the sixth to the last three decades of the fourth century B.C. have survived. It was made up of a large rectangular room with no internal partitions, with a small room at the rear, in all covering an area of about 22 × 9 m. A portico ran along one of the long sides while in the main room a square enclosure made of stone slabs, about 2 × 2 m, was added during the first quarter of the fifth century B.C.—perhaps the base of a table used for offerings, which appear to have played a central part in the celebration of the cult. Among the numerous votive offerings recovered, most notable are agricultural or woodworking tools, above all chains and iron plows. These dedications seem to be connected with the ritual of the granting of freedom to slaves under the sacred guarantee of the sanctuary—a procedure that could have been associated with Hera, as is demonstrated in the case of the famous sanctuary to the goddess near the Lacinio promontory.

The Extraurban Sanctuaries

When the Delphic Oracle instructed Myskellos to found Kroton, it gave him three topographical points of reference the Esauro River, Cape Lacinio, and the "Sacra Krimisa," which marked the territorial boundaries of the city. The latter two were linked

by historical tradition to the two most important sanctuaries, dedicated respectively to Hera and Apollo, the two leading deities of the new colony.

The Sanctuary of Hera Lakinia

The sanctuary of Hera Lakinia was situated about 7.5 miles (12 km) south of Kroton, near the present-day Cape Colonna—the ancient Lacinio promontory which was of immense importance to the small vessels that plied the Ionic coast. The presence of the sanctuary brought that stretch of the sea under the protection of the goddess. A similar attempt to invite the protection of the gods can be seen in the dedication to Zeus Meilichios (sweet as honey; benign) inscribed on an anchor found further south, near Cape Cimitti. It was dedicated at the start of the fifth century B.C. by Faillo, a famous athlete but also a courageous commander and the only one of the Western Greeks to sail his own ship to Salamis to join the fight against the Persians.

The sanctuary of Hera Lakinia, renowned in ancient times for its prestigious cult, was of fundamental importance to the religious and political life of Kroton. It contained masterpieces by famous artists and housed an immense treasure, but, above all, it was connected with the foundation of the city. According to mythical tradition, the city was founded by Herakles who brought with him the herd of cattle stolen from Gerion. He landed on the promontory in order to defend himself against a robber called Lakinio and accidentally killed his host, Kroton. To expiate his sin and celebrate the memory of Kroton, the hero predicted the foundation of a city which would bear the name of his victim. At the same time he founded the sanctuary to Hera. The myth of Gerion's herd is connected to the sacred wood that constituted the unique natural setting in which the sanctuary was built, and among whose rich pastures the goddess's sacred beasts could roam freely.

Hera was venerated under a number of aspects: patron of navigation and goddess of armaments, and at the same time protector of the birth, reproduction, and defense of the political community. In her capacity as an arms-bearing deity (hoplosmia, from the Greek hopla, arms), she protected or restored the liberty of the individual by conferring freedom. Included on some of the dedications to the goddess from the sixth and fifth centuries B.C. that have been found in the sanctuary is the title of "Liberator" (eleutheria).

The sanctuary occupied the extreme eastern part of Cape Colonna, which is now partly eroded by the sea. The area, covering the landward slope of the promontory, was protected by an imposing walled enclosure (temenos), built in two sections, 200 and 155 m long, respectively, and reinforced externally by two square towers. In addition to the sanctuary, the walls enclosed an inhabited area to the north apparently dating from the fourth century B.C.

Today one can identify traces of what, in the fourth century B.C., was probably the first phase of construction, consisting of an outer wall built of regular square stone blocks and some lattice-patterned brickwork that was built over the earlier wall during the Roman Republican era. Entrance to the sacred area was through a monumental gate in the wall, which had an inner room faced with stone blocks like those used in the earlier phase of construction. A sacred way ran from this gate to the Temple of Hera—a road that certainly predates both wall and gate because it is aligned with the earliest major building to be excavated in the sanctuary to date. In the light of this, it should be stressed that originally the sacred area must have had a larger extent than that enclosed within the perimeter of the walls.

About .6 mile (1 km) inland, archaeologists made the fortuitous discovery of a bronze tablet dating from around the middle of the fifth century B.C., which bears an inscription to Pythian Apollo; this evidently indicates that the cult also included worship of the Delphic god, who, as at the sanctuaries at Poseidonia and Metapontion, was paired with Hera.

Inside the temenos, on either side of the sacred way, are two rectangular buildings, constructed in the second half of the fourth century B.C. to house official delegations of pilgrims. They were built on the same plan, with a central inner peristyle that opened onto a courtyard and along which were a series of small square rooms, each covering an area of 15 to 20 square meters. The larger of the two buildings ("building K"), situated to the north of the road, measured about 38 × 44 m and was

obviously intended for the accommodation of pilgrims. It opened onto the road and toward the temple, which had a Doric colonnade of the same style as the stucco-clad wooden columns of the central peristyle.

The smaller building to the south of the road (building H), measured 26.3 × 29 m and consisted of fourteen rooms set around the peristyle, which was probably also supported by wooden columns. It has been recognized as a great banqueting hall, with each room capable of holding seven convivial couches ranged along the walls. Farther to the east along the sacred way was the earliest sacred building in the sanctuary, now known as "building B," a rectangular structure measuring 22 × 9 m. Two phases of construction can be discerned: one dating from the end of the seventh century B.C., with mudbrick walls and a roof made of some kind of perishable material, and a more recent one from the first half of the fifth century B.C., having a tiled roof decorated with architectural terracottas. Still preserved are the foundations of the outside walls and steps built of stone and angled blocks. On the long sides, large blocks have been placed at right angles to the foundations, perhaps during restoration work carried out in the final phase in the life of the building, believed to have been about the middle of the fifth century B.C.

Set against the far wall is a rectangular foundation built of blocks and measuring about 3 × 2.5 m which, like the one in the building at Vigna Nuova, was probably the focal point of the cult. It must have supported a wooden surface, possibly for a cult statue or else used as a table for offerings. The sacred building was built in a space whose boundaries had already been defined; inside it, about halfway along the side of the foundations, a stone stele has come to light, while the foundations rest on three column drums—probably left from the Archaic phase of the Temple of Hera—placed deliberately in order to establish it as a ritual area.

The sacred building has yielded an immense number of votive offerings of extremely high quality—perhaps the remains of the sanctuary's famous treasure that is mentioned in the historical sources. Notable items among them are the many bronze vases imported from Greece, some with figured handles or bases, but most outstanding is the exceptional repoussé guilloche diadem from the middle of the sixth century B.C., to which, at a later date were added gold myrtle leaves and berries: a charming theory holds that this was the ornament that crowned the statue of the goddess. Another item of exceptional interest is a bronze ship from Sardinia, adorned with figurines of birds of good omen. It was probably brought to Kroton by the Phoenicians, which illustrates the breadth of the connections established by the sanctuary.

Immediately to the south of building B was the Temple of Hera, of which there remain only a part of the foundations and a lone column silhouetted against the sea. In its present state, the temple dates from the second quarter of the fifth century B.C. Of the Doric order, it measured 22 × 57 m and contained a *cella* with entrance porch surrounded by a colonnade of six by fifteen columns and a room open to the rear (*opisthodomos*). The roof was covered with marble tiles, and embellished by pediments and akroteria decorated with statues, of which some fragments remain. On the same site was an earlier temple, to which the column drums reused in building B and some fragments of architectural terracottas—such as lion-head spouts—probably belonged.

Krimisa and the Sanctuary of Apollo Aleos

Ancient tradition connects the city of Krimisa to the Temple of Apollo Aleos; both were founded by Philoktetes, the infallible archer who, armed with the bow of Herakles, was responsible for the ultimate conquest of Troy. It is interesting to note how, according to ancient sources, Philoktetes joined the native Chones people, a tribe of Oinotrian origin. Historical tradition also shows that both Krimisa and the Temple of Apollo developed in the context of a collaboration between the Greeks and the native population, and were located in a marginal area which, though it came under Kroton's influence at the time of the fall of Sybaris, maintained its own cultural autonomy.

Krimisa has not yet been identified, but the Temple of Apollo Aleos was uncovered on the promontory of Punta Alice, in the district of Ciro Marina, 18.6 miles (30 km) to the north of Kroton. Two phases exist, of which only the foundations

remain. The earlier one, from the first half of the sixth century B.C., consists of an elongated *cella*, measuring about 27 × 8 m, built of mud brick, probably with a closed rear chamber (*adyton*) and a peristyle of five by fifteen columns; the *cella* was divided down the center by a line of seven columns whose bases have survived. In the *adyton* are four more bases which fairly certainly formed part of the supports surrounding the cult statue. The entablature was clad in terracotta decorated with typical Doric motifs, such as fascias, fillets, and beads.

The temple was rebuilt in the third century B.C.; the Archaic building was incorporated into the new Doric construction, of which one characteristic was an imposing peristyle with 8 × 19 columns. Between this and the *cella* was a second line of columns intended to emphasize the monument's façade.

During the construction of the new temple, the remains of two cult statues were buried in the old temple. One of these had been made using the acrolithic technique, which involved grafting a

Right: foundations of the
Temple of Apollo Aleos at Ciro
Marina, the ancient Krimisa
(Cantarazo)

sculpted marble head and marble extremities onto a wooden body, which was then clad in precious vestments. The statue, dating from shortly after the middle of the fifth century B.C., represents Apollo and was probably originally housed in the *adyton* of the temple, in the space between the four column bases. The god was depicted seated, in the act of playing the kithara, his head slightly raised in musical ecstasy. The parts of the statue that were found include the magnificent face, with concave sockets that once contained eyes made of precious materials, both feet, and one hand. Of a second, slightly earlier statue, perhaps carved entirely from wood, there remains only the bronze skullcap detailed with a rendering of hair, on which rested a laurel wreath—this, too, a symbol of Apollo.

The Territory

The size of the colony's territory seems to have varied with the centuries, influenced by the events of the city's complex history. In the earliest phase it could have covered the area between the Neto River in the north and the Tacina in the south, but after the victory against Sybaris in 510 B.C., it expanded northward as far as the river Nica. The political and economic expansion of the city from the end of the sixth and in the first half of the fifth century B.C. is reflected in a marked increase in the number of farms, determined by the allocation of land. The opposite seemed to be the case at the end of the century, when Kroton came under pressure from the native Italian peoples (the Lucanians and then the Brettii), who began settling on land that was supposedly under the colony's control.

Within this changed historical framework the Greek city set up a defensive military structure for the protection of its borders. The best-preserved example of this can be seen near the Le Castella promontory in the district of Isola di Capo Rizzuto. Beneath the fort built in the Aragonese era, one can see a long stretch of a fortified structure built in the last part of the fourth century B.C., made up of parallel walls built of alternating blocks laid in a squared pattern and the cavity between them filled with stones.

Sybaris and Thurii

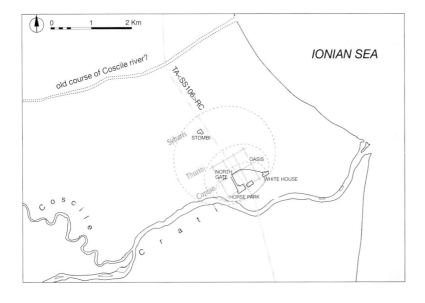

Re-creation of hypothetical extent of the cities of Sybaris, Thurii, and Copia

On opposite page: the great *plateia* A, oriented north–south, 29.5 m wide, uncovered at Parco del Cavallo. The basalt surface was laid when it was the Roman city of Copia.

History

Sybaris was founded at the end of the eighth century B.C. by colonists from the region of Achaia in the Greek Peloponnese. The leader of the expedition, according to Strabo, was called Is and was from Elis. The colonial contingent was reinforced by a group of people from Troizen, a city in the Argolid, who were subsequently expelled. Ancient tradition offers two dates for the foundation of the colony: 709–708 B.C. or 720 B.C. The former is more in line with the evidence furnished by

archaeological investigation. In antiquity the city was renowned for its wealth and for the excesses that led to its ruin. Setting aside this moralistic view, however, one must acknowledge the power accumulated by the colony, which was blessed with exceptionally fertile soil and was more than capable of the vigorous promotion of trading relationships with the Greeks and the Etruscans. Emblematic of the strength of these relationships, according to the testimony of Herodotos, was the sadness caused by the fall of Sybaris among the inhabitants of Miletos (a city in Asia Minor), who shaved their heads as a sign of mourning.

Ancient sources attribute to the colony the formation of an extended territorial empire that included "four peoples and twenty-five cities." This expansion was achieved by widening the parameters under which the right of citizenship could be granted to native communities and settlements, which then, while integrated in the community, still enjoyed distinct levels of autonomy.

Sybaris' rule extended from the mountainous inland region of Sila to the Tyrrhenian coast. In this area, the city instituted its own strongholds in the centers of Temesa, near the Savuto River to the north of the Gulf of Sant'Eufemia, Laus, in the Gulf of Scalea, and Scidrus; but, above all, it promoted the foundation of Poseidonia at the end of the seventh and start of the sixth century B.C. The expansionist aims of Sybaris also turned to the east. Around 570 B.C., together with Kroton and

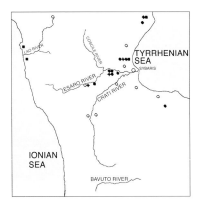

Below: Sybaris and its territory

Metapontion, it conquered Siris and, in all probability, absorbed its territory.

The exceptional brilliance achieved by the city undermined its internal stability. In the final years of the sixth century B.C. the people rose up against the domination of the aristocracy and led the way for the arrival of a tyrant, Teli, who started a war against Kroton. In 510 B.C., despite its superior military force, Sybaris suffered an irremediable defeat near the Traeis River and, after a siege, was conquered and destroyed.

According to ancient historians, Kroton, so as not to leave the rival city with a way of surviving, diverted the course of the Crati toward it; a story that, as will be seen, has been partially disproved by archaeological findings. Some of the surviving inhabitants found refuge at Scidrus and Laus. In the latter center they founded another city to which they gave the name of Sybaris. An extraordinary epigraphic document, consisting of a bronze tablet found at Olympia, memorializes the eternal friendship between the new Sybaris and the native population of the Serdaioi, who gave their permission for the city to be built there on land they owned. Guarantor of this alliance, in addition to "Zeus, Apollo, and other deities," was Poseidonia.

In the years immediately following 510 B.C. and in the course of the fifth century B.C., the remaining Sybarites tried several times to rebuild their old city, but were frustrated in every case by Kroton. Finally, in 446–445 B.C., the enterprise was successful, thanks to the help of a contingent led by Athens but comprised also of elements from the Peloponnese. This new city, however, had an ephemeral life because of conflicts between the new colonists and the old Sybarites, who demanded the best civic positions and the best land for themselves; for this reason they were either killed or obliged to flee.

Left in charge, the Athenians moved the city to a new site, thus founding Thurii. In 444–443 B.C. the colonial contingent was reinforced by an invitation extended to all the regions of Greece. This was the true foundation of the Panhellenic colony requested by Pericles, and it was led by Lampon and Xenocritos, who was already at the head of the first naval expedition. The best intellectuals of the epoch participated in the Thurii project: the architect Hippodamos of Miletos, who designed the street plan for the city; the philosopher Protagoras, who wrote the constitution; and the historian Herodotos, who was buried in the *agora* of the new colony.

The population was divided into ten tribes representing all of the Greek territories, and the land allocated to them on a proportionate basis. Thurii entered into a nonaggression pact with Kroton but immediately quarreled with Taranto over possession of Siris. In the war, the Thuriian army was led by the Spartan general Kleandridas. The conflict ended with an agreement between the parties, who repopulated the site of the former Siris with a "communal colony." In 433–432 B.C., the new settlement was transferred, under pressure from Taranto, and neighboring Herakleia was thus founded.

In the same year the Spartan Kleandridas defended the city against the native Lucanians, who had begun to put pressure on the Greek coastal city. In 434–433 B.C. the Panhellenic community of Thurii was in crisis because of difficulties arising between the colonists of Peloponnese origin and the Athenian component, whose influence on the politics of the city was seriously diminished. The crisis came to a head at the end of the fifth century B.C. on the occasion of an Athenian expedition to Sicily against Syracuse. Initially, Thurii gave its support to the military intervention; when the war failed, this provoked the expulsion of the "Athenian party" from the city. Having become a member of the Italiote League at the beginning of the fourth century B.C. in order to defend itself against Dionysios I, tyrant of Syracuse, and the Lucanians, Thurii was badly defeated by the latter in 390 B.C. near Laus, which by that time was in Lucanian hands. Nevertheless, the colony continued to resist, thus assuming for a brief period a guiding role in the league.

In the second half of the fourth century B.C., Thurii had to repulse an attack by the Italian Brettii, against whom it asked the help of Alexander the Molossan, king of Epyros and one of the foreign commanders called to Taranto to direct the military operations of the Italiote League. The

Above: silver stater incused with a bull looking backward, 530–510 B.C., from Sybaris (National Archaeological Museum, Reggio Calabria)

king formed a strong relationship with the colony and, after a disagreement with Taranto, transferred the meeting place of the league to Thurii. When he fell in battle, in 331 B.C. according to historical tradition, Thurii collected his body and gave it an honorable burial.

In 282 B.C. the city, threatened by an attack of Lucanians and Brettii, sought the help of Rome, which defeated the enemy and then installed a garrison of its own. The interference of Rome caused Taranto to react by conquering and sacking Thurii. This episode triggered the war between Rome and Taranto, the latter inviting Pyrrhos, king of Epyros, to intervene. With the defeat of Taranto in 272 B.C. Thurii entered the Roman orbit. At the time of the Second Punic War, the city was invaded by Hannibal, who, in 204 B.C., transferred its inhabitants to Kroton. In 194 B.C., the Romans repopulated the center—by then deserted—thus founding the colony of Copia.

The System of Settlement at Sybaris and Thurii

The area occupied by the Greek cities of Sybaris and Thurii, and by the Roman colony of Copia, is located near the district of Cassano Jonio, along the state highway between Taranto and Reggio Calabria.

The archaeological area is not far from the sea, at the modern confluence of the rivers Crati and Coscile (the ancient Sybaris). The countryside at that time, however, was very different from the way it is now. The Crati and Coscile rivers were then two separate entities which met the sea roughly 1.85 miles (3 km) from each other. The coastline was then further back so that, in their respective time periods, the three cities were all washed by the sea.

Excavations have shown how the placement of the inhabited areas of Sybaris, Thurii, and Copia (though different phases were superimposed) did not coincide exactly. The Archaic settlement at Sybaris extended toward the Coscile, further north than the other two which, each in their time, expanded toward the east into an area that, at the time of Sybaris, was covered by the sea. Copia, while continuing to exploit the settlement of Thurii, occupied only its southern half.

An extensive program of archaeological exploration has confirmed the interspersed relationships that existed between the three settlements. The sites that have been investigated, and are now open to the public, are named Stombi, Incrocio–Parco del Cavallo, Prolungamento Strada, and "Casa Bianca."

SYBARIS

An extensive strip of ancient Sybaris has been brought to light at the Stombi site, situated on the northern perimeter of the ancient part of the city, which was not subsequently included in the establishment of Thurii. Remains of the Sybaritic residential quarter have been discovered during deep trials beneath the levels of Thurii and Copia, 1.25 miles (2 km) further south, at the Incrocio–Parco del Cavallo and Prolungamento Strada archaeological sites. The city, therefore, seems to have extended over an enormous area, equal to fifty stadiums (a stadium measured 180 m)—the size given to it by ancient history.

At Stombi the investigators uncovered a residential quarter, probably organized on the basis of the allocation of lots. The phase that was discovered dates from the final moments in the life of Sybaris, but the urban traces date from the sixth century B.C. Also recovered were fragments of vases dating from the last two decades of the eighth century B.C. that confirm the date of the foundation of the city documented by the sources.

The houses at Stombi were of standardized size and were rectangular, generally with one room that took up half the available space and two small ones. They were built on foundations made from river stones, with walls of plaster over a base of mud brick, and they had tiled, pitched roofs. A series of wells provided the water supply, while the discovery of two kilns used for firing pottery indicated that crafts were produced there. It appears that the defeat of Sybaris, rather than involving violent destruction, entailed only the abandonment of the quarter. The houses, in fact, were empty of all contents when they were found, as if they had been stripped by their inhabitants when they were obliged to abandon the city.

Evidence of a different kind was found at the Parco del Cavallo site. Numerous large square blocks, originally from one or more of the public buildings of Sybaris, were reused in a large, semi-circular wall dating from the first century B.C., then reused again in the theater from the Imperial era, which faced the main road between Thurii and Copia. Particularly outstanding among these pieces are three stone blocks forming part of a sculpted frieze which must have decorated the elevation of a temple from the second half of the sixth century B.C. Easily recognizable is the scene of a figure playing a flute to the accompaniment of young dancing girls, a design also used in the Temple of Hera at the mouth of the Sele at Poseidonia/Paestum, and in a terracotta relief in Reggio Calabria.

THURII

The urban settlement of Thurii has an exceptionally prominent place in the history of the Greek cities. Traditional ancient history underscores its innovative character, entirely in keeping with the enormous political significance invested in the colony, whose founders were drawn from all regions of Greece.

The Thurii project was entrusted to Hippodamos of Miletos, a great urban planner who was also dedicated to political debate; this makes it understandable that the city also reflects an ideal social model. It is not surprising, therefore, that the criteria for the general layout of the urban space should have been handed down to posterity by the ancient writers; the historian Diodoros Siculos of the first century B.C. writes that the city was divided into four "wide streets" (*plateiai*) running along its length, and three across its width, and the resulting blocks were, in their turn, divided by "narrow streets" (*stenopoi*). Diodoros also gives the names of the streets: the four long *plateia* were Herakleia, Aphrodisia, Olympias, and Dionysias; the three shorter ones were Heroa, Thuria, and Thurina. Excavations have revealed some of this network of streets beneath the Copia phase. Though narrow, they continued in use throughout the whole of the Roman period of the city.

Bronze statuette of hoplite (armored foot-soldier), 530 B.C., from the sanctuary of Athena on the Timpone Mound at Francavilla Marittima, Cozenza (National Archaeological Museum of Sybarite Artifacts, Sybaris-Cosenza)

Top plan: drawing re-creating
urban settlement of Thurii

Lower plan: re-creation of
the street network of the
inhabited area

At the Parco del Cavallo and Prolungamento Strada sites, archaeologists have discovered four *plateiai* that intersect to form a block 295 m wide by 390 m long. The main artery (*plateia* A), of which a large stretch has been brought to light, was 29.5 m wide and ran north–south. East of that was a second, parallel *plateia* (C) 12.5 m wide. Two streets crossed over these *plateiai* at right angles: the one to the south (B), 14.6 m wide, goes as far as the ancient line of thes beach to the east and was found at the Casa Bianca site; the northern one (D), at least 20 m wide, is interrupted by the city wall of Copia, which means, therefore, that the northern part of the Thurii urban area lay outside this wall. In the course of an exploratory excavation to a greater depth, it was possible to see that beneath *plateia* A are earlier hard-packed road surfaces from the Sybarite phase, possibly also pertaining to an ancient street network.

The block measuring 295 × 390 m is divided up by a network of *stenopoi* 3 m wide (Diodoros Siculos' "narrow streets") running north–south and east–west. These define smaller lots of 37 × 74 m, which in turn are divided in half by a central drain.

Based on the street plan and the dimensions of the block, it is possible to make a reconstruction of the urban plan that agrees with the historical information mentioning the arrangement of four *plateiai* running lengthways and three running across. This gives the picture of a city in the form of a square, made up of two lines of three blocks, covering an area of around 173 acres (70 hectares). Then, bearing in mind that the names of the large streets running north–south pertained to Aphrodite, Zeus Olympios, Dionysios, and Herakles, it is reasonable to suppose that each of them fronted the sanctuary of the corresponding deity or hero. This is an important innovation which made greater use of city planning than did the traditional concentration of cults in one large urban sanctuary.

Finally, mention should be made of an important discovery made in the Casa Bianca site, which, as we have already pointed out, was the port zone of Thurii and of Copia. Found in this area was the last stretch of one of the east–west *plateiai*, which

led to a solid basalt platform, subdivided into numerous squares by thin lines. This was ultimately identified as the pavement of a room in one of the gates of the fortified city wall. The gate was protected by towers, originally round but subsequently rebuilt in square form. The foundations of one of these is still recognizable.

The Territory of Sybaris and Thurii

It was already mentioned above that in addition to its fertile agricultural land, Sybaris had access to a veritable territorial empire that encompassed, as the ancient historians put it, "four peoples and twenty-five cities." The archaeological evidence shows that Sybaris' dominion consisted, above all, of an advanced system of political and productive relationships set up with the inland native population—a complex network of economic exchanges and cultural interaction that failed to survive the defeat of the colony in 510 B.C.

One of Sybaris' satellite centers can be identified at Francavilla Marittima, at the foot of the hill bounding the coastal plain to the northwest, about 9.3 miles (15 km) from the colony. The settlement, inhabited by a group of Oinotrian extraction and already flourishing in the Iron Age (the ninth to the eighth centuries B.C.), occupied an upland plain surmounted by a height (the "Timpone della Motta" [the Kettledrum created by the Landslide]), which was the open-air site of a religious cult. At the time of the foundation of Sybaris, at the end of the eighth century B.C., the native settlement was not destroyed but rebuilt. The "Timpone della Motta" hill became the new settlement's acropolis, where, in a continuation of its previous use, the sanctuary was built.

In the course of the seventh century B.C. the sacred area acquired two temples (buildings III and V) and a portico (building I) built of wood, which were rebuilt in the first half of the next century in monumental form, with stone foundations, tiled roofs, and mudbrick walls. One of these buildings (III) was dedicated to Athena, who is named in a exceptional inscription on a bronze tablet from the beginning of the sixth century B.C. It mentions the offering made by an athlete called Kleombrotos who, having won a contest at

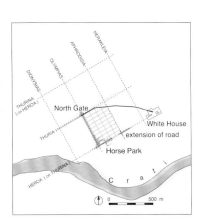

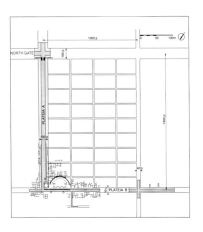

the Olympic Games, dedicated a part of his prize to the goddess in thanks.

A piece of decorated terracotta revetment from the entablature of the temple, depicting a procession on a chariot, could also refer to a ritual honoring Athena. An identical scene also occurs in the decoration of the temple at Metapontion. In the course of the sixth century B.C., two more monuments were added to the sanctuary of the "Timpone della Motta," including a small temple with *pronaos* and two columns (building II). The sacred area survived up to the time of the founding of Thurii, as is shown by numerous statuettes dedicated to Pan and to the nymphs, found in a structure resembling a portico (building IV), which dates from somewhere between the second half of the fifth and the end of the fourth century B.C.

The territory of Thurii covered a smaller area than that of Sybaris. According to a process common to all the colonies in Southern Italy, the coastal plain and the surrounding hill slopes seem to have been occupied by farms in the course of the fourth and third centuries B.C., while along the frontier facing the interior, defensive fortifications were built on the heights, in strategic positions controlling access to the plain. Among the most interesting of the items found in the colony are two large burial tumuli dating from the fourth century B.C., discovered near the village of Cogliano Calabro, 3.4 miles (5.5 km) south of the city. They still stand out in the surrounding countryside, and the local name for them is the "Timponi" (Kettledrums). The larger is 28 m in diameter and 9 m high and contained a single tomb with ashes. In the smaller one, 5 m high with a diameter of 17 m, were three bodies. All the dead were initiates of the mystical Orphic religion, and all were equipped with a small gold lamina inscribed with the necessary directions for reaching the afterlife.

View of the theater at Copia in the Parco del Cavallo (Horse Park) quarter

Siris and Herakleia

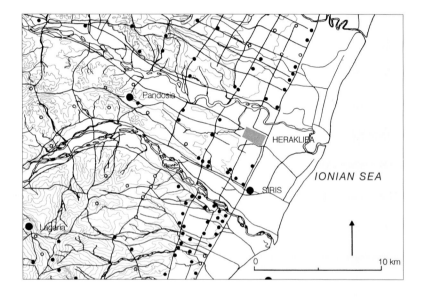

The territory of Siris and Herakleia

On opposite page: red-figured *pelike* (distinctively shaped amphora) with Athena and Poseidon, Carnee Painter, end of the fifth century B.C., from the western necropolis at Herakleia (National Archaeological Museum of Artifacts from Siris, Policoro-Matera)

History

According to Strabo, Siris took the name of the river near which it was built (the present-day Sinni). It was in essence a city of Trojan origin, but it belonged to the Oinotrian tribe known as the Chones. Its origin was confirmed by the existence of an ancient wooden statue of Athena Ilias (Trojan) which, at the moment of the violent capture of the city by Greeks from Ionia, averted its eyes while the conquerors killed a group of unarmed supplicants who had taken refuge beside it. The historian adds that the newcomers renamed the city Polieion, and were in turn forced to flee from the invasion by the Lydians. This enables us to recognize them as refugees from Kolophon, a city of Asia Minor, conquered by the famous Lydian king Gyges around the middle of the seventh century B.C.

Events referred to by traditional historians have generally been verified by archaeological exploration, which has confirmed both the eastern Greek matrix of the colonies and the existence of an early Greek settlement in the territory of Siris that predated the foundation of the colony. This dates from the period of transition between the end of the eighth and the beginning of the seventh century B.C. and was marked by a form of cooperation between the Greeks and the native population.

In the seventh century B.C. Siris was renowned for its fertile land, which the poet Archilochos characterized as "beautiful, desirable, amiable." Its richness and its ethnic diversity provoked the hostility of the nearby colonies of Achaian extraction—Metapontion, Sybaris, and Kroton—who, according to tradition, formed a coalition and conquered the city around 570 B.C. A second version of the story of the killing of the supplicants in the sanctuary of Athena Ilias refers to this event. This time the supplicants were Ionians, and the sacrilegious assassins Achaians. Following the defeat, the city lost its political autonomy and was probably integrated into the orbit of Sybaris.

On opposite page: mold of a *pinax* with a female standing before a figure reclining on a *kline*, with inscription carved in freehand before firing, fourth century B.C., from the Castello Hill at Herakleia (National Archaeological Museum of Artifacts from Siris, Policoro-Matera)

View of the central quarter from the Castello Hill at Herakleia, Policoro (Matera)

One proof of Siris' loss of independence is a silver coin of Sybarite origin, which carries the names of Siris and Pixunte (Policastro Bussentine, in the province of Salerno). The use of the Sybarite coinage demonstrates that the two centers—one on the Ionian Sea and the other on the Tyrrhenian—were both subjects of the city's wide empire, though they maintained a margin of autonomy, as shown by the use of their own name on the coins.

The question of Siris continued to be very much at the fore in the course of the fifth century B.C., after the fall of Sybaris. Herodotos records how, on the eve of the Battle of Salamis, Themistokles threatened the allies with the transfer of the Athenians to Siris, which as an Ionian city, was "ours from ancient times and the Oracles say it must be colonized by us." In the context of this historical interpretation of the facts, the foundation of Herakleia took place in the second half of the fifth century. After a prolonged contest for the possession of Siris, Thurii and Taranto agreed to a joint repopulation of Siris, with the new colony being attributed to Taranto.

In a second phase, in 433–432 B.C., the Tarantans transferred the settlement, added new colonists to it, and founded Herakleia; the old site of Siris became the port for the new settlement. In the course of the fourth century B.C., Herakleia, like the other Greek cities on the Ionian coast, was subjected to pressure by the indigenous population of the interior. It was liberated from the Lucanians by the intervention of Alexander the Molossan, king of Epyros, one of the foreign commanders called upon by Taranto to defend them against attacks by the Italian population in 334–331 B.C. The king, his relations with Taranto in crisis, transferred the seat of assembly of the Italiote League from Herakleia to Thurii, and fortified the locality beside the river Acalandro (now the Cavone) where the communal meetings took place.

In 280 B.C. the first battle between the Romans and Pyrrhos occurred near the city; in 212 B.C. Herakleia aligned itself with Hannibal. Archaeological evidence shows that the center continued to be vital right up until its final moment in the second century B.C.

The Settlement System in Siris and Herakleia

It has already been explained that historical tradition places Siris at the mouth of the river Sinni, in the vicinity of the sanctuary of Athena Ilias. This makes the site of the Archaic colony palpably distinct from that of Herakleia; at the time of Herakleia's foundation Siris became the port for the new city. It is possible to compare this information with data furnished by archaeological exploration.

The city of Herakleia was discovered below a hill immediately to the north of the center of present-day Policoro. It was built on top of an extensive earlier settlement dating from the end of the eighth century B.C., which, while it relates to the Siris phase, cannot be associated with the earlier colony situated at the mouth of the river.

One tends to favor the theory that Siris did not consist of a single centralized settlement, but was arranged as a number of sites, including that of Policoro, organized around the real political and religious center of the colony—the still-to-be identified sanctuary of Athena on the Sinni. The economy of the nuclear settlements that made up Siris was not based on acquiring and exploiting agricultural land but instead relied on trade with the native population. These Greeks did not discriminate against the indigenous people, unlike the other colonies, to whom the acquisition and defense of an extensive area of territory were seen as essential.

Apart from the site at Policoro, other nuclear settlements have been found that existed from the end of the eighth century B.C. onward, and relate to the particular model of Siris. One of these, consisting of huts partially dug into the ground, was uncovered in the area subsequently occupied by the urban settlement of Metapontion. Another, more extensively explored one was found on the Incoronata Hill, overlooking a stretch of the Basento River about 4.3 miles (7 km) to the west of that city. The bases of numerous huts similar to those found at Metapontion have come to light there, also square rooms with stone foundations and walls of mud brick; these rooms contained splendid clay table services and amphoras for storing precious commodities such as oil and wine, imported from various regions in Greece. Both these settlements were destroyed in the seventh century B.C., at the time of the foundation of Metapontion and the related organization of the territory.

The ancient settlement of Policoro and that of Herakleia, from the Classical period, occupied a long, narrow hill on the right bank of the Agri River that controlled the coastal plain between there and the river Sinni. Dominated on the eastern slope by the so-called Baron's Castle, built in the eighteenth century, the hill part of the inhabited area was bounded on the southern slope by a small valley separating it from the larger plateau where the modern town of Policoro now stands. This plateau and the valley were also occupied, though in slightly different ways, both by the settlement existing during the Siris phase and by that of Herakleia.

SIRIS

The earliest evidence from the Archaic settlement of Siris dates to the end of the eighth century B.C. and, therefore, to the time before the colony was founded, around the middle of the seventh century B.C. It consisted of groups of huts, which were discovered both on the level plain of the Baron's Hill where they were interspersed with burial places, and in two external nuclei which subsequently became part of the fortifications and the Hellenistic burial ground of Herakleia. Another possible inhabited area is indicated by some tombs which came to light about 1.25 miles (2 km) away, between the mouth of the Sinni and the hill that housed the residential quarter.

Two big burial grounds situated to the west and the southwest of the plain were connected with the main settlement on Castle Hill. Alongside the tombs of the colonists were graves belonging to the native population, with bodies buried in the foetal position. This shared burial place clearly indicates the degree of integration between the Greeks and the local people, which distinguishes Siris from other Greek settlements.

In the final part of the seventh century B.C.— the true colonial phase of Siris—the settlement on Castle Hill was fortified by a surrounding mud-brick wall, which enclosed an area of about 59 acres (24 hectares). At the same time, both on the plain and beyond it, the huts were replaced by houses with stone foundations and tiled roofs. The best preserved of these has an area of about 115 square meters, with three rooms opening onto a portico; this was found in the outer area, which later became associated with the necropolis of Herakleia.

As early as this period the intervening valley between Castle Hill and the terrace of Policoro was destined to be the site of the sacred area, associated, it seems, with one or more female deities. In the earliest phase, the cult was arranged around small shrines with columns and entablatures in wood, decorated with figured terracotta friezes like those adorning the oldest temples at Metapontion.

One last important change occurred after the middle of the sixth century B.C., when Siris, defeated by the alliance of the Achaian colonies, was absorbed into the territory of the Sybarites. The eastern sector of the plain was reserved for cult purposes; near the castle, excavations have revealed foundations on three levels, built from

Dinos (vessel for mixing wine and water) with horses facing each other, mid-seventh century B.C., from the acropolis at Herakleia (National Archaeological Museum of Artifacts from Siris, Policoro-Matera)

On opposite page: figured *dinos* with Bellerophon, mid-seventh century B.C., from Incoronata di Pisticci, Matera (National Archaeological Museum, Metapontion-Matera)

stone blocks, which clearly formed part of a temple building. A second wall from a monument built around this in the course of the fourth century B.C. confirms that the area continued to be used as a public place throughout the Herakleia phase.

More shrines were built in the underlying valley, with roofs decorated with antefixes depicting gorgon heads; on the slopes of the terrace at Policoro a sanctuary dedicated to Demeter was built over an earlier cult area next to a spring. The entire territory shows traces of occupation, signaled by small cult areas and a few farms; the small inhabited areas around Castle Hill had ceased to exist. Based on archaeological evidence, the Archaic inhabited area seems to have survived until the start of the fifth century B.C.

HERAKLEIA

In the Heraklean phase, urban plans were implemented in the three sectors involved in the extension of the earlier inhabited area: Castle Hill, the valley in between, and the southern plain of Policoro. It should be stressed that this work took place in the second quarter of the fourth century B.C., that is to say about fifty years after the date the colony was founded, around 433–432 B.C. The life of the settlement seems to have continued until the end of the second century B.C., with a final revival in the first century B.C.

Castle Hill

The hill was surrounded by a wall built of stone blocks which served as a fortification on the north, east, and west sides, while on the south slope, facing the valley, the defenses were incorporated into the terracing. On the plateau are traces of a main east–west road (*plateia*), about 10 m wide, running lengthwise across the center of the inhabited area. On both sides of this artery, at right angles to it, were minor roads between 4.5 and 8 m wide, forming blocks whose lengths varied with the distance to the edge of the plateau. It has been possible to establish that, despite the limitations imposed by the terrain, the roads and blocks divided the space into plots all measuring 41 m wide.

The urban plan greatly modified the physical appearance of the western sector of the plateau. In order to build the main transverse artery a cut was made through the central axis of the hill, lowering the level; the inhabited areas were thus raised to a higher level than the *plateia*, so that the *stenopoi* which connected with them ran downhill. The existence of different levels assisted the drainage of the surface water onto the central plateau, from which it discharged on to the western edge. The unusual deployment of the *stenopoi* on either side of the main road could also have been a measure to assist drainage; they did not go straight across the *plateia* but joined it at 15 m intervals which were staggered in order to distribute the discharged water along the whole length of the *plateia*.

Within the blocks, subdivided into lots, the plans of the houses varied over time. Those dating from the end of the fourth and start of the third centuries B.C. had an open inner courtyard and occupied an area of about 220–250 square meters. In the course of the third and second centuries B.C. the houses became larger, with the inner courtyard transformed into a kind of atrium surrounded on all four sides by a portico. Of the kind of houses that had a large garden surrounded by a portico (peristyle), fewer have been found, even though they were from the same period.

In the rooms surrounding the courtyard of one of the houses in the central sector of the inhabited area were kilns and a cache connected with metalworking. The subsequent discovery of a splendid terracotta bust of Hephaistos, the deity protecting metalworkers, confirmed the purpose of the complex. In the western sector was found a block of small, identical houses facing onto the colonnade along the large *plateia*. At the rear of each of these was a room recognizable as a shop which faced toward the street. Complexes such as this are evidence of the existence of small family craft businesses, of a type combining shop and living quarters. In addition to these, there were zones reserved exclusively for craft activities. A potters' quarter was found on the western edge of the hill; in use from the second half of the fourth century B.C. right through the second century B.C., it occupied a block that had ample open spaces, kilns, and

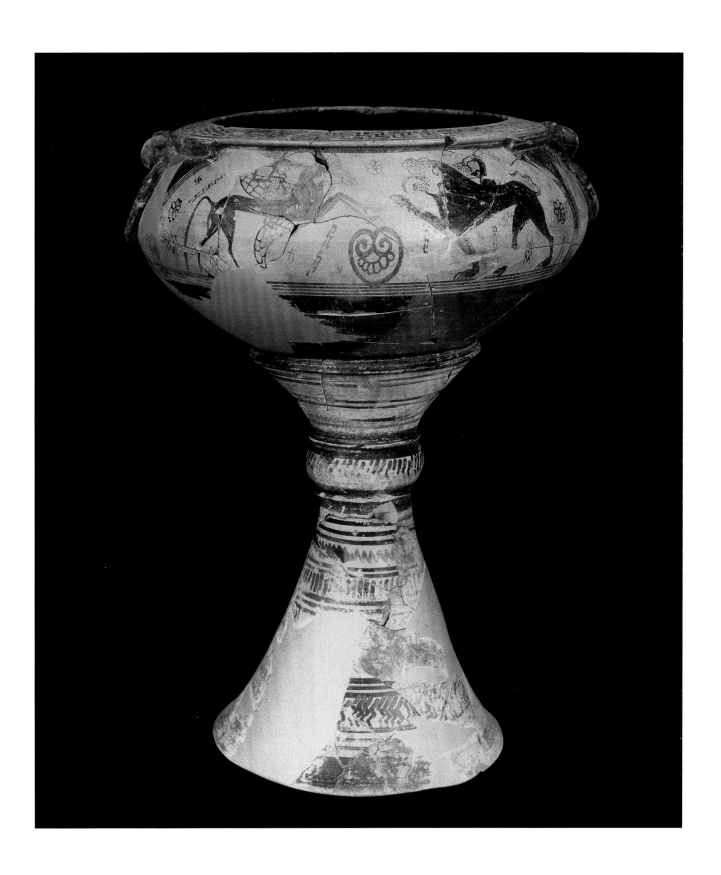

a series of rooms for the storage or sale of goods—vases and terracotta votives, judging from the numerous molds and fragments found.

The eastern sector of Castle Hill seems to have been a kind of acropolis reserved for public functions of a sacred nature, as it had been in the Archaic phase of Siris. Already mentioned was the continuous use of what was probably a cult building close to the site now occupied by the eighteenth-century castle; on the opposite, western side, near the inhabited area, the space occupied by the "acropolis" seems to have been divided into large open areas, one of them bordered by colonnades.

The Valley

A similar continuity of use can also be seen in the valley to the south close to the plain, which contained the sacred areas and quite probably the *agora* of Herakleia as well. Even the way this "nerve sector" of the inhabited area was organized seems to date from the second quarter of the fourth century B.C. The main cult area was situated on the southern slope of the valley and the lower slopes of the Policoro plateau. It was divided into two large terraces, the main one being occupied by a temple of which only the foundations remain. The sacred building, built on an east–west axis, contained a *cella* with entrance porch (*pronaos*) surrounded by a *peristasis*. Its date can be fixed as the fourth century B.C., even though the existence of an earlier phase from the Siris era cannot be excluded.

The second terrace of the sanctuary was situated immediately to the south of that on which the temple stood, at a slightly higher level. It was surrounded on three sides by a boundary wall, probably lined with porticoes. Found inside was an altar built of stone blocks, inscribed with the name of the god Dionysos and containing a small niche to hold the cult statue. Other inscriptions indicate the existence of a dedication to Aphrodite and probably also Asklepios, while Artemis is represented by a number of terracotta figurines. Found inside the sacred area were a number of hearths with the remains of food consumed in the course of rituals. Finally, there was a large banqueting room backing on to the external façade of the wall overlooking the temple terrace. It is believed that this room was reserved for the meals served to the city magistrates.

To the southeast of the sanctuary of Dionysos was the previously mentioned sanctuary of Demeter which, in the course of the fourth century B.C., was divided into a series of small shrines on small terraces within a single wall. A sacred well formed the central element of the cult. The image of the goddess was reproduced in a number of figurines, which featured a piglet, her favorite sacrificial victim, and crossed flaming torches, an essential part of the nocturnal celebration of the cult. The same torch symbol is depicted on the little water pots (*hydriai*) dedicated by the faithful on the occasion of rites carried out near the spring in the sacred area.

A third sacred area has been identified to the west of the sanctuaries to Dionysos and Demeter; only partially investigated, it is thought to have been associated with a deity overseeing health, possibly Apollo.

The Southern Terrace

The southern zone, occupied in the Archaic period by the groups of nuclear settlements of Siris, was enclosed by a wall, built in the first half of the fourth century B.C. and rebuilt in the course of the third century B.C. It consisted of two parallel lines of masonry, built of blocks, and filled internally, and was protected on the south side by circular towers. The wall was divided into three straight sections and linked to the fortifications of Castle Hill, encircling the intermediate valley. It enclosed an area of about 348 acres (141 hectares). Outside the wall, on all three sides, were *necropoleis* from the Heraklean phase.

The inhabited sector of the southern plain was organized and oriented differently from that of Castle Hill. The street plan consisted of roads set at right angles, parallel with the line of the city wall; eight running east–west have been identified and at least six oriented north–south, producing blocks with a 55 m frontage.

The Territory

Exceptional documentary evidence that permitted the reconstruction of a plan of the city has been provided by the "Tablets of Herakleia," discovered in the eighteenth century A.D. They consist of two long Greek texts inscribed on bronze tablets dating from around the middle of the fourth century B.C. One of the tablets had subsequently been used for the purpose of transcribing a law in Latin. The tablets were found in an area at the extreme edge of the Heraklean territory at the confluence of the Cavone and Salandrella rivers, which may have been where the Italiote League meetings were held. The two inscriptions report the measures taken by the government of the city to regain possession of, and reorganize, the terrain belonging to the sanctuaries of Athena Polias and Dionysos (undoubtedly those discovered by excavators) that had been illegally appropriated by private individuals. The sacred property was confiscated, subdivided into lots, and reallocated in the form of concessions. The texts prescribe the rules for the payment of rents, the type of cultivation, and the improvements to be made to the property by the addition of stables, granaries, and haystacks.

Information furnished by archaeological excavation, combined with the data furnished by the tablets, has proved the existence of farms and rural sanctuaries—particularly before the fourth century B.C.—in outlying areas of the hills; greater numbers of them were also present beside the Sinni River, at the mouth of which was the port area. One of these farms was discovered in the region of Masseria del Concio, 1.9 miles (3 km) south of Herakleia; the foundations of the circular granary, built from big stone blocks, and possibly also of its associated mill, have been preserved. The territory was defended by a network of little forts, intended to protect both the road system and the natural boundaries provided by the rivers.

Clay *perirrhanterion* with decoration in relief, from the second half of the seventh century B.C., from Incoronata di Pisticci, Matera (National Archaeological Museum Metapontion-Matera)

On opposite page: bronze tablets containing the two decrees from the mid-fourth century B.C., relating to the boundaries and location of sanctuaries of Dionysos and Athena Polias, found in 1732 on the shore of the Salandrella stream between Herakleia and Metapontion (National Archaeological Museum, Naples)

Metapontion

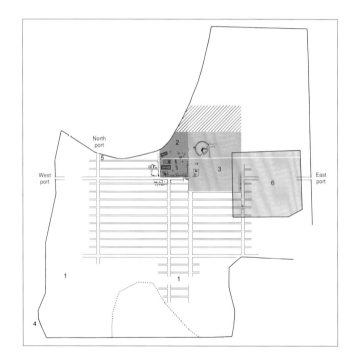

Theoretical reconstruction of the urban settlement at Metapontion

On opposite page: remains of extraurban Doric temple dedicated to Hera, known as the "Tavole Palatine"

History

According to the historian Antiochos of Syracuse, the foundation of Metapontion was promoted by Sybaris. This powerful city sent a group of colonists, who originated from Achaia, its own native region, to occupy territory on the borders of Taranto, in order to block its expansion. The historian records that Metapontion was developed on the site of a previous settlement which was connected with either the city of Siris or an indigenous group—a statement substantially confirmed by the available archaeological evidence. The results of excavations also provide precise chronological information about the foundation of the colony, which dates from the very end of the seventh century B.C. The rivalry with Siris came to an end around 570 B.C., when Metapontion joined forces with Sybaris and Kroton to form the coalition that destroyed the city drawn from Ionic stock.

Metapontion was renowned in ancient tradition for the prosperity of its agricultural territory; the choice of the symbol of the ear of corn stamped on its coins was not an arbitrary one, and its gift of a golden sheaf of corn to the sanctuary of Apollo at Delphi was famous.

The city's prosperity fostered the development of an aristocracy, some of whose extraordinarily rich tombs have recently been brought to light. At the same time, historical tradition reveals the existence of deep internal conflict that resulted in experiments with tyranny. In the second half of the fifth century B.C., Metapontion underwent a revision in the extent of its political authority; one of the most obvious reasons for this was the foundation of Herakleia, jointly promoted by Taranto and Thurii in 434–433 B.C., on the not-too-distant site of the old Siris. Metapontion joined with Thurii in 413 B.C. to support the expedition of the Athenian fleet against Syracuse.

Female statuette in Daedalic style, end of the seventh century B.C., from Metapontion (National Archaeological Museum, Metapontion-Matera)

On opposite page:
above: slab from a frieze showing a cult cortege, 575–550 B.C., from Temple C in the urban sanctuary (National Archaeological Museum, Metapontion-Matera)
below: slab from a frieze depicting a departure, 650–625 B.C., from the sanctuary of San Biagio della Venella, at Bernalda, Matera (National Archaeological Museum, Metapontion-Matera)

The history of the city in the second half of the fifth century B.C. is characterized by its struggle against the Lucanians, the local Italic population. On several occasions Metapontion asked the help of the Greek commanders, called to Italy by the Italiote League headed by Taranto: first Alexander the Molossan, king of Epyros, then Kleonymos, king of Sparta (304–302 B.C.). After the fall of Taranto (272 B.C.) Metapontion was absorbed into the sphere of Rome and became one of its naval allies.

During the Second Punic War, the city welcomed Hannibal, who set up his headquarters there but then transferred the entire population when he was obliged to retreat; the ancient Greek colony never recovered from the devastation of that war.

The Layout of the City and Its Surrounding Territory

Metapontion was built on the Ionic coast of Basilicata, a fertile alluvial plain. The Greek city covered an area of about 370 acres (150 hectares) and was originally close to the sea and bounded on the north by the Bradano River and on the south by the Basento, the mouth of which provided a natural port for the urban settlement. Today the river follows a different course. In Roman times, from the third century B.C. onward, the settlement was limited to the so-called *Castrum,* which occupied a narrow sector of the eastern part of the earlier urban area. The inhabited area was already occupied at the end of the eighth century B.C., by scattered groups of huts that were part of the territorial arrangement laid out by the previous colony of Siris; these were destroyed at the time of Metapontion's foundation.

From the start, the act of foundation provided for the division of the urban space and the organization of the territory: the first priority was to separate the public sectors from the private and commercial ones; the second saw the creation of sanctuaries for the protection of the borders.

The Urban Settlement

Because of its proximity to the sea and its position between two rivers, the territory on which the city was founded contained marshy depressions and higher areas of sand dunes. The presence of this adjacent marshland obliged the ancient city to take constant measures to drain off the excess water. Inevitably, the sand dunes, which were higher and drier, were the first choice of location when the public areas and groups of housing were organized.

The public zone consisted of the sanctuary and the great square (*agora*), situated beside each other at the southern extremity of the urban space. The houses, separated by wide open areas, were scattered in small groups around the public area. The larger areas to be occupied by housing were connected by paths, which formed the basis of the roads built later, around the middle of the sixth century B.C.

At the beginning of the sixth century B.C., the first perimeter walls were built around the city, constructed in mud brick on a stone plinth. The walls followed a route dictated by the terrain; on the north slope and on the one to the southeast, the line of the wall curved sharply inward; these changes in course corresponded to the loops in the Bradano and the Basento rivers.

Work began in the sanctuary and the *agora* on the first of the religious buildings and those connected with political activities from the moment the city was founded. In the sanctuary, excavations have revealed traces of small wooden cult buildings. In the square, beneath the Hellenistic theater and the *ekklesiasterion* (meeting place of the popular assembly), built between the sixth and the fifth centuries B.C., archaeologists have discovered the remains of a platform, also in wood, which appears to have been part of the early primitive building used for meetings.

Around 600 B.C. the first buildings built with stone foundations were constructed. The sanctuary area was surrounded by a wall. At the southeast corner of the area was a small rectangular temple oriented east–west (Temple C, phase 1); only its foundations and a corner of the first course of a *cella* wall have survived. The building was decorated with terracotta slabs depicting a procession of women on chariots in molded bas-relief. Because identical slabs have been found both in the

sanctuary of Athena at Francavilla, in Sybarite territory, and at Policoro, in Siris's territory, it is probable that the Temple at Metapontion was dedicated to same goddess. Dating from the same period as Temple C1 is a second sacred building found at the opposite, northeast, corner of the sanctuary, beneath the fifth-century B.C. phase of Temple D, which was dedicated to Artemis.

In the second quarter of the sixth century B.C. work was begun on the Temple of Hera, immedi-ately to the north of that of Athena and with the same orientation. The sacred building (Temple A, phase 1), however, never progressed beyond the laying of the foundations of the *peristasis* (the colonnade destined to encircle the four sides of the *cella*). The building work was probably interrupted by the impressive construction program that was taking place throughout the inhabited area, to the detriment, particularly, of work in the public sector.

During this phase the first roads in beaten earth were constructed following the tracks of the old link roads: a main artery (*plateia* IV) 22 m wide, running north–south, crossed the entire city, arriving at the public area at the point between the sanctuary and the *agora*. The *agora* was bordered to the east by a second artery (*plateia* V), 13 m wide and parallel to the first, marking out a space 263 m wide that covered the enormous area of about 17.25 acres (7 hectares). The southern limits of the sanctuary

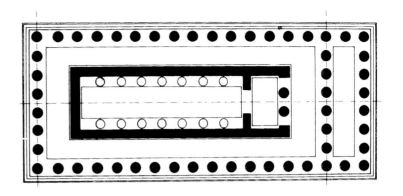

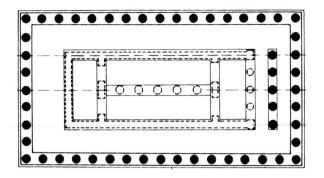

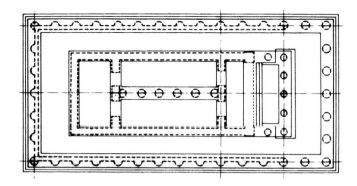

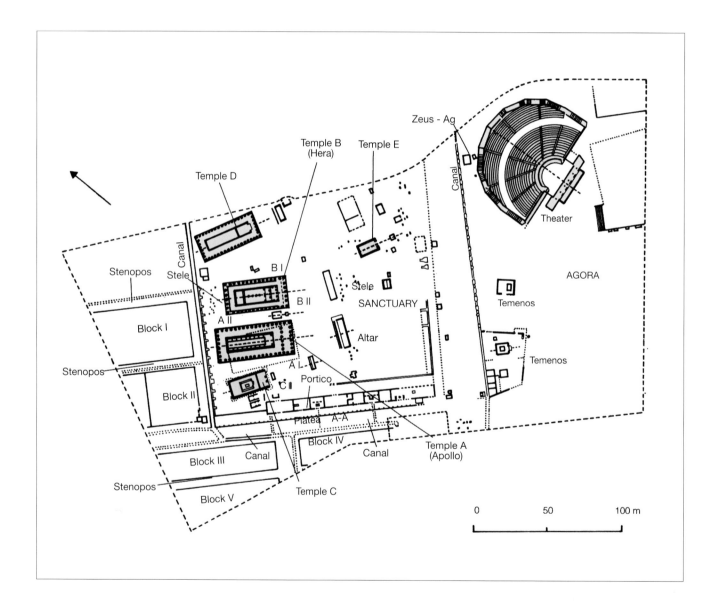

Temple D

Temple B (Hera)

Temple E

Zeus - Ag

Canal

Theater

Stenopos

Canal

Stele

B I

B II

A II

Stele

SANCTUARY

AGORA

Block I

Temenos

Stenopos

Altar

A I

Block II

Temenos

C I

Portico

C II

Platea

A-A

Block IV

Canal

Temple A (Apollo)

Block III

Canal

Stenopos

Temple C

Block V

0   50   100 m

were bounded by a third, smaller road (*stenopos*) which crossed the main *plateia* at right angles and created a narrow strip outside the perimeter wall. This strip was absorbed, in the first half of the fifth century B.C., into a *plateia* oriented east–west (*plateia* A), which led toward the west gate of the city.

The housing blocks were originally built only along the two sides of the imposing north–south artery, which seems to have been the focus of the entire road system; the blocks were bounded by *stenopoi* running east–west and their frontage measured 35 m. It is interesting to note how the road network seems to have been extended throughout the whole of the city only during the second half of the fourth century B.C.

The Temple of Hera was rebuilt in the sanctuary (Temple A, phase 2) and a new temple building added further to the north (Temple B); both were of the Doric order and were oriented, unlike

Detail of a capital from the Ionic temple in the urban sanctuary (Temple D) Metapontion (Matera)

On opposite page:
above left: plan of Temple B, of Apollo, first phase (B1)
above right: plan of Temple B, of Apollo, second phase (B2)
below: plan of the urban sanctuary and the *agora* at Metapontion

Top of page 138: the theater-*ekklesiasterion* of Metapontion

Bottom of page 138: part of the external walls of the theater-*ekklesiasterion* of Metapontion

On page 139: the *cavea* and orchestra of the theater at Metapontion, detail

the older sacred buildings, with the road. The older of the two temples, Temple B, was dedicated to Apollo. A stone stele bearing an inscription to Apollo and giving him the name "Lyceos" (having the nature of a wolf), together with a number of stone stelai, roughly squared and sharpened to a point, was found embedded in the ground near the altar at the front of the temple façade.

Like the earlier Temple of Hera (A1), the Temple of Apollo shows signs of a first phase of construction (B1) that was never completed. During the rebuilding that took place immediately afterwards (B2), the building was extended to a length of 40 m and a width of 18 m. It was built on exactly the same plan as the original—a long, narrow *cella*, an entrance porch (*pronaos*), and room to the rear (*adyton*) surrounded by a *peristasis*. A second line of columns was inserted at the front between the *peristasis* and the *pronaos*. The *cella* was divided along its length by a central line of columns, while the *peristasis* was enclosed by a continuous wall with seven half-columns on the short sides and fifteen on the longer sides.

The construction of the Temple of Hera (A2) was completed shortly after the middle of the sixth century B.C.; it covered an area 6 m long and 23 m wide. The temple, furnished with a *peristasis* of eight by seventeen columns, was made up of a very deep *cella* and an entrance porch (*pronaos*) with antas. Close to the long walls of the *cella* were probably two lines of columns, built to support the weight of the entablature. The elevation of the temple was reconstructed along the eastern façade of the sacred building: it is possible to see the combination—typical of the Doric order—of capitals, with very flattened echinus and four-sided abacus, and a frieze with alternating triglyphs and metopes.

On the temple façade was an inscription of which only the words "for himself and his family" have been preserved. This was perhaps a commemorative dedication put there by some exceptionally powerful political figure, who sought to claim the prestige of being associated with the construction of the temple.

The roofs of both temples were decorated with polychrome architectural terracottas; particularly

Red-figured Italiote *hydria* attributed to the Amykos Painter, depicting Theseus and Pirithoos chasing women, end of the fifth century B.C., from Metapontion (National Archaeological Museum, Metapontion-Matera)

outstanding was the covering of the entablature and the cornices, decorated with braid motifs and repetitive designs, and the *cyma*, decorated with chains of palmettes and lotus buds. The roof was replaced in the second quarter of the fifth century B.C., at which time the *cyma* were embellished with splendid lion-head spouts.

Around 480 B.C., the temples of Athena (C2) and Artemis (D) were rebuilt. The two buildings were no longer aligned with the road network, but were given the same orientation as the earlier sacred buildings. In the case of Temple C, the oldest shrine (C1) was subsumed by a large building, of which only a part of the foundations, made from stone blocks, has survived; among those fragments left of the actual building, it is possible to see that the roof tiles, akroteria, and eaves were of marble. Still remaining of Temple D, situated in the northern sector of the sacred area, are foundations, on two levels, measuring about 14 × 38 m. The temple contained a long, narrow *cella* with a deep porch (*pronaos*), probably with antas, and was in the center of a *peristasis* of eight by twenty columns. The elevation was built in the Ionic order, with some modifications. The columns set on high bases, the upper part of their shafts decorated with floral and geometric motifs and their capitals with wide volutes covered in leaf motifs. Crowning the architrave was a frieze of palmettes and lotus buds. The eaves were decorated with geometric patterns with gorgon-head antefixes.

Around the middle of the sixth century B.C. in the *agora*, a new building was constructed on top of the ancient wooden platform; it served the duplicate function of theater and political assembly hall (*ekklesiasterion*). It was a circular building, 62 m in diameter, capable of holding 8,000 spectators, and consisted of two facing semicircular tiers of seating (*cavea*), built into embankments supported by containing walls. In the center was a rectangular open space that was reached by symmetrical passages; this was the orchestra, used as a stage for the production of plays or as a platform for orators. At the beginning of the fifth century B.C. the *ekklesiasterion* was rebuilt, with the access to the tiers and the seating made of stone.

At the northwest corner of the monumental circular building was a rectangular enclosure dating from the Archaic period, with a central altar. Two stone stelai were found there that had been inscribed in the sixth and the fifth centuries B.C. On the first is written "*agora* of Zeus" and on the other, "Luminous Zeus" (*aglaos*), an epithet which, as will be seen, also applied to the extraurban sanctuary of San Biagio alla Venella. The supreme male deity was, therefore, charged with the protection of the political space of the city, emblematic of which was the *ekklesiasterion*. Because of its crucial importance to the city, the enclosure around the sanctuary of Zeus survived until at least the third century B.C., undergoing much reconstruction during that time.

In the second half of the fourth century B.C. the urban settlement was comprehensively restructured. The fortifications were reconstructed with double parallel lines of masonry built of blocks, and a outer ditch was added. The route the wall took, however, was unchanged from that of the earlier walls. The street network was extended to cover the whole urban area and two main arteries were added, running north–south (*plateiai* I and III), toward, respectively, the north gate and the sanctuary; in the southern sector of the city a third avenue (*plateia* C) was constructed at right angles to the others. At the opposite, northern, sector, in the strip running along the walls, another north–south road was built, intersected by *stenopoi* at right angles, along which were blocks of houses with atrium and peristyle. Beside this road was a large sewer that collected the water from two main sewers and ran along beside the perimeter of the sanctuary to the north, where it discharged into the ditch outside the city walls.

Work in the public area concentrated above all on the *agora*. On the west side, a series of stone stelai were set up in a line along the extension of the big, central north–south *plateia*, marking the boundary between the *agora* and the area of the urban sanctuary. The opposite side was bordered by a two-story portico (*stoa*).

It is known that in the southwest section of the *agora* there was a large trapezoidal enclosure encircling a shrine dating from the end of the third cen-

tury B.C., the foundations of which are still there. The shrine included an earlier altar associated with a well, around which numerous bronze laurel leaves have been found. Immediately to the south of the altar, from the same phase, was a large plinth made of stone blocks, possibly the base of a statue. According to one very appealing theory, the identity of the altar/plinth complex is revealed in a statement by Herodotos. The great historian records the existence at Metapontion of an altar dedicated to Apollo in his capacity as the god of prophesies, and a statue of his inspired priest, Aristeas of Proconneso, dedicated in the *agora* with the same designation, Aristeas. The cult is a manifestation of Metapontion's powerful attachment to the Pythagorean doctrine. The city was the last refuge of the philosopher after he was exiled from Kroton, and an enduring tradition of study and political activities based on the philosophy of the great thinker grew up there.

The largest building in the *agora* was certainly the great theater built on top of the *ekklesiasterion*, of which an extensive sector of the façade has been reconstructed. The monument, which always served the dual purpose of place of entertainment and political meeting place, consisted of semicircular tiers of seating set on an artificial embankment supported by an imposing retaining wall. In front of this supporting structure was placed the actual façade of the building: a polygonal wall with ten sides, crowned by a Doric colonnade with a frieze of triglyphs and metopes. Inside, in front of the tiers, which were subdivided into five sectors, was the circular orchestra.

The Extraurban Sanctuaries

From the earliest years of the settlement, the boundaries of the extensive territory of Metapontion were protected by two important sanctuaries. The first, dedicated to Hera, was built about 1.9 miles (3 km) to the northeast of the old city, and dominated the course of the river Bradano, beyond which was the territory of Taranto. The second, connected with Zeus, Athena, and Artemis, was in the San Biagio alla Vella locality, about 3.8 miles (6 km) to the west of the city, not far from the left bank of the Basento.

Small sculpture in whitish sandstone, depicting Helen emerging from the egg, 425–400 B.C., from a collection of grave goods in the Torretta area (National Archaeological Museum, Metapontion-Matera)

On opposite page: statuette of a winged female with a faun, probably representing Artemis, 525–500 B.C., from the extraurban sanctuary of San Biagio alla Venella, at Bernalda (National Archaeological Museum, Metapontion-Matera)

The Temple of Hera (the "Tavole Palatine") dates from 540–530 B.C. It was built on stepped foundations on three levels measuring about 34 × 16 m and was divided into a *cella*, a porch (*pronaos*), and a closed room to the rear (*adyton*) surrounded by a *peristasis* of six by twelve Doric columns, well preserved on both of the long sides. The architrave was decorated with the usual frieze of metopes and triglyphs; the roof, like those in the temples in the urban sanctuary, was lined with terracottas decorated with double braids, and eaves ornamented with palmettes and false lion-head spouts molded in relief. The last course of tiles on the pitched roof was retained by antefixes with palmettes and lotus buds.

The sanctuary of San Biagio alla Venella can be identified with that of Artemis on the Kasas (the ancient name for the Basento), mentioned in a poem written by the poet Bacchylides in honor of Alexidamos of Metapontion, victor in the Delphic Games. Recently identified in the sacred area is a monumental building, dating from the fourth century B.C., which consists of a small peripteral temple measuring perhaps 16 × 19 m, of which only a few bits of the foundations have survived.

Further to the east was a rectangular structure, the so-called fountain shrine, located near a spring. The earliest phase dates from the seventh century B.C., making it the earliest evidence of the existence of large buildings in the colony. Belonging to it was molded clay frieze, representing a warrior—probably Achilles—mounting a chariot drawn by a pair of winged horses. The monument shows signs of successive stages of reconstruction in the sixth century B.C., and also in the fourth century B.C., when it was embellished with a basin to collect the water from the spring. Found in the sanctuary was a stone stele inscribed in the Archaic period which mentions Zeus Aglaos (luminous)—the same epithet with which the god was venerated later in the enclosure near the *ekklesiasterion*.

The Territory

The old city extended its control over a wide agricultural territory including the coastal alluvial plain and the hills beyond, watered by the Bradano, Cavone, and Basento rivers and their subsidiaries. While the plain was obviously ideal for the cultivation of cereals, the stretch of uplands was the sector preferred by those setting up farms, especially in the second half of the fourth century B.C.; the area had good pastures and was suitable for the specialized cultivation of vines and olives.

The older farming settlements, going back to the first half of the sixth century B.C., were located in the valleys of the Bradano and the Basento, but over the course of the second half of the same century the exploitation of the agricultural land became increasingly widespread, a trend which peaked in the fourth century B.C., at which time there were possibly a thousand farms.

At the end of the sixth century B.C., an extraordinary process used to divide up the agricultural land left deep marks on the landscape—so deep that they were first noticed in the course of aerial photography. The strip of land between the Bradano and Cavone rivers, and perhaps even further south, as far as the river Agri, was crisscrossed, over a distance of 9.3 miles (15 km) toward the interior, by a system of roads and canals running east–west toward the coastline. These axes were arranged at a distance of about 210–215 m from each other and were intersected by other, transverse ones, marking out large lots of, on average, about 44.5 acres (18 hectares). The few farm complexes that have been explored to date were either constructed on a square plan, with a single story, small rooms, and no courtyard, or were of a larger size, with two stories and a central courtyard and granary.

Scattered over the landscape was a network of little rural sanctuaries, placed not far from each other; located along the highways, in places suited to the making of contacts and exchanges, these were the essential sites that united the rural population. The one that has been the most systematically explored is in the Pantanello region, a small monument at the mouth of a spring in use since the Archaic period.

Taranto

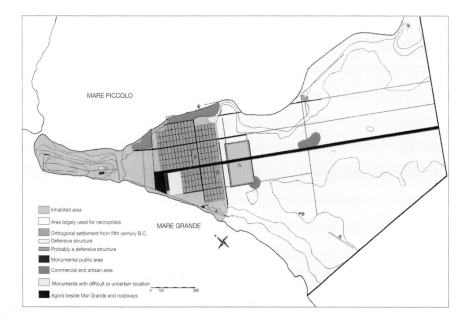

Plan of Taranto

On opposite page: female
head in Parian marble, first
century B.C., from Taranto
(National Archaeological Museum,
Taranto)

History

According to historical tradition, Taranto was
founded in the year 706 B.C., by colonists from
Lakonia, a Greek region in the southeast part of the
Peloponnese, of which Sparta is the capital. The
foundation was carried out by a group of exiles
called the "Parteni" (born of virgins), who were
expelled from Sparta after the Messenian War was
brought to a victorious conclusion. According to

one version, the "Parteni" were the dishonored
sons of those who, having taken no part in the war,
were made into slaves; according to another, the
"Parteni" were born of illicit unions between the
Spartan women and the young warriors who, having left for the war, were sent back home when the
conflict was prolonged in order to procreate and
avoid the risk of a future shortage of men. Even in
this case, though, once the war was over, the sons
born of these illegitimate unions were denied the
rights accorded to other citizens.

In both cases, their subordinate status provoked them into starting a rebellion, which was
put down; to overcome the crisis and find a place
for them, it was decided to send Phalantos, the
leader of the rebellion, to consult the oracle at
Delphi, who gave the following response: "I give
you Saturo and the fertile land of Taranto, to be
the 'scourge of the Iapygians.'" The oracle's prophesy defined the focal points of the territory of the
colony: the urban center and its eastern outpost,
which, as will be seen, came into being at the
foundation of Taranto; also the mention of the
Iapygians anticipated the struggle against the
native population that the city would have to face
throughout its history.

The news of the conquest of the Iapygian city
of Carbina (perhaps the modern Carovigno) came
in the first decades of the fifth century B.C.; during
this conflict the Tarantans' reputation was sullied
by cruel outrages perpetrated against women and

children. At around the same time, two gifts were dedicated to Delphi, attributed to the sculptors Argos and Onatas of Aegina: the first depicted horses and female Messapian prisoners, and the second, the mythical fathers of the city, Taras and Phalantos, towering above the native king, Opis. At some time between 473 and 467 B.C., the fates were reversed and the army of Taranto, allied to that of Rhegion, suffered a terrible defeat, chronicled by Herodotos, who defined it as "the greatest slaughter ever suffered by Greeks." The backlash of the defeat rebounded on the political order of the colony, and the aristocratic government was ousted in favor of a more democratic regime.

In the second half of the fifth century B.C., profiting from the growing weakness of Metapontion and Kroton, the city turned its own expansionist aims toward the territory of Siris, engaging in battle with the recently founded Thurii; as already mentioned, the conflict ended up with the creation of a common settlement and, later, with the foundation of Herakleia under the control of Taranto. When the Athenians sent an expedition to Sicily, the city took the side of Syracuse and that of the mother city, Sparta, while in 413 B.C., in the opposite camp, the native king Arta supplied the Athenians with 600 archers.

The fourth century B.C. was a period of great magnificence for the city, which assumed an influential role among the other Greek colonies and became one of the most important centers of culture in the Mediterranean. The history of Taranto in the first half of the century was marked by the extraordinary personality of the Pythagorean Archytas: philosopher, mathematician, and friend and host to Plato on his voyages to the West in 388, 366, and 361 B.C. At the same time, he assumed a prominent role in the political life of the city, where for seven consecutive years, from 367 to 361 B.C., he held the most important magistrate's role.

Archytas, together with Plato, entered into a very close relationship with the tyrant of Syracuse, Dionysios II, seeking vainly to convert him to their own philosophical ideals. They did manage, however, to dissuade him from his alliance with the Lucanians, thus obtaining a period of peace for the

Greek city. It was in this context that Taranto, after the decline of Kroton, assumed the leadership of the Italiote League and transferred its seat to Herakleia. At the death of Archytas, the delicate political balance that the philosopher had succeeded in creating crumbled. The city was not able to resist the pressure from the indigenous populations and was obliged to call upon foreign princes for help.

The first of these, in 342 B.C., was the king of Sparta, Archidamos, who died in Manduria, fighting against the Lucanians and the Messapians in 338 B.C. In 334 B.C., it was the turn of Alexander the Molossan, king of Epyros. At first the commander won important victories, coming by the Tyrrhenian Sea as far as Paestum, but then he broke with Taranto and transferred the seat of the Italiote League from Herakleia to Thurii. Finally he was killed in an encounter with the Lucanians in 331 B.C., near the river Acheronte. In the years immediately following, Taranto found itself for the first time faced with the menace of Roman expansionism. In 327 B.C., together with the Samnites, it sent an ambassador to Naples to seek an alliance against Rome. The signing of this alliance was the forerunner to the Second Samnite War (327–304 B.C.), during which Rome succeeded in establishing a stronghold in Puglia with the foundation of a colony at Lucera (314 B.C.).

To defend itself from the Lucanians, Taranto continued to call on the aid of foreign commanders; in 304 B.C. it asked the assistance of Kleonymos, younger son of the king of Sparta and, a few years later, that of Agathokles, tyrant of Syracuse. In the meantime, Rome signed a treaty of nonaggression with the city, in which it agreed not to sail its fleet beyond Cape Lacinio (now Cape Colonna). In 282 B.C. the decisive battle between Rome and Taranto for supremacy in Southern Italy began. Rome, in violation of the treaty which required it not to take an armed fleet beyond Cape Lacinio, intervened in defense of Thurii, threatened by Lucanians and Brettii, and shortly after sent a naval squadron into the waters off Taranto. The Greek city reacted by accepting the declaration of war and asked the help of Pyrrhos, king of Epyros, who arrived in Italy in 280 B.C. After some

Top: gold stater with head of Hera on obverse and a horseman on reverse, 340–334 B.C., from Taranto (National Archaeological Museum, Taranto)

Below: clay acroterion from a shrine, end of the sixth century B.C., from Taranto (National Archaeological Museum, Taranto)

important initial victories, and having vainly attempted to wrest Sicily from the Carthaginians, Pyrrhos suffered a serious defeat against the Romans in 275 B.C., at Benevento and, in the same year, was obliged to return to Greece, where he died in 273 B.C. The next year Taranto surrendered to Rome, becoming a part of its naval alliance. During the Second Punic War, in 213 B.C., the city sided with Hannibal, forcing the Roman garrison of the city to take up a defensive position on the acropolis (the area of the present Old City), where it faced a long siege. In 209 B.C., the Roman army, led by Fabius Maximus, reconquered the city, knocking down the walls, plundering its treasure, and deporting the inhabitants. According to the ancient historians, in Taranto there remained only "the angry ones."

In 122 B.C. the city was renamed Neptunia, a Roman colony.

The Layout of the Inhabited Area in the Archaic Period

The ancient city was established in an exceptionally fine strategic position, on the narrow peninsula between the Mare Grande (Great Sea) and the lagoon known as the Mare Piccolo (Small Sea),

which in ancient times was a secure port. Because of its favorable geographical position, the city represented an obligatory point of passage on the routes that connected Greece first to Italy and then to the Adriatic; for this reason it was not surprising that there had already been an important native settlement there, which was destroyed at the time the colony was founded.

At the time of foundation, which, according to the oldest evidence found, dates from the end of the eighth century B.C., the city was divided into two quarters: one situated in the area of the present-day Old City; and the other in the strip of the Borgo, just to the east of the navigable canal.

The countryside in ancient times was very different from the way it is now. The islet of the Old City, now reached by a swing bridge, was originally connected to the mainland by an isthmus, and was separated from it in medieval times by the creation of a ditch, which in 1887 was transformed into a navigable canal. The isthmus overlooked a hollow that separated the area of the Old City from the rest of the settlement. This natural defense was subsequently reinforced by the construction of a ditch.

In ancient times the peninsula of the Old City covered an area of about 39.5 acres (16 hectares), less than the modern city, which was extended in the tenth century A.D. by a stretch of alluvial reclamation along the basin of the Mare Piccolo. Its present road network follows the ancient one, with the modern Via Duomo retracing the route of the main artery (*plateia*), which crossed the entire length of the peninsula. Leading off that road, of which strata from several periods have been uncovered, were the little transverse roads (*stenopoi*) that are still recognizable in the modern street network.

Because of its favorable geographic site, protected by the sea and in a dominant position relative to the rest of the settlement, the peninsula became the acropolis of the Old City in the Archaic period, and was enclosed within a protective wall; it housed the principal cult site, which contained splendid offerings like the colossal bronze statue of Herakles, a work by the sculptor Lysippos that was transported to Rome to celebrate the triumph after the conquest of the city in 209 B.C.

At the entrance to the acropolis, in the Piazza Castello immediately to the south of Via Duomo, one can see the ruins of a great temple of the Doric order; these consist of a part of the *peristasis* with three columns, two of which have been preserved in their entirety. The form of the capitals, which are similar to examples in Corfu and therefore suggest a date of around the first quarter of the sixth century B.C., would make the Tarantan temple the oldest stone building in Magna Graecia.

In medieval times the temple was used as a source of stone, and was subsequently assimilated into the structure of the Church of the Trinità and the convent of the Celestini; during this phase, kilns and wells were built that eventually damaged the fabric of the monument. The present condition of the building is the result of a radical town-planning project during which the medieval structures built over the ancient sites were demolished. The tormented history of the temple explains its precarious state of conservation. There remain, apart from those sections of the colonnade still standing, only a few traces of the outer wall and the ruins of what may perhaps have been an altar. There is no trace, however, of a *cella*, which, at a guess, could have been built—at least initially—of mud brick. Also uncertain is the identity of the deity, probably female, to whom the cult was ascribed.

The other side of the Via Duomo, opposite the Church of Sant'Agostino, may have been the site of another sacred building, indicated by the discovery of a series of altars belonging to the cult of Aphrodite. Another cult structure has also been identified beneath the cathedral of San Cataldo, while at the western end of the peninsula excavations carried out under the Gothic church of San Domenica and to the side of San Martin have revealed elements of the *peristasis* and the *cella* of a temple from the first half of the fifth century B.C., constructed over an even older monument from the Archaic period.

The main square of the city—the *agora* in the Greek phase and the Forum of the subsequent Roman settlement—was located outside the acropolis quarter. The historian Strabo emphasized its huge dimensions and recalled how it

housed the bronze Zeus that was also the work of Lysippos, and was second in size only to the Colossus of Rhodes. According to scholarly tradition, the statue was still standing at the time of St. Peter's visit to Taranto, when the apostle's faith caused the pagan idol to fall. The site of the *agora* has not yet been identified; it must have been

Statue of Zeus in bronze, around 500 B.C., from Ugento, Lecce (National Archaeological Museum, Taranto)

already determined at the time of foundation, which would place it near the area of the isthmus.

Along the shore of the Mare Piccolo two important sanctuaries have been found, both in use as early as the Archaic period. One of them is in the area of the Military Hospital and near the Naval Arsenal; there, in the first years of the twentieth century, a sacred *aedicula*, or wall recess, was discovered, probably dating from the first century B.C., characterized by the presence of an altar and some stone stelai placed along the walls. It was built over another, older, structure consisting of terracing made from blocks, from which two flights of steps led to the beach. Arranged in the same way, probably from the fourth to the third centuries B.C., were the buildings in an older sacred area that, from the material recovered, could date from the sixth century B.C.

In the same area numerous deposits of votive terracottas were found, the most conspicuous among them being the Fondo Giovinazzi, discovered at the end of the nineteenth century. The majority of the items it contains are figures of diners at a banquet, reclining on a couch and with various items such as goblets, lyres, and cornucopias. These are related to the wide variety of types in use from the second half of the sixth century B.C. right through to the end of the fourth century B.C. In these images one can usually identify divine (Zeus, Dionysos, Hades) or heroic figures linked to one of the chthonic cults. A recent suggestion is that they simply represented the donors themselves, enjoying the activities of the symposium and confirming their position as citizens and free men. The sacred area grew up near the port basin, which was situated in a wide semicircular creek, protected by two jetties built of stone blocks; these were discovered during the last century.

A second important sanctuary was located outside the city, on the Pizzone promontory, in the internal area of the lagoon of the Mare Piccolo. In this area extensive deposits of votives have been found, dating from the middle of the seventh to the fourth centuries B.C., dedicated to a chthonic deity similar to Persephone. A vase inscription from the sixth century B.C. states that the goddess was

venerated under the name of Gaia (the Earth), according to a cult that was particularly important also in the mother city, Sparta. Dedicated to her are prestigious ceramic figurines, miniature vases, and, above all, thousands of statuettes in terracotta: female figures, nude or seated; standing figures; statuettes of mother and child; busts with typical attributes of the cult of Demeter, like piglets or crossed torches.

On the east side, the boundary of the Archaic city is marked by a swathe of *necropoleis,* which start less than 0.6 miles (1 km) from the line of the navigable canal. In the densely occupied cemetery, the tombs were found to contain small family groups, spread over three or four generations. Further from the city the tombs clustered in little groups placed along the sides of the main road. Even further away the graves probably belonged to small villages remote from the urban center.

Among the graves from the Archaic period was a small group of monumental tombs dating from the middle of the sixth to the first decades of the fifth century B.C. These were underground chambers, lined with stone slabs, with one or two columns supporting a pitched roof. Stone sarcophagi were set around the interior wall. One appealing theory maintains that the plan of the chamber, and the arrangement of the sarcophagi around the walls, was an evocation of the way the banqueting room is arranged, with its couches convivially placed around the walls of the room. The tomb architecture seems to attempt to replicate the experience of the symposium—the symposium being, as Greek poetry tells us, that prestigious occasion used by the aristocracy to promote friendship and form relationships and alliances.

Urban Changes in the Fifth Century B.C.

In the course of the fifth century B.C., the urban settlement underwent a radical change that modified the order of the city. An enormous expansion took place in the quarter outside the acropolis of the Old City, surrounding it with an imposing perimeter wall 6.8 miles (11 km) long, which enclosed an area of 1,359.5 acres (530 hectares). On the east side, the wall described a sharp angle, from the Mare Piccolo to the Mare Grande around the marshy depression of the so-called Small Salt-flat—reclaimed in recent years—which constituted a natural defense.

Remains of the wall are recognizable in the areas of Masseria Carmine, Collepasso, and Solito. Built as a double line of masonry in sandstone blocks, it is a little more than 4 m wide and furnished with towers and an outer ditch 11 m wide. The blocks bear many letters of the Greek alphabet, which were used as quarry marks. The wall was built over tombs from the sixth century B.C., which sets the upper date limit for the construction at around the middle of the fifth century B.C. But what were the conditions that were responsible for this impressive reconstruction of the urban area? The most likely circumstance, historically, was the political upheaval caused by the serious defeat of the city by the Messapians between 473 and 467 B.C., which occasioned the fall of the previous aristocratic regime and replaced it with a democratic government. The new institutional order included the extension of political rights with a consequent enlargement of the citizen community. The increase in the urban space could, therefore, have been connected to the need for further urban accommodation incurred because greater numbers were able to participate in the political life of the city.

The "democratic" reconstruction of the city also meant the reorganization the urban layout involving the planning of a regular road network. A number of traces of this have been found and, in all probability, they continued to be used by the subsequent network created during the Roman period. In this context the historian Polybios mentioned the existence of two main arteries—the "Low Road" and the "Savior"—which led from the city walls to the Forum and were linked by a terrace at right angles to the isthmus of the Old City.

Regarding the housing blocks, it has been possible to reconstruct a model about 32.5 × 54 m in size, originally subdivided into six lots. When it was extended, the inhabited area was built on top

of the earliest burial grounds, and even the contemporary *necropoleis* were inside the perimeter wall. The tombs were moved to the eastern urban periphery, in a zone not occupied by houses, which started from what is now Via Duca degli Abruzzi. The location of the tombs inside the walls ran very much contrary to historical tradition; by way of explanation, Polybios tells of an oracle which foretold the future of the Tarantan people: "if these had lived among the majority."

A strip of the necropolis has recently been investigated and labeled for visitors in an archaeological area in Via Marche, near the Palace of Justice. The area, used for funeral purposes in the Archaic period, was part of an urban reorganization during the fifth century B.C., when it was divided into blocks, marked out by roads. Within these blocks the tombs were arranged in family lots until the third century B.C. From the first half of the fourth century B.C. until the second century B.C., *aedicula* were put into the tombs in the form of small temples (*naiskoi*) destined to contain the statue of the deceased. They were decorated with elaborate sculptural adornments (pediments, friezes, metopes) made in an expressive style, rich in movement, which reflected the most up-to-date techniques of the great contemporary sculptural tradition. There was a variety of themes illustrated in scenes either of a funereal nature or of combat. Frequently they involved a horseman striking down an enemy, modeled on the traditional heroic image of Alexander the Great. Another typical scene was of two figures (women, warriors, figures in oriental costume) fleeing in opposite directions.

The Territory

In the oracle of foundation, given to Phalantos at Delphi, the territory of the colony was defined as being between the two principal strong points of Taranto and Satyrion, or "Saturo." The prophesy stressed that the colony should not consist of a single urban center but required the simultaneous foundation of two stable settlements capable from the start of ensuring the defense of a territory surrounded by a hostile native population.

Top: woman's head in clay, 360–340 B.C., from Taranto (National Archaeological Museum, Taranto)
Bottom: black-figured Kalchedian *hydria* with facing sphinxes, 530–520 B.C., from tomb 1 in Via Palma n. 72 at Taranto (National Archaeological Museum, Taranto)

On pages 152–53: clay statuettes of dancers, fourth to third centuries B.C., from Taranto (National Archaeological Museum, Taranto)

The Greek name Satyrion has been preserved in the modern one of Saturo, 7.45 miles (12 km) to the east of Taranto. The site, before the foundation of the colony, was occupied by a large native settlement that was destroyed by the Greeks, who replaced it with a large village, as is confirmed by the existence of a necropolis that was already begun in the seventh century B.C. The acropolis of the settlement was developed on a low hill situated between the bay of Saturo and Porto Perone. Excavation has uncovered foundations surrounded by part of a flagged floor that were part of a shrine from the Hellenistic period. The building of this monument obliterated an earlier deposit of votive material dating from the second half of the seventh century B.C. Based on epigraphic data, the sanctuary has been attributed to the cult of Athena.

In the valley below the acropolis, between the coast road and the sea, near the ancient port, was a second sanctuary associated with a spring that nowadays flows into a large basin. It included a shrine, perhaps dating from the middle of the fourth century B.C., that contained a statue related to one of the female cults and a stone box, possibly intended for valuable offerings. A second stone box, found outside the shrine, contained numerous coins and gold artifacts.

In the sanctuary were very rich deposits of votives—heavily plundered by clandestine excavation—dating from an extended period running from the middle of the seventh to the third century B.C. The inscriptions confirm that the cult was dedicated to great female goddesses such as Gaia, whom we already met in the sanctuary of Pizzone, and Aphrodite, who was venerated with the title Basilis (Queen), the same title with which she was celebrated in Sparta. Beside these two goddesses was another figure, probably that of the local nymph Satyria, to whom the shrine by the spring may have been dedicated.

Apart from Saturo, an extensive network of farming villages occupied the plain right up to the spurs of the Murge hills. They developed right from the first years of the life of the colonial settlement and are mostly indicated by the presence of groups of tombs. The only center that has been extensively investigated is that of L'Amastuola,

8.7 miles (14 km) northwest of Taranto, in the district of Crispiano. The village already existed during the first decades of the seventh century B.C. and survived to the beginning of the following one. It grew up on a plateau dominating the coastal plain, protected by an embankment. About 700 m from there, a necropolis containing thousands of tombs has been found. Within the inhabited area, houses have come to light dating from the earliest time of the settlement and rebuilt at the end of the seventh century B.C. They were constructed on a very simple plan, on a plinth of stones with walls of mud brick and a roof of some kind of perishable material, and contained a single square room opening onto a large courtyard. At the edges of the territory, at Campomarino near Maruggio, and in the region of Torricella, sanctuaries marking the boundaries of the Greek city were established from the Archaic period onward. A significant number of them were dedicated to Artemis, goddess of the wild.

The system of land occupation developed in the course of the seventh and sixth centuries B.C. went into crisis in the fifth century B.C. The areas farthest from Taranto were abandoned, and farming continued only in the strip around the city. This change coincided with the democratic reformation of the city, to which the enlargement of the city has already been attributed. The political upheaval must, in fact, have had repercussions on the estates of landowners, so that the crisis also affected that part of the aristocracy that lived permanently on the land.

As in other Greek colonies, it was only in the fourth century B.C. that the agrarian space became intensively populated—a situation linked to the development of specialized agriculture such as vines and olives. Indications of this are found in the establishment of a network of farms and larger nuclear settlements that stretched right to the Murges and to the northern limit of the river Bradano.

The territory of the colony was defended by a fortified encircling wall, built between the fifth and fourth centuries B.C., along the strip of the Murges and the heights that bordered the Tarantan plain to the north.

Hollow tubular earring with spiral twist ending in two forward-facing female heads with Phrygian bonnets, end of the fourth to the beginning of the third century B.C., from Via Principe Amedeo at Taranto (National Archaeological Museum, Taranto)

On opposite page: gold earring with a disk decorated with a rosette and a hollow pendant of a woman's head, Hellenistic period, from Crispiano, Taranto (National Archaeological Museum, Taranto)

Naxos

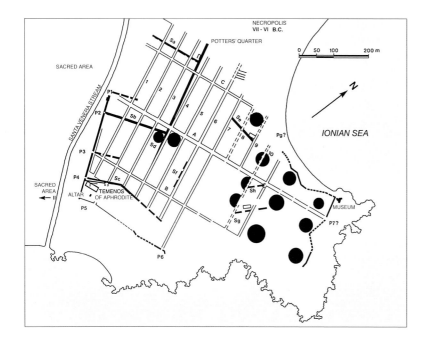

Plan of Naxos

On opposite page: perimeter wall of the *temenos* of Aphrodite

History

The ancient sources offer a somewhat controversial picture of the events surrounding the foundation of Naxos.

According to Thucydides, Naxos was oldest of the Greek colonies in Sicily, founded around 834 B.C. by Kalchedians from the island of Euboia, led by the *ekistes* (founder of the colony) Theocles.

Almost as soon as they arrived the colonists would have erected an altar to Apollo Archegetes, the guiding deity of the expedition, to whom the *teoroi* (sacred messengers) offered sacrifices before departing on their missions. In the historian's time (the fifth century B.C.), this altar was located outside the walls of the colony. Ephoros also considered Naxos to be the oldest of the Greek colonies in Sicily, though he maintains that it was founded at the same time as Megara Hyblaia, ten generations after the Trojan War (that is, around 834 B.C.), by colonists from Kalchedon, together with a group of Ionians and Dorians. Finally, Hellanicos maintained that some of the colonists who founded Naxos were from Kalchedon, and others from the island of Naxos, in the Cyclades, from which, appropriately enough, the Sicilian colony took its name. The archaeological evidence goes only part of the way toward answering the questions set by these literary sources.

The oldest finds, dating from between 740 and 730 B.C., seem to support Thucydides' version of the timeline—on the whole a more coherent account than that put forward by Ephoros. However, the items, mostly imported ceramics, are not actually older than those found in other Siciliote cities, such as Megara or Syracuse, where there is evidence of a permanent Greek presence around 750 B.C. On the other hand, the discovery of imported ceramics more or less contemporary with those found in other Euboian colonies, like

Zankle, Katane, and Leontinoi, seems to demonstrate that the colonies of this group of settlements were all founded at substantially the same time. At any rate, Naxos must certainly have represented an early port of call when one considers that it was the first secure landing place for ships from the eastern Mediterranean bound for the West.

The location of the city probably explains the appearance of coins connected with the port's economic activities (customs duties, tolls, etc.) around 530 B.C. The first series of coins, the oldest in Sicily, had the head of a bearded Dionysos on the obverse,

Wall in polygonal work, part of fortifications

while the reverse carried a bunch of grapes, referring, evidently, to the importance of wine production on soil that was ill-suited to growing cereals.

As far as the ethnic makeup of the colony is concerned, the abundant amount of Euboian ceramics, either imported or, especially, produced locally, indicates that the colonists were of Euboian extraction. To date, no imports from the island of Naxos

have been found. The recent discovery of a marble stele dating from the seventh century B.C., with an inscription dedicating it to the goddess Enyo in characters resembling the alphabet used on the island of Naxos, would, however, appear to confirm the theory that the foundation of Naxos was indeed influenced by the island of Naxos in the Cyclades.

Naxos remained a colony of modest size but was nevertheless an important departure point for Greeks traveling into native territory. Groups left from Naxos to found Leontinoi and Katane, and in addition, according to the sources, Naxos founded the subcolony of Kallipolis, a site that still remains to be identified. After an initial powerful attack launched by Hippokrates, tyrant of Gela, at the beginning of the fifth century B.C., the city fell victim to the expansionist aims of the Deinomenides, lords of Syracuse. In 476 B.C. the tyrant Hieron destroyed it, deporting the inhabitants, together with those of Katane, to Leontinoi. Only in 460 B.C., after the fall of the Deinomenides and the restoration of democracy in Syracuse, could the inhabitants of Naxos return to their city and enjoy thirty years of peace. The renewed independence of Naxos was marked by the issuing of a new series of silver coins, stamped with a bearded head of Dionysios on the obverse and, on the reverse, a depiction of a drunken Silenos, one of the finest artistic expressions in Greek numismatics.

In the course of the Peloponnesian War during the first (427–424 B.C.) and the second (415–413 B.C.) Athenian expeditions to Sicily, the Ionic Naxos allied itself with Athens. After a heavy defeat was suffered by the Athenian army, the city fell victim to the vengeance of Syracuse; in 403 B.C., Dionysios I, aided by a traitor and the use of trickery, razed it to the ground, confiscating the land to distribute among the Sicels and selling the inhabitants into slavery.

Albeit in a much reduced form, life on the site started again, concentrated mainly on the area closest to the bay; it was probably from there that, for a short time, coins were minted bearing the name Neapolis (new city). But the real heir to old Naxos was Tauromenion (now Taormina), the new city which the survivors and descendants of the citizens of Naxos founded in 358 B.C., under the leadership of Andromachos, father of the historian Timaios. At any rate, the site was not depopulated; in the small inhabited area around the bay, probably dating from the first two centuries of the Roman Empire, one could possibly recognize the *mansio* (staging post for horses) which the *Itinerarium Antonini* mentions in connection with the name of Naxos.

The Foundation of the Colony and the Creation of the Urban Settlement

The Euboian settlement was established on the slopes of Mount Tauro, on a lava rock terrace a little above sea level on the peninsula of Schiso, which encloses a wide bay to the southeast—the city's natural port. To the west, the Santa Venera stream, whose course runs close to the walls, defines the boundary of the inhabited area toward the interior.

Due to its favorable position and the natural advantages it offered, the site was occupied by native settlements from Neolithic times onward and was still inhabited at the time the Euboian colonists arrived, as is shown by the fragments of pottery contained in the mixture of detritus from the Iron Age found in the deeper strata in various parts of the city. For the rest, the sources indicate that when the Greeks disembarked, the Sicels currently occupying the zone withdrew to the mountainous spurs of Mount Tauro.

The settlement in the eighth century B.C. occupied only the eastern side, concentrated near Cape Schiso and the bay, and covered an area not greater than 24.7 acres (10 hectares). Traceable to this earliest phase are just two roads, oriented northeast–southwest and running parallel to the coast, and one house consisting of a single, square room, equipped with a stone bench along one side, matching the type of dwelling found in many parts of Sicily (Megara, Syracuse) and in the Greek homeland (Chios and Andros).

In the middle of the seventh century B.C., the settlement spread out over the whole peninsula, to occupy an area of 99 acres (40 hectares), with an urban plan centered on roads oriented north–south, which linked the city with the hinterland. The minor roads, which crossed at right angles to the main roads running north–south, had a different orientation in the eastern part—the most recently urbanized—from that of the west, and seem to have outlined an urban system based on quarters. Various buildings, both sacred and private, faced onto the roads. Among them was a sizeable dwelling of the *a pastas* type (that is, having a portico which serves as a link between the closed rooms and the exterior), which, on account of large area of its floor plan—rare in the Archaic period—would seem to have been occupied by a person of high rank, possibly a priest.

At the end of the sixth century B.C., perhaps under the threat of an attack by Hippokrates of Gela, the urban area was ringed by an imposing fortification made up of a double line of masonry built of blocks of igneous rock laid in polygonal work. It is possible to the trace the route of these city walls, which followed the coastline in the eastern and southern areas of the peninsula and ran for some distance beside the Santa Venera stream to the west. On that side, the imposing width of the fortification (about 5 m) leads one to suppose that it also served as an embankment against the frequent overflow of the nearby stream.

The Classical City

At the beginning of the fifth century B.C., the face of the city was radically changed by the creation of a new urban settlement, which was built over the long-disused Archaic one. The new urban installation, the result of a unification project, can reasonably be attributed to Hieron of Syracuse, who, after he conquered Naxos in 476 B.C., could well have initiated a real refounding of the city, reconstructing the urban network and repopulating it with citizens of Doric origin, probably mercenaries.

The Classical city was redesigned according to a modular urban plan, of the Hippodamian type, crisscrossed by three *plateiai* running east–west—of which the wider central one functioned as the main artery of the system—with intersecting smaller roads (*stenopoi*) set at right angles to them. One of the latter, the one that followed the route of the old road to Zankle (*stenopos 6*) was wider than the others. Every point where the *plateiai* and the *stenopoi* intersected was marked by a post consisting of a square altar base; all were of the same size, and were made from blocks of lava rock; these must certainly have served some sort of sacred function in addition to acting as measuring rods. The network of streets marked out regular rectangular blocks, of a basic model measuring 156–158 × 39 m, except for those which, because of the conformation of the ground, or some prior installation (like the southern sanctuary), were smaller.

Within the regular blocks the houses were arranged in groups of four, separated by narrow passages (*ambitus*) that served to drain away the water. The houses were, for the most part, very small, having an internal courtyard with an atrium, often covered. Still uncertain, however, is the location of the public space, the *agora,* which a recent theory suggests may have been located in an area free of buildings at the crossing point of *plateia* C (the most northerly one) and *stenopos* 6. The position of the square between the two major roads leading to Katana and Zankle, respectively, and in proximity to the port would, if the theory is correct, have been in accordance with the maritime and commercial activities of the city.

The Sacred Areas

Within the urban network of the Archaic city there were many cult areas, consisting for the most part of simple square buildings without external columns (shrines E and F), often only indicated today by finds of the architectural terracottas that served to decorate and protect the wooden structures. Dating from the end of the seventh century B.C. was a small temple (temple C) in the eastern sector of the peninsula, which contained an elongated *cella in antis.*

The most important of the urban sanctuaries was, however, the one situated on the extreme southwest boundary of the city, near the left bank of the Santa Venere, noted as the *temenos* (sanctuary) of Aphrodite. It was built in the second half of the seventh century B.C., and at the end of that century the sanctuary was enclosed by a boundary wall skillfully and meticulously built in polygonal work. The sacred area had two entrances, one of them to the south, toward the beach and the sea and the other to the north, a true *propylaia* (mon-

umental entrance). When, toward the end of the sixth century B.C., this boundary wall was subsumed by the fortified city walls, the southern entrance became one of the gates of the city, while the one to the north constituted the monumental entrance leading from the inhabited area.

Inside the *temenos,* the remains of a shrine (shrine A) oriented northeast–southwest, date from the earliest phase, at the end of the seventh century B.C., as do a similarly oriented shrine to the south, a square altar with three steps, and several small altars scattered over the southern side of the boundary. Also from the same period are two kilns—one rectangular for firing tiles, the other circular, for vases—which provided for the needs of the cult. At the end of the sixth century B.C., a large building resembling a temple (shrine B) was superimposed on shrine A. This one, unlike the preceding one, was oriented east–west, in line with the urban street plan of the Classical period.

The fairly controversial proposition advanced by a number of experts was that the sanctuary was the *Aphrodision,* mentioned by the sources, which was in fact located on the sea (*epithalassion*); according to another theory, it was a sanctuary of Hera, as shown by the inscription of the goddess's name on a fragment of a *hydria* (water container). Immediately outside the area, along the right bank of the Santa Venera, excavations uncovered two important Archaic sacred complexes, which, by their position on the boundary, marked some kind of consecrated area between the city and the surrounding land.

The sanctuary nearest the coast was built on the La Musa property, not far from the mouth of the stream, and seems to have reached its maximum period of development between the seventh century and the first half of the sixth centuries B.C. Its presence was revealed by numerous pieces of architectural terracottas, which gave no clue to the identity of the deity to whom it was dedicated. The other complex was on the Scalia-Malprovvido property, a little farther west and a short distance from one of the city gates (gate A); it appears to have been particularly significant, both for the wealth of items it contained and for its cultural implications. Among the things brought to light inside the vast *temenos*, active from the end of the seventh century until the Hellenistic period, are the remains of a shrine (shrine A) and two small temples (H and I) dating from some time during the first half of the sixth century, and an exceptional amount of architectural terracottas, also from the Archaic period, which indicate the likely presence of other destroyed or unknown buildings.

Given the vastness of the sacred area and its layout, which appears to be an aggregation of other neighboring *temene,* it is probable that other divinities were venerated there in addition to the particular one or ones for whom the cult was named. According to one theory, for the moment unconfirmed, this was probably the Temple of Apollo Archegetes, founded by the colonists when they disembarked, which would have been near the mouth of the Santa Venera and not on Cape Schiso, as is usually claimed. But it was certainly attributed to the cult of Enyo—a rather archaic divine personage with warlike features—as was proved by the discovery of a stone with an inscribed dedication, and also to that of Athena, given the designation *promachos* on some votive statuettes.

The Potters' Quarter

Naxos had an important ceramic tradition, both in the production of vases, as is proved by the abundant quantity of local pottery of the Euboian type, produced between the end of the eighth and the seventh centuries B.C., and in the production of terracotta figurines. In particular, the production of architectural sheathing materials in clay was notable for both its quality and the variety of influences and inspired ideas. The clay needed for the manufacture of these products was found in the hills behind the bay, in an area northeast of the city.

Although some of the earliest kilns discovered in Naxos were found inside the urban perimeter, in the *temenos* of Aphrodite and linked to the activities of the sanctuary, the quarters containing the workshops were located essentially in the peripheral areas, as was the custom in Greek cities. The most important quarter for the production of vases and similar items was on the Larunchi hill on the northern periphery of the city, where there

were rich deposits of clay; it continued to be so from the end of the sixth century throughout the whole of the fifth century B.C. The complex consisted of three kilns and rooms for working the clay lining two streets running at right angles to each other. To judge from the numerous fragments left from the work, the workshops produced vases and tiles, clay figurines, and antefixes with Silen heads—a form of architectural terracotta quite common in Naxos.

A similar establishment was found to the west of the city, also in a marginal area, between the Santa Venera stream and Alcantara. From the fragments that have come to light in that area, it seems to have been active during the whole of the fifth century B.C. Here, too, separate rooms were arranged along two streets set at right angles, but no kilns were found.

The Necropolis

The largest cemetery area was located to the north of the city, in the strip behind the bay of Schiso, and along the main road, which ran from Naxos to Zankle-Messana (route retraced within the perimeter by *stenopos* 6). The necropolis came into being during the earliest days of the colony—as is proven by the discovery of twenty or so tombs dating from the eighth century B.C.—and remained in use, with one or two gaps, until the Hellenistic period. The area it covered varied notably with the passage of time; while in the Archaic period the same space was used for successive burials, in the Hellenistic period the tombs, regrouped in little clusters, seem to have been dispersed over a wider area, at a greater distance from the inhabited zone.

Another area used as a cemetery was also located to the west of the inhabited area, half way between the Santa Venere and the Alcantara River, serving the extraurban development of *plateia* B. The necropolis was installed at the beginning of the fifth century, at the time Hieron was establishing the new city, and was in use throughout the Classical period. In the Hellenistic period the space seems, however, to have been abandoned and the dead buried in the old necropolis to the north and in a new area, also to the west of the inhabited area, near the suburban sanctuary on the La Musa property.

Taormina (Tauromenion)

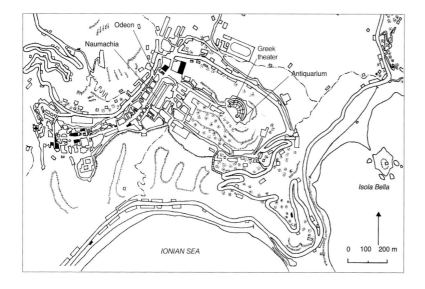

Odeon
Naumachia
Greek
theater
Antiquarium

Isola Bella

IONIAN SEA

0   100   200 m

Plan of Taormina

On opposite page and pages 164–65: the theater at Taormina

History

From the beginning, the history of the ancient center of Tauromenion, the modern Taormina, seems to have been closely linked with that of Naxos; virtually nothing about its earliest phase, however, is recorded in historical sources, and archaeological evidence is not available in sufficient quantity, nor is it of the right kind, to fill the gaps in our knowledge.

At the time the colonists arrived in Naxos, the area around Mount Tauro was occupied by Sicels,

as the grave goods found in the tombs and grottoes of Coccolonazzo di Mola, next to Tauromenion, show. The necropolis continued in use for several decades, which seems to indicate that, at least for a time, newcomers and natives existed peacefully side by side. Very soon, however, the favorable position of the area, which dominated the landing sites between Cape Taormina and Cape Schiso, thus controlling the route along the northeast coast of the island, attracted the interest of the neighboring Euboian colony.

Recent finds of Kalchedian ware and two antefixes from the Archaic period—one with palmettes and the other decorated with representations of heads of black people—almost certainly made at Naxos, probably point to an early conquest by Naxos, which thus gained a valuable outpost on the borders of its own sphere of influence.

There is no further information about the center until the late Classical period, when, according to Diodoros, the Sicels (to whom the tyrant Dionysios I had granted the area, confiscated from Naxos after the conquest in 403 B.C.), with the support of the Carthaginian commander Himilco, settled on Mount Tauro in 396 B.C. and founded the city of Tauromenion there. A few years later Dionysios, thanks to an agreement with the Carthaginians, succeeded in conquering the Sicel fortress and ousting most of the inhabitants, replacing them with mercenaries loyal to himself. The city was then refounded in 358 B.C. by

Andromachos, father of the historian Timaios, who installed a colony populated by survivors of the destruction of Naxos in 403 B.C. The center thus inherited the legacy of the old Euboian colony; the Tauromenian coins bore the image of Apollo Archegetes, the god who had guided the Euboian colonists to Sicily.

The new city came within the political orbit of Syracuse and remained connected with that city until the Roman conquest. In fact, in 345 B.C. Tauromenion fought on the side of Timoleon

during the encounter with the Carthaginians and, during the reign of Agathokles, was directly annexed by Syracuse. It was Agathokles who exiled the historian Timaios, son of the founder of the colony and his political adversary. When Rome appeared on the political scene in Sicily, in the course of the First Punic War, Tauromenion followed the lead of Syracuse, then governed by Hieron II, and allied itself with the Romans. The city then became one of the strongholds of the rebel slaves in the course of the first of their wars, and was conquered in 132 B.C., after a prolonged siege.

Under Caesar, Tauromenion became a Latin *municipium*. Finally, Augustus, at the end of the first century B.C., ousted the original inhabitants, who had been hostile to him during his war against Sextus Pompeius, and created a new colony in its place.

The Settlement

The city of Tauromenion was established on one of the terraces of Mount Tauro, about 200 m above sea level. Little is known about the appearance of the old center, which was built over by the medieval and modern cities. The disappearance of the old ring of fortifications, large parts of which were still visible at the start of the twentieth century, has also seriously compromised any possibility there may have been of recording the topography of the old inhabited area.

The settlement must have covered the strip of plain bounded on the east by Theater Hill and dominated, inland, by Castle Hill. From Diodoros' description of the failed siege attempt by Dionysios I, in 395 B.C., it would seem that both these heights served as acropolises.

The political and administrative center of the Roman city, the Forum, must have been located near the modern Piazza Vittorio Emmanuele II, and was most probably built on top of the old *agora* from the Hellenistic period. Nothing, however, is known about the street plan, though it is probable that the present Via del Teatro and the Corso Umberto I follow long-established routes. The city archives also seem to have been located a short distance from the Forum/*agora*, or so it would appear from the discovery in that area of inscriptions of an administrative nature dating from the Hellenistic period. These include important documents that list the names of public officials (*strategoi* and teachers) and monthly financial reports, which offer invaluable information about the administration of the city, especially financial. It seems possible, however, that the philosophical school was located in the other sector of the city, to the southeast of the theater, where brief inscriptions on plaster have been found, dating from the Hellenistic period, which quote summaries of the works of Greek historians of the time (among them Fabius Pictor, author of the earliest Roman annals—written, however, in Greek) and were almost certainly displayed in a library, probably one attached to the school.

Finally, among the buildings of a public nature was an imposing bath complex from the late Imperial period, which stood back-to-back with the Forum. The complex was made up of three major rooms, flanked by smaller rooms, and built in perforated brickwork with a lining of marble *crustae* on the walls.

The Sacred Buildings

The remains of two ancient sacred buildings have been preserved, incorporated, as often occurred, within a Christian edifice. Beneath the church of Santa Caterina, near Piazza Vittorio Emmanuele II, is the stylobate from a small fourth-century B.C. temple, which is richly decorated with marble in the Ionic order. The location of the building, near the Forum/*agora,* is an indication of the importance of the cult, but the name of the deity to whom it was dedicated has not been identified. However, the square building behind it, dating from the Hellenistic period, was dedicated to Isis and Serapis; remains of it have been located beneath the Church of San Pancrazio, just outside the Messina gate. The identity of the cult was confirmed by the discovery of two inscriptions containing dedications to the two deities, one in Greek and the other in Latin, and a statue of Isis.

The Theater

The most significant and best preserved of all the monuments of the ancient city is the theater. Built on the southern slope of the hill, Tauromenion's theater was the second largest in Sicily

after the one in Syracuse. It was built during the Hellenistic period, but only a few remains of stone walls beneath the stage, and a few steps, carved with a Greek inscription mentioning Philistide, the wife of Hieron II, have survived from that phase.

The building that now occupies the site is a reconstruction from the Imperial period, which was notably larger than the earlier building, as indicated by the fact that one part of it covers the remains of a small Hellenistic temple. The *cavea,*

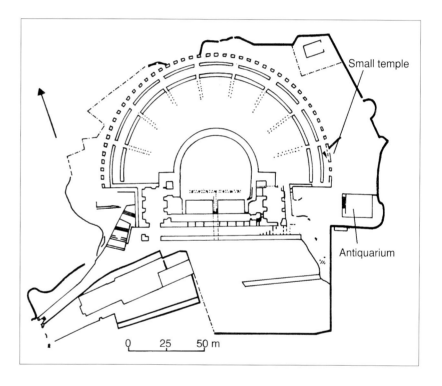

109 m in diameter, was crowned by a covered double colonnade, reached from the tiers of seating, which were divided into nine sectors by flights of steps. Access to the stage from the orchestra was gained by way of passages lined with niches framed by columns.

Lentini (Leontinoi) and Catania (Katane)

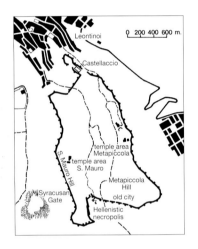

Plan of Leontinoi

On opposite page: southern urban gate (Syracusan Gate)

Lentini (Leontinoi)

History

According to the writings of Thucydides, Theocles and the inhabitants of Naxos founded the colony of Leontinoi five years after the foundation of Syracuse in 729 B.C., after they had expelled the Sicels by force of arms. However, Polyenos' account of their connections with the Sicels is somewhat different; he maintains that there was a period of peaceful coexistence between the colonists and the native people that lasted until the latter were forcibly removed by colonists who arrived at Leontinoi from Megara Hyblaia, following Lamis.

The existence of a settlement in the pre-Hellenistic era has been confirmed by archaeological research, which brought to light the remains of a native inhabited area on the Metapiccola hill, probably identifiable as belonging to the Xouthia, who are mentioned in the ancient sources. The village, consisting of rectangular huts built around a clearing, only came into existence at the end of the eighth century B.C., and so seems to point to a period of cohabitation between Greeks and Sicels. However, the city soon began to expand, at the expense of the natives, who were expelled from the site in the course of the seventh and sixth centuries B.C. and from the surrounding land also, as is shown by the destruction of many indigenous settlements in the outlying areas beyond Leontinoi.

Up until the end of the Classical period very little is known about the history of the city. At the start of the sixth century B.C., after the outbreak of a civil war, power was seized by a person called Panezio, who appointed himself tyrant. At the start of the fifth century B.C. the expansionist policies of the Deinomenides drew Leontinoi into the political orbit of Syracuse, as is demonstrated by the first emissions of coins, dating from the second quarter of the fifth century B.C., bearing a Sicilian version of a quadriga (a chariot drawn by four horses) on the obverse and, on the reverse, an embossed lion's head—living symbol of the city—surrounded by four stalks of barley. In 476 B.C., Hieron, after he destroyed the cities of Naxos and Katane, deported their inhabitants to Leontinoi.

After the fall of the Deinomenides, Leontinoi tried to break free of the Syracusan hegemony. The city entered into an alliance with other Kalchedian cities and with Athens, which, at the time of an attack by Syracuse in 426 B.C., was persuaded by the greatest orator of the time, the Sophist Gorgyas of Leontinoi, to come to the aid of its old ally. Nonetheless, the congress of the Siciliote League, held at Gela in 424 B.C., ratified a truce for the whole island, forcing Athens to withdraw. Leontinoi again came within the sphere of influence of Syracuse, but a serious social crisis revived the conflict. The city was split between the big landowners, who favored Syracuse, and the democratic party, which again appealed for help from the Athenians. This was the pretext for a second Athenian expedition to Sicily (415–413 B.C.),

Top: clay bust of goddess,
first half of the fifth century
B.C., from the plain of
Catania (Civic Museum, Adrano)

Below: marble head of a
kouros (standing Greek
male), beginning of the fifth
century B.C., from Leontinoi
(Civic Museum, Castello Ursino,
Catania)

which ended in the defeat of the Athenian army near Syracuse.

Leontinoi then became a kind of *phrourion* (outpost) of Syracuse, inhabited by foreigners and exiles, involved in the turbulent events that characterized the last two centuries of the autonomy of the great Siciliote *polis* before the Roman conquest. Occupied in 406 B.C. by citizens of Agrigento fleeing from the Carthaginian advance, it was repopulated by Dionysios I around 396 B.C., with 10,000 mercenaries who, in lieu of pay, were given the territory belonging to the old Euboian city.

Around the middle of the fourth century B.C., under the government of the tyrant Hiketas—who first supported and then became the enemy of Timoleon—the city was conquered by the latter, who deported the inhabitants to Syracuse. Then, in company with Taormina, Katane, and Kamarina, it was punished by Agathokles for having taken the side of the Carthaginians. Finally, in the course of the Second Punic War, the killing of a number of Romans gave Marcellus a pretext for attacking the city, sacking it, and massacring the inhabitants. From that point on there followed an unstoppable period of decline for Leontinoi; by the time of Cicero, the ancient Euboian colony had been reduced to a miserable village.

The Settlement

The colony of Leontinoi was established on a group of hills to the south of the plain of Etna, in territory renowned in antiquity for the fertility of its soil—the famous "Leontinoian fields." The inhabited area extended over two hills, San Mauro and Metapiccola, separated by the deep San Mauro valley.

The first Greek settlement occupied the San Mauro hill and, in the course of the sixth century B.C., was extended eastward onto the adjacent hill of Metapiccola, which had previously been the site of a native settlement. According to the description handed down to us by Polybios, the inhabited quarter and the sanctuaries were on the heights, while the valley held the *agora* and the public buildings. The city had, at that time, two gates, one at the southern extremity of the valley, in the direction of Syracuse; on the opposite side, toward the north, the other gate opened on to the "Leontinoian Fields." At the foot of the hill to the west, beyond the

bank of the river Lixos (now the San Eligio) was another inhabited area. Archaeological research seems to confirm the information passed on by Polybios.

On the San Mauro hill, finds were made of architectural terracottas which must have decorated a great temple that dominated the height and the remains of a Greek edifice, set into the rock, dating from between the eighth and seventh centuries B.C. On the adjacent Metapiccola hill, foundations were uncovered of a sixth century B.C. temple and, along the western slope, a deposit of votives was found containing terracotta and Attic and Corinthian ceramics from the second half of the sixth century B.C.

The Fortifications

Of the imposing city wall that protected the inhabited area, investigations have brought to light a large stretch of the southern sector, which includes the Syracusan gate described by Polybios.

The part of the wall that has been preserved enclosed the southern and eastern slopes of the San Mauro hill and ran down into the valley, describing a wide indentation of about 160 m, then climbing back up toward the east, along the western slope of the Metapiccola. The gate, protected on the east side by a square tower, was set in the oldest part of the fortifications and was of the "pincer" type. This was a type of defense quite common in Sicily—examples have been found in Megara Hyblaia, Syracuse, Naxos, Eloro, and Tindari—which gave greater control over the entrances to the city. The walls were built at the beginning of the sixth century B.C., first enclosing just the San Mauro hill, seat of the earliest habitation, then later taking in the Metapiccolo area too. Around the middle of the fifth century the walls were subject to extensive rebuilding, which also included extending the earlier system.

Finally, toward the end of the third century B.C., probably occasioned by the events of the Second Punic War, the defensive system was again reinforced.

The *Necropoleis*

The city's largest burial ground so far uncovered was located just outside the southern gate, along the road leading to Syracuse. The necropolis was in use from the Archaic period until the end of the third century B.C. During the earliest period—the last half of the sixth and the whole of the fifth century B.C.—the dead were cremated and the tombs used to hold the ashes, with little in the way of embellishments; the end of the fourth and the beginning of the third century B.C., however, saw the appearance of many *epitymbiai,* monumental tombs with stairs. The final period, between the second quarter and the end of the third century B.C., seems to indicate a break with the previous state of affairs. The tombs from this phase are very poor indeed, arranged in a very casual way, often amid the ruins of the fortifications.

Another consistent cluster of *necropoleis,* in use during the Classical period, was found in the Piscitello district, in the area to the north of the modern residential quarter. The tombs that have been investigated are of the trench type, covered by large slabs, and date from the second quarter of the fifth to the first half of the fourth century B.C.

CATANIA (KATANE)

History

The city of Katane was founded by a group of Kalchedian colonists who left Naxos shortly after the foundation of Leontinoi, around 729 B.C., under the leadership of the *ekistes* (founder of the colony) Evarcos. Literary sources make no mention of any native settlement existing prior to the arrival of the Greeks—unlike what is known about Naxos, Leontinoi, Syracuse, and other colonies that were settled nearby. Even the archaeological research, which revealed the occupation of the site in very ancient times (the Neolithic, Eneolithic, and, to some extent, the Bronze Age), seems to uphold the ancient authors' silence on this subject. However, the gradual conquest of the outlying territory, spreading out along the river valleys, must surely have taken place at the expense of the Sicels; judging from the archaeological evidence, it was fairly violent.

Almost nothing is known of the earliest history, but in the sixth century B.C. Carondas, one of the most famous legislators of the Greek world, whose laws were adopted not only in his own country but

also in the other Kalchedian cities in Sicily and Southern Italy, was a resident of Katane.

Like Naxos and Leontinoi, at the start of the fifth century B.C. Katane, too, was a victim of the expansionist policies of the Syracuse of the Deinominides. In 476 B.C. the tyrant Hieron, after conquering Leontinoi, deported its population and refounded Katane under the name of Aitna, repopulating it with 10,000 inhabitants of Doric origin, many of them probably mercenaries, coming from Syracuse and the Peloponnese.

The new city minted coins and was celebrated by Pindar in the famous *Pythian* I, written in Hieron's honor, and by Aeschylos, in his lost tragedy, *The People of Aitna.* Quite soon, however, with the death of Hieron and the restoration of democracy in Syracuse (461 B.C.), the new inhabitants were forced to flee the city and take refuge in the Sicel center at Inessa, which in turn assumed the name of Aitna, while the original inhabitants returned to Katane, which reverted to its original name.

In the encounter between Athens and Syracuse, during the second Athenian expedition to Sicily (415–413 B.C.), after an initial period of vacillation Katane ranged itself on the side of Athens, becoming a support base for the Athenian encampment. At the end of the fifth century B.C., Dionysios I's accession to power and the encounter with the Carthaginians marked a tortured page in the history of the city. In 403 B.C., the Syracusan tyrant succeeded in conquering it, selling some of its inhabitants into slavery, and repopulating it once again with mercenaries, this time from Campania. One of these, the Sabellian Mamerco, became tyrant of the city in 354 B.C. Having first allied himself with Timoleon, and then going over to the Carthaginian side, he was captured by Syracusans in 338 B.C. and crucified in the city's theater.

With the First Punic War, Katane entered the political orbit of Rome; among the booty taken from the city was, so Pliny tells us, a great sundial which was taken from its place in the Assembly and sent directly to adorn a temple in Rome. During the period of Roman domination, the city of Katane was one of the more flourishing centers on the island. This is made evident by its depiction in the ancient sources as "extremely wealthy" (Cicero, *Verrine Orations,* II.3.10) and from its appearance, if the

Silver tetradrachm with *auriga* crowned with Nike on obverse and head of Apollo on reverse, around 480–470 B.C., from Leontinoi (National Archaeological Museum, Naples)

numerous monuments that embellished the urban center—some of them still there today—are any indication.

The Countryside in Ancient Times and the Settlement

The colony of Katane was established on the west coast of Sicily, on the lower southern slopes of Mount Etna, on the margins of the very fertile plain that surrounds the foot of the volcano. The superimposition of the modern city and the profound changes that have occurred—some of them caused by natural forces, like the lava flow of 1669 which filled up a large area of the old harbor basin, and the earthquake of 1693—make a reconstruction of the physical appearance of the old center difficult to achieve, particularly the Greek center. However, again thanks to the newest research, it is now possible to define the topography of the ancient city, at least along general lines. The first settlement of the colonists occupied the Montevergine hill—present site of the eighteenth-century Benedictine convent—which took on the

function of an acropolis. In fact, its height looked out over a wide expanse of plain that extended to the north and the south, crossed by the river Amenado—to the south of the city, corresponding to the present Via Etnea—and an ample port, bounded by the promontory on which the Castello Ursino now stands.

The Acropolis

The earliest settlement on the hill has left behind only the imported ceramics (from Corinth, Euboia, Rhodes, and Attica) found in the deepest layers, and a few isolated remains of walls. In the middle of the sixth century B.C., the acropolis seems to have been organized to form an urban plan. While no arterial roads have been found, the houses that have come to light, containing many relatively small rooms, were consistently oriented southwest–northeast, like the slope of the hill.

In the first quarter of the fifth century B.C., the area suffered radical destruction, perhaps as a result of its conquest by Hieron in 476 B.C. Not until the fourth century B.C. was there a new

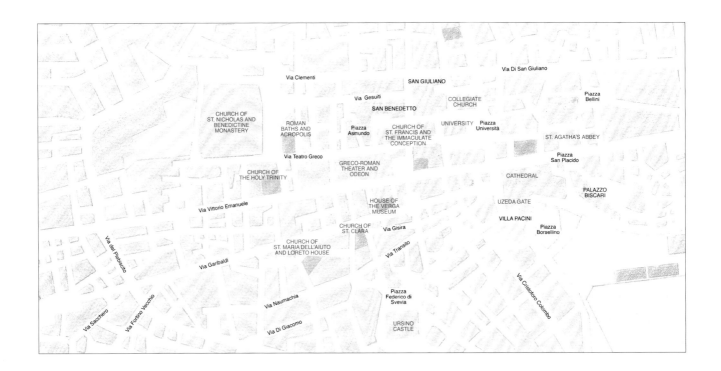

urban reorganization involving the whole of the hill of the acropolis. The new plan placed the buildings according to a north–south orientation that did not follow the natural contour of the terrain, superimposing them in a haphazard way on the Archaic system. Beside the housing area there was also a building devoted to sacred use, probably connected with the cult of Demeter as indicated by finds of statuettes of devotees with torches and piglets.

Finally, in the first decades of the third century B.C., around the time of the Roman conquest in 263 B.C., the whole area was reorganized and a group of houses was built on terraces, with plastered and painted walls and paved floors, which demonstrate the wealth of the city in Roman times.

The Lower City

We hardly know anything about the lower city in the earliest period. The single defining element of the inhabited area consisted of an expanse, now gone, of the Archaic walled enclosure discovered in the Indirizzo quarter (Via Zappala Gemelli), to the southeast of the city. At this point, the line of the wall took in the river Amenano, going on to join up with the point of the promontory of Castello Ursine.

At the foot of the acropolis, to the south, in the area of Piazza San Francesco, was the sanctuary of Demeter, mentioned in the sources, and the site of the discovery of a rich deposit of votives, among them molded terracottas and ceramics dating from the first years of the sixth to the end of the fourth century B.C.

It is also possible that the public square of the Hellenistic period, the *agora,* was nearby, in what is now the bustling Via Vittorio Emanuele, where the Forum stood in the time of the Roman city. Along the same road, which probably retraces a part of an important ancient way, were the theater, rebuilt in the Imperial epoch on the site of an older edifice from the Greek era, of which a few traces still survive, and the *odeion,* placed beside it, as in Naples and Pompeii. At the opposite end of the city, near Piazza Stesicoro, the northern boundary of the city, one finds the amphitheater, a building 125 m long which could accommodate around 15,000 spectators.

Zankle/Messina and Milazzo (Mylai)

View of the Straits of Messina

ZANKLE/MESSINA

History

According to an account by Thucydides—the main source of information about events surrounding the foundation of many of the Greek colonies in Sicily—the foundation of Zankle happened in two stages. The colony was originally founded by pirates (*lestai*) from the Kalchedian city of Cumae in Opicia, and only subsequently were they joined by a contingent from Kalchis and the rest of Euboia. In fact, the first settlement, that of the "pirates" from Cumae, cannot have been a real *apoikia* (colony) but was rather the occupation of a strategic point on the route to the West at a time preceding the political foundation of the city. The finds uncovered by archaeologists seem to place this presence in a setting that is still precolonial. For this reason, some scholars prefer to attribute the original initiative to the Kalchedians from Pithekoussai, rather than to the "pirates" from Cumae, since that city was founded only at a later date.

The foundation of the *polis* happened with the arrival of the real colonial expedition from Euboia, whose date is placed by archaeological evidence at around 730 B.C., in the same period as the foundation of Rhegion and a number of other ancient Siciliote cities. The colony was given the name Zankle, derived from a Sicel word meaning "sickle" (*danklion*), which alludes to the arc-shape of the port; the choice of the sickle stamped on the earliest issue of coins was thus not an arbitrary one, since it represented the port and the fundamental role it played in the economy of the city.

The expanse of agricultural land surrounding the site was not sufficient to sustain the community and its development. To make up for this deficiency, Zankle expanded to the west; at the end of the eighth century B.C. it founded the subcolony of Mylai (Milazzo) and later, around the middle of the seventh century B.C., also that of Himera. At the beginning of the seventh century B.C. the city also managed to take over the territory on the opposite side of the Strait, where it established the colony of Metaurus, now Gioia Tauro, which was later to come under Lokroian influence. Additional motives for the foundation of Mylai and Metauros are to be found in a desire to occupy key points of the Strait, thus creating a "system" capable of controlling navigation between the Ionian and lower Tyrrhenian seas.

We have very little information about the events occurring in the city in the Late Archaic period, but archaeological evidence shows a picture of a quite prosperous center, open to the traffic in the Strait. Between the late sixth and the early part of the fifth centuries B.C., this picture changed. Zankle went through a crisis to similar that which overtook the Kalchedian colonies of northeast Sicily, as it was prey first to the expansionist policies of Hippokrates of Gela—whose assaults forced the surrender of the city—and later to those of the Deinominedes of Syracuse.

Following the Persian victory at Lade in 494 B.C., some groups of Esuli, who came from Samos and the rest of Ionia, took over the city but were expelled a short time later by the tyrant Anaxilas, who took Zankle in the furtherance of an ambitious project to create an "Empire of the Strait." The tyrant installed a contingent of colonists in the city who came from Messene, his own place of origin, in honor of which the name of the Euboian colony was changed to Messana. The profound political changes that followed were reflected in the coinage, which in this period carried a lion's head on the obverse and a calf's head on the reverse. The same design was adopted in Rhegion, the only difference being the word "Reginon," which replaced "Messenion."

The "Empire of the Strait" did not, however, survive beyond the death of Anaxilas; the inhabitants of both Rhegion and Zankle expelled the tyrant's sons and set up a constitution along democratic lines (461 B.C.). The slow decline the city seems to have experienced in the course of the fifth

century B.C. accelerated sharply at the start of the next century, when the city was conquered by the Carthaginian army in 396 B.C. and razed to the ground. Repopulated in the same year by Dionysios I, who installed a mixed citizenship made up of 1,000 Lokroians, 4,000 Medmei, and 600 Messanians, the city finally fell into the hands of the Mamertines (named from *Mamers,* the Oscan name for Mars), mercenaries from Campania enlisted by Agathokles, who in 288 B.C. traitorously took possession of the city and exterminated most of the population. It was these same Mamertines who, having clashed with Hieron II of Syracuse, called for the help of Rome, thus starting the First Punic War in 264 B.C.

The Settlement

The colony of Zankle was established near the Strait, above a wide area of plain furrowed by streams, at the edge of which lay the sickle-shaped peninsula of San Rainieri, which formed a natural port. The site, although it had been occupied for its strategic position by a native settlement since the Neolithic period, seems to have been deserted at the time of the arrival of the Euboian colonists. Such knowledge as we have of the planning of the ancient inhabited area is seriously affected by the superimposition of the modern city, which, moreover, was devastated by the terrible earthquake of 1908. However, archaeological finds have shown that the early inhabited area, until the end of the fifth century B.C., occupied only a small part of the coastal plain, bounded on the north by the river Portalegna and on the south by the river Zaera. The peninsula of San Rainieri does not seem ever to have been completely urbanized, and contained nothing but a few sacred areas.

The old residential quarter seems to have been organized, at least from the sixth century onward, according to a regular plan, with blocks aligned northwest–southeast; the blocks probably followed the orientation of the arterial road which, being at right angles to the coast and parallel to the rivers, followed the natural gradient of the land, thus assisting the drainage of surface water. From the start of the fifth century B.C., the settlement seems to have begun to scale back and to move toward the

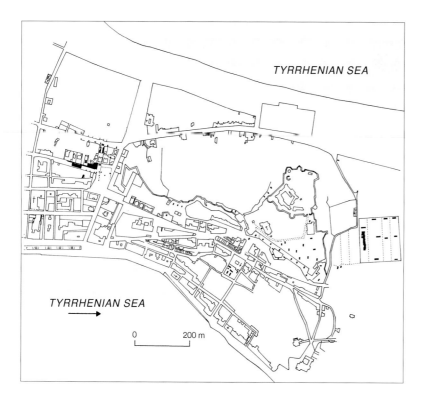

them very ancient indeed—which abound in the religious heritage of the Euboian colonies.

On the Sicilian shore of the Strait, the most ancient and meaningful cults seem to have been concerned with extraurban matters; in the *chora* at Zankle, near Mylai, there was a famous sanctuary to Artemis Phacelitis, guardian deity of "passings," both physical and symbolic. On Cape Peloro there used to be a sanctuary to Poseidon, erected by the giant Orion, symbol of the primordial forces of nature. However, there is no archaeological evidence concerning these cult areas, so the location of the temple, dedicated in the fifth century B.C. by the Messanian Manticlo, to Herakles, the hero who had crossed the Strait with the cattle of Gerion, has not been found.

Even regarding the urban cult sites our knowledge is fragmentary; a deposit of votives found at the end of the San Rainieri peninsula, with materials dating from between the eighth and the sixth centuries B.C., has been tentatively linked to the nymph Pelorias, while there are some deposits of votives which came from the area near to the Hellenistic necropolis at Orti della Maddalena.

interior and the north, and concentrated, during the Imperial period, in an area north of the Portalegna River.

The burial grounds were spread, as always, around the edges of the inhabited area. The only necropolis in use in the Archaic period (the end of the seventh to the first half of the fifth century B.C.) seems to have been some distance from the residential quarter, to the south, near the San Cosimo River, while several groups of tombs from the Classical period have been found some way to the west and southwest of the inhabited part of the city. In the late Classical and the Hellenistic periods, however, a vast cemetery was in use to the southwest of the inhabited area (Orti della Maddelena).

The Cults and Sacred Areas

The whole of the Strait area, on account of its symbolic standing as a liminal zone, a place of passage, is riddled with myths and cults—some of

MILAZZO (MYLAI)

History

The subcolony of Mylai was founded by Kalchedians from Zankle in the last quarter of the eighth century B.C. The ancient sources agree that it was simply an outpost of the main settlement and never became an independent *polis*. Thucydides, moreover, speaks of Himera—the other colony founded by Zankle—as the only Greek city on the north coast of Sicily, while Diodoros categorizes Milazzo as a *phrourion* (fortress). The ancient traditional version of events is indeed upheld by numismatic evidence: Mylai never coined its own money.

The foundation of Mylai was certainly motivated by Zankle's need to secure a larger hinterland for agricultural purposes, but what must not be undervalued is the role it played as one of the pivots, together with Metauros (Gioia Tauro), of that "Empire of the Strait" that controlled navigation between the Ionian and the Tyrrhenian seas. In addition, the settlement performed a defensive role, situated as it was in a strategic position that gave Zankle protection from a possible attack coming from the mountainous area at its back.

All the subsequent history of Mylai, consequently, was strictly linked with that of its founding city, for which it played at all times a most important role; this is demonstrated by the attacks it suffered during the most fragile moments of crisis involving Zankle and Messana. In the course of the Peloponnesian War, during the first Athenian expedition to Sicily, Mylai was besieged and conquered by the Athenians when Messana, first allied with the Athenians, detached itself and went over to the enemy.

Under Dionysios I, Mylai was taken by Rhegion in the war against the tyrant of Syracuse, and repopulated by fugitives from Naxos and Katane, only to be reconquered by Dionysios. The fortress was stormed by Agathokles in 315 B.C., and by Hieron II in 274 B.C. during the encounter with the Mamertines.

During the First Punic War, it was in the waters off Mylai that the Roman fleet carried a great naval victory over the Carthaginians (260 B.C.). Finally, Mylai was one of the bases of Sextus Pompeius at the time of the conflict with Octavius. In 36 B.C., at Nauloco, near Milazzo, the fleet, commanded by Agrippa, won a decisive victory against the enemy.

The Settlement

The settlement at Mylai was established on a narrow peninsula that reached out into the Tyrrhenian Sea in the direction of the island of Aeolia, to which it formed a natural bridge. One of the characteristics of the eastern slope of the peninsula was a wide creek that provided a sheltered, safe harbor basin. Like the island of Aeolia, it was the site of a native settlement in the Middle and Late Bronze Age but does not seem to have been occupied when the colonists arrived.

Our knowledge of the physical appearance of the colonial settlement is sketchy. The earliest inhabited area, or at least a part of it, was probably established on the rock where the Swabian Castle now stands, which had all the characteristics of a fortified acropolis; it was then extended during the Hellenistic and Roman eras onto the eastern slopes that ran down toward the port. It is probable, however, that the plain that rose up at the point of the Cape, a quite large and naturally well protected area, that also contained elements of the Archaic inhabited area. The necropolis was located to the south of the acropolis, on the margins of the inhabited area.

Almost nothing is known of the occupation of the *chora*, the fertility of which was so renowned in antiquity that it was referred to as the "Pastures of the Cattle of the Sun." It seems, however, that the boundary of the territory of Mylai in the Archaic period ran to the west by the river Mela, beyond which were native settlements. On account of its position as a border post, it was not by chance that it contained the sanctuary of Artemis Phacelitis, a deity with liminal elements, linked to the complex universe of physical and symbolic passings.

The *Necropoleis*

The burial grounds extended from the Isthmus to occupy a large part of the flat hinterland. The space given over to necropoleis spread out progressively from the north to the south. The earliest necropolis, in fact, occupied only a limited strip behind the Castle (known as the necropolis of the Isthmus, between Piazza Roma and the Via XX Settembre) and continued along the sides of a main road which linked the inhabited area with the plain. From the sixth century B.C. onward, however, the necropolis tended to spread southward until it had engulfed the San Giovanni quarter.

The most frequently performed rite was that of cremation, with the charred remains of the body collected in a clay container, but there were also plenty of bodies buried in graves dug in the earth, sometimes lined with stones or tiles, and burials in *enchytrismos* (burial in urns, generally used for small children). The grave goods accompanying the bodies were mostly of poor quality and did not seem to represent significant differences in socio-economic position (or perhaps this was a distinction they did not choose to make).

Silver tetradrachm with a chariot drawn by two mules on obverse and hare on reverse, from the era of Anaxilas, around 480 B.C., from Messina

Lipari (Lipara)

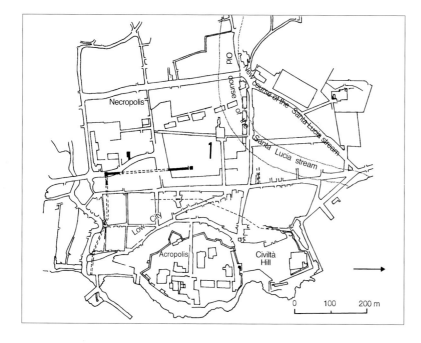

History

The origin of the name Lipari is connected, in ancient tradition, with the saga of Liparos, son of Ausone—king of the homonymous people, the Ausonians of Campania—who, having fled Italy following a quarrel with his brothers, landed on the island and founded the city that bears a version of his name. There he was joined by Aeolos, the eponym of the Aeolian peninsula, to whom he gave his daughter Kyane in marriage. According to one theory, this mythical tradition is the reflection of something that happened in another historical era. Lipari, in fact, like the other islands of the archipelago, beginning in the Neolithic period, was constantly occupied by particularly affluent native peoples, who benefited from trade in obsidian and, later, from trade with the Mycenaean world. In the Late Bronze Age, these groups were supplanted by new groups of people whose material culture had been influenced by contact with that of the population of central Italy. Mythical tradition centering on the figure of Liparos can therefore be seen to celebrates the memory of the migration of human groups from the peninsula toward Aeolia and Sicily.

The history of Greek Lipara started, however, much later. The colony was founded in fact around 580 B.C., by colonists from Knidos and from Rhodes who, after trying in vain to colonize Lilybaion under the leadership of the Heraklean, Pentathlos, embarked for Lipara following the death of their leader. Notwithstanding the reports by the ancient sources of a group of five hundred natives, descendants of Aeolos, who welcomed the new colonists and peacefully coexisted with them, archaeologists have found no signs of native occupation contemporary with the arrival of the Knidians.

Clay mask of Hekuba from Euripides' *Trojans,* first half of fourth century B.C., from Lipari (Regional Aeolian Archaeological Museum, Lipari)

Unlike what happened in other colonies—where the division of the land and its allocation constituted the act of foundation of the city—it seems that at Lipara they set up an unusual, communist-type economy. Tradition tells us that the Liparans worked together on the common cultivation of the land on their own island and that of other neighboring small islands. Only sometime later was the land parceled and allocated for private use, but the other islands of the peninsula continued to be cultivated by the whole community.

Another source of income for the economy of Lipara was the activities of the fleet, which over time evolved from commerce to piracy. These profits, too, were shared out among the citizens. The Liparan fleet, in fact, ruled the waters of the lower Tyrrhenian Sea, finding itself frequently in conflict with the Etruscans, who were pirates also. Three large gifts donated to the sanctuary of Apollo at Delphi record victories won by the Liparans against the Etruscans.

Lipara maintained a fairly marginal position in respect to the events affecting Sicily. From the fifth century B.C. onward, however, it allied itself with Syracuse—a choice for which it suffered when it was besieged by Athens in 427 B.C., and again later by the Carthaginians, led by Himilco, in 397 B.C. At any rate, the Carthaginian siege constituted the only moment of crisis in a long period of peace and prosperity, easily seen in the progressive expansion of the living areas, the lavishness of the tombs, and the flourishing craft production.

At the end of the fourth century B.C., the traditional alliance with Syracuse crumbled; in 309 B.C. Agathokles attacked the city and forcibly removed sacred objects dedicated to Aeolos and Hephaistos, the principal gods of the city. Lipara then went over to the side of the Carthaginians and, as their ally, was besieged in the course of the Punic War and conquered by the Romans in 252–251 B.C. The destruction must have been extreme, and it brought about a serious economic and cultural breakdown in the city, which began to show signs of recovery only in the course of the following century.

The Aeolian islands finally were the scene of the seaborne encounter between Sextus Pompeius and Octavian; allied with the former, the Liparans were deported to Campania by Octavius before Agrippa's final victory at Cape Nauloco, in 36 B.C.

The Settlement

The colony was established on the Castle promontory and very soon after expanded toward the area of plain that extended out from the foot of the promontory. Nothing is known about the layout of the urban settlement in the Greek era. From the end of the sixth century B.C., both the acropolis and the low city were ringed by a fortified wall An expanse of the wall that has come to light near to the present Piazza Monfalcone marks the extent of the Archaic settlement toward the west.

In the course of the next two centuries, the low city expanded still farther to the west, right to the limits of the modern city, as is shown by the new line of the fortifications built in the fourth century B.C. The new fortifications were constructed with a double line of masonry and fortified with towers near the gates of the city and north of the acropolis.

More is known, however, about the Roman period settlement. In the middle of the second century B.C. the city seems to have been reconstructed according to a regular urban plan, with a few main arteries that ran north–south, intersected at right angles by minor roads. The urban perimeter was not altered but simply reinforced with a new city wall at the time of the confrontation between Sextus Pompeius and Octavian.

Cults and Sacred Areas

The main sanctuary of the city was located on the acropolis and was dedicated to Aeolos. There are no buildings left in the area, only a great *bothros* (votive well), almost 7 m deep, the lower part of which was carved out of the rock above a natural ravine across which one can feel the wind blowing from the direction of Greece. The *bothros* was sealed by a circular cover made of solidified lava, surmounted by a recumbent lion of the Ionic style, sculpted around the middle of the sixth century B.C., with two holes at the sides into which the votive offerings were thrown.

The votive material consisted of pottery dating from the middle of the sixth century to the end of the fifth century B.C., among which were a beautiful black-figured Attic *dinos* by the Antimenes Painter, a small narrow-necked vase with a single handle and dedicated to Aeolos in graffiti, and some figured terracottas.

Within the city, other important deities, such as Hephaistos and Aphrodite, were venerated, as is shown by literary tradition and by inscriptions, while an important extraurban sacred area has been found near the necropolis at Predio Maggiore. Within that *temenos* was an altar that was built in the fourth century B.C. over the remains of a previous structure from the fifth century B.C. Next to this were numerous pits filled to the brim with votive material, largely figured terracottas, including busts and statuettes of Demeter and Kore, the powerful chthonic deities to whom the sanctuary was dedicated.

The *Necropoleis*

The main necropolis, used continuously from the middle of the sixth century B.C. to the late Imperial era, extended over a wide area of the plain to the north of the city, in the Diana quarter. From the end of the Archaic period to the Hellenistic period, the most prevalent funeral rite was burial, with the body placed in characteristic terracotta tub-shaped sarcophagi, or in ones constructed from mud brick and stone slabs. Cremation was also used, and the ashes collected in clay containers, while babies and small children were buried in amphoras.

Burials were always accompanied by grave goods, which seem to have been quite rich in the Hellenistic period. The pottery deposited with the bodies was either imported or locally made, like the beautiful vases from the workshop of the Lipara Painter, whose work is recognizable from the use of bright polychrome and from the artist's predilection for terracotta vessels associated with the female sphere: pyxides (small cosmetic boxes), *lekanides* (see illustration below), and hemispherical nuptial drinking vessels. Of the objects deposited in tombs in this period, the most interesting are the terracottas representing theatrical objects, such as clay masks like those worn by actors during performances of comedies or tragedies, and statuettes of comic actors, satyrs or dancers, acrobats, and jugglers.

On page 182: red-figured krater depicting a Dionysiac scene, mid-fourth century B.C., from the necropolis at Lipari (Regional Aeolian Archaeological Museum, Lipari)

On page 183: red-figured krater depicting a theatrical scene—Dionysos with actors and jugglers—attributed to Asteas, mid-fourth century B.C., from the necropolis at Lipari (Regional Aeolian Archaeological Museum, Lipari)

Below left: *lekanis* with a scene of a *gynaeceum* by the Lipari Painter, 325–280 B.C., from Lipari (Regional Aeolian Archaeological Museum, Lipari)

Tindari

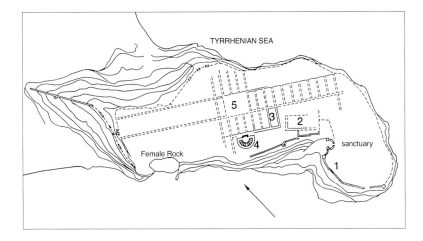

TYRRHENIAN SEA

5

3

2

4

Female Rock

sanctuary

1

Plan of Tindari
1. Wall with towers
2. School
3. House from Timoleon's era
4. Theater
5. *Agora*

On opposite page: the theater
at Tindari

History

The foundation of Tindari was set against the background of the massive movements of people that occurred in the east-central part of Greek Sicily between the fifth and fourth centuries B.C. This was initiated by the tyrants of Syracuse, whose aggressive policy of territorial expansion changed the old settlement picture, destroying and repopulating the old cities and founding new ones. The city was founded in 396 B.C., after the Carthaginians were defeated by Dionysios I of Syracuse, who settled a group of exiles from Messina there; these colonists, in honor of the Lakonian hero Tindaros, husband of Leda and putative father of Dioskouros, gave the colony the name of Tindari.

Tindari entered the political orbit of Syracuse, with whom it was allied in the course of the encounter with the Carthaginians and, later, against the Mamertines of Messina. During the First Punic War, it transferred its allegiance to the Romans. The city remained faithful to the new masters of the island, who, though they imposed the payment of tribute on it as a *decumana* (tithe-paying) city, nevertheless conceded to it also the honor of belonging to the circle of seventeen cities that were permitted to offer a crown to the sanctuary of Venus Ericina, a goddess particularly venerated by the Romans.

Involved in the encounter between Sextus Pompeius and Augustus, the city was conquered by Agrippa in 36 B.C., then occupied next by a colony that received the name Colonia Augusta Tyndaritanorum. A little later, at the start of the Imperial era, a terrible disaster struck: according to Pliny the Elder, one half of the city slipped into the sea.

The Urban Settlement

The colony was established on the northwest coast of Sicily, on a rocky promontory 230 m above sea level, which gave it the appearance of a natural fortress.

The city occupied a plateau that sloped toward the northeast and was set out according to a regular

urban plan crossed by three large roads (*plateia*) running northwest–southeast, intersected at right angles by small roads (*stenopoi*). Such a *per strigas* arrangement produced blocks about 78 m long, set at right angles to the coast. Within each block the houses were built on terraces artificially constructed to level the natural gradient of the plain. The only block as yet excavated, in the extreme south of the city, was occupied on its highest part by a bath complex from the Imperial era, with richly decorated mosaic pavements in geometric designs and figures, one of which shows the *pilei* (caps) of the Dioskouroi, protectors of the city. The terraces lower down contained two houses centered on a large area with peristyle, built during the Hellenistic period, while the last terrace of all, which faced the large *plateia,* contained a number of *tabernae* (stalls or booths), some of which had a shop at the back.

The public area of the city, containing the *agora* and the main public buildings, was set in the southern sector of the plain, down from the highest *plateia,* dominated by rock spurs on which the sanctuary of the Virgin of Tindari stood, very probably the seat of the ancient acropolis.

The Fortifications

Right from the time of its foundation, the city was surrounded by a wall that followed the natural lie of the land. A wide stretch is visible on the southwestern side of the city. The walls dating from the time of Dionysios were built in a haphazard way,

with a coating of plaster, and appear to have been reinforced at irregular intervals by square towers.

At the start of the third century B.C., the fortifications were rebuilt in squared stonework, with double lines of masonry and *emplekton* (an in-fill made from stone chips mixed with mud poured between two elements). Dating from the same time was the great "pincer" device that protected the main gate of the city, located to the south, a little below the modern residential quarter. The actual access door opened at the back of a deep recess, concave in profile, which was further protected by towers to each side.

The Theater

The most important public building in Tindari to come to light to date is the theater, found to the west of the highest *plateia,* a little way in from the line of the wall. The building, which had a diameter of 63 m, was built at the end of the fourth century B.C., although it was rebuilt and restored several times in the Roman period. The *cavea* was for the most part carved entirely out of the hill and was divided into eleven sectors by flights of steps; at the center was the orchestra—access to which was gained by narrow lateral passages (*paradoi*). These were greatly modified in Roman times when the building was used for gladiatorial games. At the front, the *cavea* faced a high, two-story building containing the stage, made up of a central façade with projecting wings, decorated with columns and an entablature in the Doric order.

On opposite page: walls at Tindari

Himera

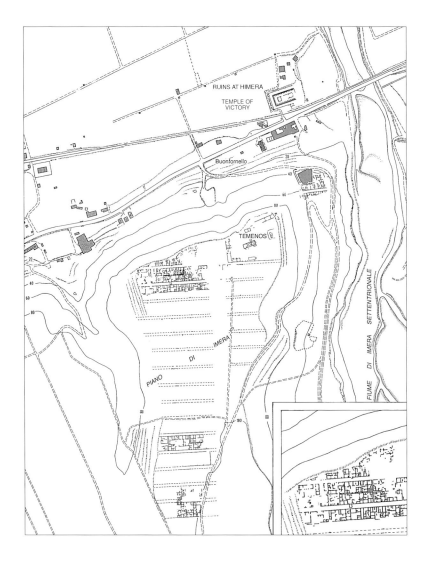

RUINS AT HIMERA

TEMPLE OF
VICTORY

Buonfornello

TEMENOS

PIANO DI IMERA

FIUME DI IMERA SETTENTRIONALE

History

Himera was founded during in the second phase of Greek colonization in the West, which was promoted, for the most part, by the old colonists, who came out in the course of the eighth century B.C. searching for new places to populate.

The city, in fact, was founded in 649 B.C. by Zankle, with the help of a group of exiles from Syracuse, called *Myletidi,* together with a contingent coming from Kalchis in Euboia, the old metropolis of Zankle. It is probable that the three *ekistes* (founders of the colony) recorded by the sources, Euclid, Simos, and Sacone, were each the leader of one of the three different groups of colonists. The mixed composition of the expedition was reflected in the language spoken in the colony, a mixed dialect of Ionian and Doric, while the institutions were Kalchedian.

The city was built on the northern coast of Sicily as the most westerly Greek outpost, near the Carthaginian *epikrateia* (possession), in a frontier position that was to determine the course of its subsequent history. The history of the colony was soon marked by a conflict with neighboring Agrigento, located at a similar height above sea level on the facing southern slope of the island. By the time of the tyranny of Phalaris (around 580–550 B.C.) Agrigento was nurturing expansionist aims toward the north, targeting Himera, which was in an ideal position both to control the traffic on the Tyrrhenian Sea, and to check and contain

On page 188: plan of Himera

On page 189: details of the *peristasis* of the Temple of Victory

Silver drachm with cock on obverse and incused square on reverse, beginning of the fifth century B.C., from Himera (Service for Cultural and Environmental Artifacts, Numismatic Dept., Syracuse)

On opposite page: The sanctuary of Athena

the influence of Carthage. The conflict reached crisis point when, a century later, Theryllos, tyrant of Himera, was threatened by Theron, tyrant of Agrigento and bound to the Deinomenides of Syracuse by a solid dynastic alliance and by a common desire to achieve political and military supremacy over the whole of Sicily. Theryllos' call for aid from the Carthaginians provoked the first weighty encounter between the Punic army and that of Syracuse/Agrigento. The Carthaginians, led by Hamilcar, were defeated near the river Himera, at the Battle of Himera (480 B.C.), which an orator of that time called the Western equivalent of the Battle of Salamis, thus placing the victories of the Greeks over the "barbarians" of the East (the Persians) and over those of the West (the Carthaginians) on the same level.

The victory of 480 B.C. was followed by the conquest of the city by Theron of Agrigento, who installed his son Trasydeos as tyrant. The revolt in which the people of Himera attempted to expel the new tyrant was severely punished by Theron who, following the usual procedure of tyrannies in the Classical period, ordered the refoundation of the city and repopulated it with citizens of Doric origin (476 B.C.). Only with the death of Theron in 472 B.C. and the collapse of the tyranny of the Emminidi at Agrigento did Himera succeed in freeing itself from Agrigentan domination and then setting up a democratic type of government.

The long period of stability the city seems to have enjoyed afterward came to an abrupt end in 409 B.C., when Himera was attacked by Carthaginians commanded by Hannibal—a descendent of the general defeated in 480 B.C.—and totally destroyed; at the site of the death of his forebear Hamilcar, Hannibal carried out a rite of expiation, sacrificing three thousand Himeran prisoners.

From then on the site remained deserted, but two years after its destruction by the Carthaginians, in 407 B.C., a new settlement was formed about 7.45 miles (12 km) to the west and given the name Thermai Himerai (now Termini Imerese)—a reference to the hot springs that existed in the area. The new colony, it would seem, was founded by Carthaginians but, according to Cicero, also welcomed exiles from the old Greek Himera.

The Settlement

The colony was established along the left bank of the similarly named river Himera, a short distance from the coast on the edge of a small alluvial plain, bordered on the interior by a range of hills. At the time the colonists arrived the site was uninhabited, although it probably formed part of the territory controlled by a nearby native community.

The living area was arranged in two distinct sectors: the elongated and narrow high plain, called the Plain of Himera, and the Buonfornello plain, which extended to the northern slopes. It is probable that the earlier settlement had shown a preference for the coastal plain because of the presence of the river, where the city's port was established, and because of the good, easily cultivated land. On the northern slopes of the Tamburino Plain, further south, in the region of Sciacciapidocchi, were two *necropoleis* that served the inhabited area on the upper plain, while the cemetery for the low city was situated on the right bank of the Himera, on the plain of Pestavecchia.

Archaeological research conducted largely in the area around the upper city has demonstrated the existence of two different urban settlements linked to two different periods in the city's history. The earlier urban plan seems to have been put in place in the course of the seventh century B.C. by the second generation of colonists, and remained in use until the second quarter of the sixth century B.C. (around 580–560 B.C.), when the city was reorganized in accordance with a new and coherent scheme which seems to have remained virtually unchanged until its destruction in 409 B.C.

The Upper City

The earliest phase of the part of the city built on the hill seems to date from the end of the seventh century B.C., when the whole of the Plain of Himera area was covered with housing; this is demonstrated by the remains brought to light on the edge of the plain (the north, south, and east quarters). The houses of this era were built on plinths of river stones, with mudbrick walls and straw roofs, all oriented northwest–southeast, which indicates a deliberate attempt at implementing a coherent and integrated plan for the

Bronze statuette of Athena, beginning of the sixth century B.C., from Himera
(The "A. Salinas" Regional Archaeological Museum, Palermo)

organization of the available space. Also dating from this time was the layout of the functional areas, and the setting aside of the whole northeastern sector of the upland plain for the *temenos* containing the cults dedicated to the city's guardian deities. The *agora* probably occupied the area that remained open immediately to the west of the sanctuary.

The possibility cannot be excluded that the city in this phase was protected by a ring of fortifications independent of the one on the plain, but the few remains that have been preserved—a stretch of wall built of mud brick near the northern boundary of the hill, and another piece of wall built of large stones at the opposite southern end—cannot for the moment be dated.

In the second quarter of the sixth century B.C., the living area was reorganized in accordance with a new urban scheme centered around one main, north–south *plateia* running through the center of the plain, intersected by sixteen minor east–west roads which defined regular blocks, 132 × 64 m in size. Each block was divided lengthwise by a narrow *ambitus* (passage) while another transverse *ambitus* subdivided the space into square lots, each containing a single housing unit. These houses consisted of a large courtyard around which were several rooms, including a meeting room in which the men could hold banquets (*andron*).

The Northeast *Temenos*

The sanctuary of the city's goddess-protector, Athena, was situated at the northeastern extremity of the plain, in a prominent position facing the sea; this is confirmed by the sources and by archaeological finds (inscriptions and statuettes). We do not know the location of the *peribolos* during the earliest phase, but the oldest cult building, Temple A, dates from the late Archaic period. The temple, built at the end of the seventh century B.C., consisted of a deep *naos* (another word for *cella*) and a square *sekos*, at the center of which a square base presumably supported a statue of the deity.

With the new urban arrangement that took place in the second quarter of the fourth century B.C., the *temenos*, too, was reorganized; the south-

ern boundary was modified to conform with the new direction of the city blocks and Temple B was built on top of the ruins of Temple A, keeping, nevertheless, to the old orientation. The new building was a *hekatompedon*, that is, a construction measuring one hundred feet (30.7 m), without portico and tripartite. It was decorated with clay friezes depicting the Labors of Herakles, the hero protected by Athena, to whom the people of Himera entrusted the recognition of their own political identity and of the legitimacy of their claim to the territory. According to the etiological myth, it was precisely at the moment that Herakles passed through the territory that the Nymphs introduced the hot springs, in order to restore him.

Between the end of the sixth and the beginning of the fifth century B.C. the sanctuary was again renovated, with the addition of two small buildings, Temple C—a *megaron* with *naos* and *sekos,* placed to the north of the main building and similarly oriented—and Temple D—a simple *megaron,* not quite parallel, at the southern boundary of the *temenos*. Both were decorated with architectural terracottas of the kind used in Campania, indicative of the settlement's Tyrrhenian contacts and its position on the trade routes.

Finally, the sacred area was redefined by the construction near the north and west boundaries of a long building subdivided into several rooms, which were probably used for public ceremonies.

The Low City

While archaeological research here has been less widespread than that carried out in the Plain of Himera, by now it seems certain that this area, right from the time of foundation, was developed very quickly. Of the earliest phase, only a few remains of buildings have been preserved, but more evidence has been found relating to the settlement in the Late Archaic period, which probably dates from the same time as that of the upper city (580–560 B.C.); when compared with upper city, however, the lower city exhibits some unusual characteristics. On the plain, in fact, the line of the coast and the course of the river Himera influenced the northwest–southeast orientation of the city blocks, which were about 41 m wide, appreciably larger than those found in the upper city. The reasons for this difference in the allocation of the space could be found in practical factors like the morphology of the terrain, but it more probably comes down to socioeconomic causes. A study of house types in Himera seems to indicate a marked socioeconomic difference between the inhabitants of the hill sector of the city, who appear to have belonged to the middle level of the landowning class, and the groups who lived in the houses in the lower city, who are more likely to have been craftsmen and traders, activities obviously helped by the presence of the riverport nearby.

The economic importance represented by this sector of the city appears to have been emphasized by the construction of a great temple called the "Temple of Victory"—the only stone monument in the whole of the colony. Probably built in an area expropriated from the inhabited quarter, the temple followed the orientation of the sacred buildings in the *temenos* of the upper city. It was erected between 470 and 460 B.C., in the canonical form of Doric architecture, with a *peristasis* of six by fourteen columns and a *cella* with *pronaos* and *opisthodomos*. The deity to whom the temple was dedicated is still unknown, and its connection with the "Victory" of 480 B.C., has been arbitrarily decided in modern times, but the impressiveness and grandeur of the building would seem to be a manifestation of the ambitious political tyranny of the Emminidi after the victory over the Carthaginians.

Plan and view of the Temple of Victory

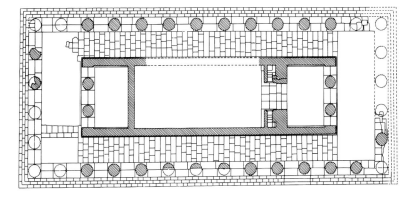

Megara Hyblaia

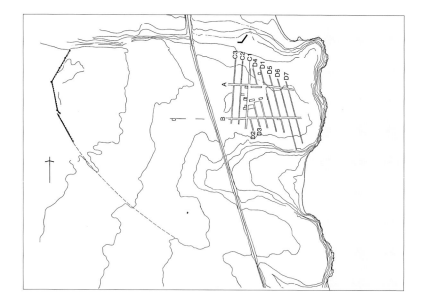

Plan of Megara Hyblaia

On opposite page: sandstone statue of a goddess suckling two infants (*kourotrophos*), around 550 B.C., from the southern necropolis at Megara Hyblaia (The "Paolo Orsi" Regional Archaeological Museum, Syracuse)

For students of town planning, the site of Megara Hyblaia is an exemplary model of an urban settlement in a city of the Archaic period. The city, dating from the final decades of the eighth century B.C., was actually completely destroyed and abandoned at the beginning of the fifth century B.C., to be reoccupied, for scarcely more than a hundred years, between the fourth and third centuries B.C. This reoccupation, at least initially, involved only a small part of the plain and made no changes to the earlier layout of the city; this

fact is what allows us to have such a good picture of the original settlement.

Excavations, already partly under way in the nineteenth century, have been systematically conducted by a French archaeological expedition since the end of the Second World War. The investigations, while furnishing data of immense relevance to the study of the city in the Archaic period, have also created a real archaeological oasis on the coastal plain between Augusta and Syracuse, which has otherwise been given over to industrial enterprises. The site consists of a area that can be explored by visitors and a small *antiquarium* containing illustrations of some of the results of the investigations and an exhibition of some of the items found; the rest are in the Regional Archaeological Museum in Syracuse.

History

Megara Hyblaia, together with Naxos, Leontini, and Katane, is one of the oldest cities in Sicily, and was colonized by people from Megara Nisea, a city facing the Saron Gulf, halfway between Corinth and Athens. The events surrounding its foundation are related by Thucydides. The expedition, led by Lamis, settled first at Trotilon, near the river Pantacio, then at Leontinoi, where the Kalchedian population first made it welcome, only to expel the settlers soon after. The exiles settled for a brief period on the island of Thapsos, north of Syracuse, but after the death of Lamis they founded the city

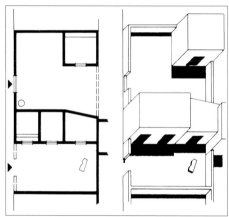

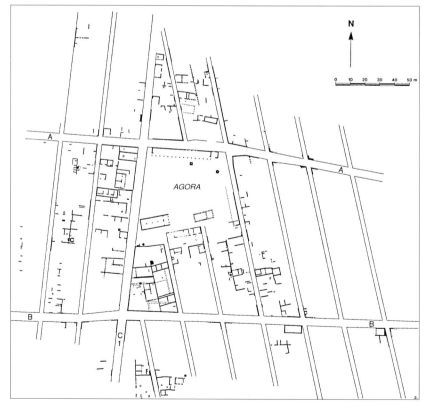

Top: inhabited area at Megara
Hyblaia (Syracuse)

Above: floor plan and
axionometric diagram of
houses in the eighth and
seventh centuries B.C.

Right: plan of the
agora quarter in the
mid-sixth century B.C.

of Megara, calling it Hyblaia, from Iblon, the name of the Sicel king who donated the land on which the city was built. About a century later, the young city was involved in promoting the foundation of Selinunte, in the eastern part of the island.

The war against Gelon, tyrant of Syracuse, had fatal consequences for the city, which was razed to the ground in 483 B.C. Diverse fates were reserved for the population, however; the affluent—those that Herodotos called *pachys*, the wealthy, well-fed ones, the very people who had sought the war against the tyrant of Syracuse—were spared and transferred to Syracuse, where they were given citizenship; the rest of the inhabitants—the lower classes, whom Gelon did not trust, though they were in no way responsible for the conflict—were sold into slavery.

Again in 415 B.C., as Thucydides records, the city was deserted; only a few buildings remained, belonging to a small fort the Syracusans built for the defense of their own city during the expedition mounted by the Athenians. The upper plain was occupied again from 340 B.C., around which time the city was partially rebuilt and repopulated at the instigation of Timoleon.

After more than a century the new city suffered the same fate as its predecessor. The encounter between the Roman army and Syracuse did not, indeed, spare Megara, which was sacked and destroyed in 214 B.C.

The General Topographical Picture

The settlement was built on an upland plain divided into two plateaus by a deep hollow that tended to level out toward the interior. The site, barely more than 20 m above sea level, was close to the sea on the east side and bordered on the north and south sides by the Cantera valley. The inhabited area, which was absolutely level and therefore without an acropolis, was encircled by an imposing wall.

The territory controlled by the city extended to the north, probably as far as the low valley of Marcellino, or to the Mulinello valley, slightly further to the north, near which a number of small Greek settlements from the Archaic period have been located. Toward the south, the territory probably did not go beyond Thapsos. The territories of Megara and Syracuse were linked by a coast road, dating from the Archaic period, which ran slightly to the east of the present-day railway.

Of particular interest was the northern plain where the caves of Melilli and Intagliata were found, while toward the interior, the city's control did not extend for much more than half a mile, not quite reaching the Hyblaian hills and their surroundings.

The City in the Archaic Period

The urban space was well defined right from the time the city was founded, as can be seen by the siting of the earliest houses—planned, effectively, in the second half of the seventh century B.C.; their position and orientation remained unchanged in all the successive blocks.

The inhabited area covered the whole of the plain, which was quite extensive: 0.6 of a mile (1 km) across in an east–west direction, and almost half a mile (800 m) from north to south. The new arrivals quickly divided the territory into lots, using these as a basis for apportioning the available space into areas destined for private use (plots of land with associated dwelling), and for public purposes (roads, religious areas, and civic assemblies). Each block was 12 m wide, and the houses built within them by the first citizens took up no more than 15–20 square meters, each with a space of 100–120 square meters which served as a garden.

Over the course of the seventh century B.C. the dwelling area was increased and a second and even a third residential quarter was added, and a type of house emerged that became the quintessential house of the Archaic period; it consisted of three small rooms set in line, with a door to the south where the courtyard was located.

The French archaeological expedition's excavations from 1948 onward provided data which permitted the recreation of the urban plan in a wide sector of the city corresponding to the area of the *agora*. Here, the part of the urban settlement which was brought to light was divided by three main arteries: two east–west roads (A and B), and one north–south (C1). These main roads (*plateiai*) were between 5 and 6 m wide. The blocks to the east

and west of *plateia* C1 were formed by the intersections of a series of smaller roads. The most significant aspect of the urban network thus created was produced by the varying orientation of these small roads; those to the west of *plateia* C1 were parallel to it (those being roads indicated by the letter C: C1, C2, C3), while those to the east, about 3 m wide, deviated toward the west by 21° (these roads indicated by D: D1, D2, D3).

This arrangement resulted in blocks of various lengths: 25 m for the more or less regular blocks to the west, but from 23 to 25 m for those to the east. The roads, originally simple tracks between the various properties, were retained in the subsequent urban development, which included blocks that were not only bounded by a wall but also divided in half lengthways by a center wall. At the point where the different orientations described above came together, near road C, was the site of the *agora,* which will be dealt with in detail later. Some indications lead one to believe that there were other public spaces too, at least in the earlier phase, but it is impossible to draw valid conclusions in the absence of systematic excavation in other sectors of the city.

For the present, no area of any great size has been found that was reserved for sanctuaries. The sacred areas were limited to altars and small temples integrated into the living areas. One exception was the sanctuary excavated on the west side of the southern plain, which contained the remains of a small temple (Temple A), and an enclosure (D) where various votive offerings were found. Another temple was located to the northeast of the *agora,* on the eastern slope, close to the coast.

A fortified wall was built around the urban area not many years after the foundation—assuming that some of the earliest stretches do indeed date from the middle of the seventh century B.C. The defensive system consisted of a wall—the earliest one built of the local low-quality limestone—and a ditch. In the sixth century B.C., the fortifications were substantially rebuilt using stone from the caves of Melilli. In this second phase the fortification wall was about 1.9 miles (3 km) long and 9 or 10 m wide, with a ditch 1.75 m wide. The walls were reinforced by

five semicircular towers, which are among the oldest in the Greek world.

The location of artisan activities, and in particular the workshops of the potters and those who worked in bronze, was indicated by finds of kilns in various parts of the city—near the *agora,* in the north and south sectors, and outside the walls. These potters' workshops in the seventh century B.C. produced a type of ceramic decorated with figures done in a polychrome technique that had a fairly ephemeral lifespan. One piece in particular, preserved in the Regional Archaeological Museum in Syracuse, consists of fragments of a large *dinos,* a vessel that sat on a stand of terracotta or metal and was used to contain wine; running across the fragments is a frieze with five men engaged in pulling on a rope to which, perhaps, was attached the great horse of Troy.

The city certainly had a port, which underwater research and some of the topographic indications tend to place at the mouth of the river Cantera, immediately to the north of the walls.

The burial areas were, as was usual, located just outside the inhabited area, more precisely, to the northwest, where the tombs essentially date from the sixth and the fifth centuries B.C., and along the road leading to Syracuse, beyond the San Cusumanno stream, with tombs dating from the seventh and sixth centuries B.C. The extensive use made of these *necropoleis* in the course of the centuries makes it difficult to understand the changes in the way the burial areas developed throughout the centuries. However, what does appear to be very interesting is the layout of the necropolis to the south, with tombs, many of them containing infants buried in amphora, located along various arterial roads. In many cases big stone vessels were used for burial or cremation.

Some of the grave goods from the 1,500 tombs excavated from the end of the nineteenth century onward are displayed in the Regional Archaeological Museum in Syracuse. The richness of some of these is borne out by the remains of some tomb markers, like two famous sculptures from around the middle of the sixth century B.C.: the renowned statue, in limestone, of a goddess suckling a pair of infants (*kourotrophos*) found in the

northern necropolis, and the headless statue which represents—as one can read in the inscription on its hip—the doctor Sombrotias, son of Mandrokles. This was discovered quite by chance in the southern necropolis.

Very different from the small house with garden within the urban area was the true agrarian lot, *kleros,* situated in an area whose boundaries, as we have already said, are difficult to define with any degree of certainty. The assumption that there must have been farms located beyond the city is based on evidence of tombs near the bank of the river Mulinello, in this particular case located in the same area as an earlier native necropolis.

The Civic Area

This is the area of the city that has been the most thoroughly investigated, because it is here that the French expedition concentrated its activities, including the production of a series of volumes dedicated to the *agora.* The area destined for this seems to have been determined by the intersection of various road axes and, by extension, by variously oriented blocks. Several religious and political buildings that were built gradually over the course of the seventh century B.C. helped to define the area. In actual fact, the function some of these buildings served is uncertain; however, comparison with other cities supports some of the theories that have been advanced to date.

Before we go on to a detailed examination of them, however, let us take a closer look at this space. Trapezoidal in shape, the *agora* covered an area of 2,370 square meters and seems to have remained without buildings from the end of the eighth century B.C. to the middle of the seventh. It was bounded by roads to the east, west, and north (D1, 3 m wide; C1 and A, 5 m wide). On the south side, the perimeter of the square was marked by three blocks with their relevant roads (D3 and D4) that linked the *agora* to a *plateia* 5,m wide, like the other two main roads (A and C1). At the end of the seventh century B.C. the *agora* was bounded to the north and east by two long, colonnaded buildings, *stoas;* the colonnades were made of wood and covered by a simple roof. This type of building, first used in the Archaic period, was frequently found

in sanctuaries, where it served as a shelter for the faithful.

The first example of a *stoa* used in a lay context was found precisely at Megara Hyblaia to the north of the *agora;* it was 40 m long and about 6 m wide, and was built in the third quarter of the seventh century B.C. A gap cut through it, perfectly aligned with the northwest—southeast axis of the road that ran immediately to the north, provided an unusual solution to the problem of access from that direction by allowing the road to continue on into the square.

The two roads that gave onto the south of the *agora* were blocked by the presence of two sacred buildings, of which a few scant traces remain. As will be seen, in those cases where it has not been possible to identify the deity to whom they were dedicated, these small temples have been allocated letters.

The building to the east, labeled "i," dates from the third quarter of the seventh century B.C. It consisted of a *cella* with a single nave and a deep entrance porch, or *pronaos,* while the one on the west, building "h," dating from the last quarter of the seventh century B.C., had a shallow *pronaos* with two doors that led to the *cella.* This was divided into two sections by a line of three columns down the center.

Immediately to the north of the two temples were some houses; the ones nearest to the temples were probably demolished to make room for the building of a boundary wall around the square. The same fate befell the houses built on the south side, demolished later to make room for the east portico. Strictly linked to the *agora* were some buildings found in the block immediately to the west of the square and separated from it by *plateia* C. The most important of them was undoubtedly the structure built in the third quarter of the seventh century B.C., in the northeast corner of the block, consisting of two square chambers side by side. In the one to the north, near the eastern entrance, fragments of an SOS amphora were found set in the rock and containing ashes, while on the west side was an empty square pit, lined with vertically placed slabs. Two similar pits, both empty, were found to the east and west inside the southern chamber. They were, in all probability, hearths, and must have had something to do with the purpose of the structure. Of particular interest also is a series of six little holes set at regular intervals on the threshold of the southern chamber. An examination of the plan of the building indicates that it was a temple with two *cellas*. It was very probably the kind of cult place that most scholars would class as a *heroon,* a burial place destined for a founding hero, as illustrated by literary and archaeological sources in other Greek cities (a case in point, for example, being that of Poseidonia).

A little farther south of the probable *heroon,* in the same block, there was another building, built about a century later (530 B.C.), on top of an older one. Judging from the characteristics of the complex, made up of three adjoining square chambers, each able to accommodate seven couches (*klinai*), and preceded by a very narrow portico facing on to a courtyard measuring 12.65 × 5.8 m, it would seem to have been a banqueting hall—a *prytanikon.* This was the building which housed the *prytaneis*—the most important magistrates of a Greek city—who entertained foreign visitors there. Also of considerable interest is the great trapezoid complex from 640–630 B.C., denominated by the letter "i," which occupied the whole of the block to the southwest of the square; this too is identifiable as a building for some sort of public use.

The City in the Fourth and Third Centuries

After being almost totally abandoned for a long period, the city was partly repopulated at the instigation of Timoleon; for practical reasons, the city kept the Archaic urban network, with small modifications that were made necessary by the construction of some buildings and that involved the creation of slightly more irregular blocks and streets. The space occupied by the *agora* was reduced to about half its previous size. Bordered on the north by a long portico, rebuilt a little further back from the previous one, the south part of the public area was taken up by a bathing establishment consisting of a series of square rooms, heated by a furnace and lined with benches along the sides. These rooms gave onto a round hall containing tubs for hot baths and to two smaller chambers also furnished with benches.

Between the dwelling houses of this period there are signs, at the northwest corner of the square, of a large house built in the third century B.C., with shops, of which all but the central one had a room to the rear. The house was arranged around a large courtyard with rooms along the sides: three rooms facing onto a wooden portico on the north side and two, one with a staircase to an upper floor, to the west. In the center of the courtyard are the remains of an earlier dwelling, dating from the eighth century B.C., consisting of a single chamber to which a second had been added in the course of the seventh century B.C.

The fortress made up of an imposing wall 2.5 m wide, made from double parallel lines of masonry filled internally, dates from the time of the war against Marcellus. Its construction cut the northern plain in half, leaving a part of the inhabited area undefended.

Syracuse

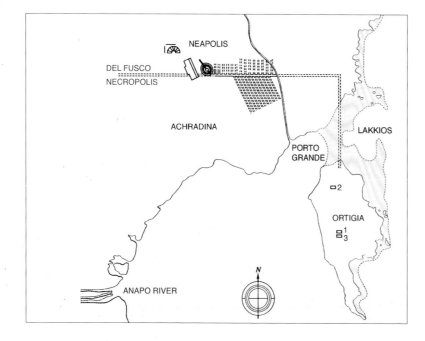

Schematic plan of Syracuse

On opposite page: slab in painted terracotta depicting a gorgon, 570 B.C., from the *temenos* of the *Athenaion* at Ortygia (The "Paolo Orsi" Regional Archaeological Museum, Syracuse)

History

Archaeological evidence confirms the date of the foundation of Syracuse given by the literary sources as 733 B.C. and attributed to a group of Corinthians led by Archytas. Ancient literature refers to the journey to Delphi of Archytas, together with Myskellos, the future founder of Kroton, to find out about the voyage that they were to undertake. When the oracle asked them whether they wanted riches or health, Archytas chose riches, and Myskellos chose health.

Tensions and social clashes, well documented in Syracuse in the course of the seventh and sixth centuries B.C., were at the root of expulsions, like that of the oligarchic faction of the *Myletidai,* or the foundation of the new city at Kamarina, on the southwest coast, at the end of the sixth century B.C. Syracuse also established settlements toward the interior—Acre, in 664 B.C., and Kasmenai, twenty years later—created for the precise purpose of defending its territory.

In power throughout this phase were the *Gamoroi,* landowners who derived their wealth from their property; opposed to them, at the start of the fifth century B.C., was the rest of the population, consisting of free men (*demos*) and slaves (*kylliroi*), who joined forces and succeeded in expelling the wealthy landowners. Having taken refuge at Leontinoi, the latter found a way to return, helped by the tyrant of Gela. A member of the noble Deinomenides family, Gelon, once he had established himself as tyrant of Gela, beat the Syracusans in the Battle of Eloro and occupied their city, to which he transferred not only his command but also a part of the population of the cities he had conquered. The tyranny of Gelon was marked by a substantial urban development project, which involved the building of new housing quarters. In 480 B.C. Gelon's Syracusan army and that of Theron of Agrigento defeated the

Silver tetradrachm, 500–480 B.C. (National Archaeological Museum, Naples)

Opposite page, top: silver tetradrachm of Agathokles, 310–304 B.C., head of Kore-Persephone on obverse and Nike on reverse (The "Paolo Orsi" Regional Archaeological Museum, Syracuse)

Opposite page, bottom: plan of the Ortygia peninsula with indications of the ancient road axes revealed by the latest excavations

Carthaginians at Himera, a victory which greatly increased the fame of the city, and also that of Agrigento. After his death, Gelon was succeeded by his brother, Hieron, who turned his attentions toward eastern Sicily and to Italy, where he enjoyed considerable political success following his great naval victory, in 474 B.C., against the Etruscans.

The power of the Deinomenides came to an end with the death of Hieron. Thrasybulos, brother of the former tyrant, was defeated shortly after by the democratic party and by a coalition of Sicilian cities which honored this victory by erecting a statue to Zeus Eleutherios, the Liberator.

The second half of the fifth century B.C. was marked by conflict with the Athenians, who intervened several times in Sicily. In the last clash, that of 415–413 B.C., Syracuse defeated the Athenian navy, massacring its men on the banks of the Assinaro River; even worse was the fate of the survivors, left to die imprisoned in the caves.

A few years later, the Carthaginians, led by Hannibal, nephew of Hamilcar, who was beaten in the Battle of Himera in 480 B.C., landed in Sicily and conquered and destroyed Selinunte, Himera, and Agrigento in quick succession. Syracuse was threatened and suffered several defeats in its attempt to stop the Punic advance on the city. After the conquest of Agrigento in 406–405 B.C., Dionysios, follower of Hermokrates, the hero of the defense of Syracuse against the Athenians, managed to get himself proclaimed supreme commander of the army. Dionysios was unable to save Gela and Kamarina, both of which were destroyed, but he was successful, assisted by a plague that struck the enemy camp, in negotiating a peace. Syracuse, thanks to Dionysios, was thus guaranteed control of eastern Sicily. The new tyrant, in the succeeding years, consolidated the fortification system of the city and reinforced the fleet, preparing Syracuse for a new encounter with Carthage. The war went on for several years with various ups and downs, until the peace of 392 B.C., with which Syracuse consolidated its control over the indigenous centers, so guaranteeing the Greek cities' independence from Carthage.

Once secure in the island, Dionysios turned his sights on Italy; between 389 and 388 B.C. he con-

quered Rhegion and in the following years founded Ancona, Adria, and Lissa in the middle and upper Adriatic, and was not above incursions and pillaging in Corsica and Etruria.

In 369 B.C., the tyrant reopened the war against the Carthaginians. A first encounter ended in the defeat of Syracuse, which ceded the cities of Selinunte and Agrigento to Carthage. A subsequent intervention ended in the death of Dionysios and the signing of a peace treaty underwritten by the son of the tyrant, Dionysios II. The constant internal struggles for power which broke out in the following years (including the assassination of Dion, who succeeded Dionysios II in 354 B.C.) were responsible for the arrival in Syracuse, in 344 B.C., of the Corinthian general Timoleon, called upon to resolve the violent clashes between citizens.

Having reached Sicily, the general did not find a favorable climate, but nevertheless managed to make a victorious entry into the city, destroying the fortifications, the palace of the Ortygia, built by Dionysios the elder, and the tombs of the tyrants. Proclaiming himself *strategos*, Timoleon governed the city for eight years, defending Syracuse from a new and powerful Carthaginian expedition in 339 B.C. At the end of that time the old general retired from politics. When he died, his tomb, like that of the city's founder, was placed within the *agora*, the civic and political heart of the city.

Subsequent events were marked by new clashes between the oligarchs—by this time the leaders of the city—and the democrats. The latter found a leader in Agathokles who, having been elected strategos in 318 B.C., took a step toward the acquisition of power, which he achieved eight years later with a coup d'état, which he followed by wiping out the entire oligarchic council of six hundred citizens. First among the dynasties of Syracuse, Agathokles had himself nominated king, making himself the equal of his contemporaries, the kings of the Hellenistic states that had been created from the dismembered Macedonian Empire of Alexander the Great.

The reign of Agathokles was marked by the war against Carthage. After several victories in Africa in 306 B.C., he was defeated and obliged to sign a peace treaty which nevertheless left him in control of Sicily. After his death, the history of the city was marked by new political clashes and by the harsh tyranny of Hiketas, which lasted for nine years. The next new encounter with the Carthaginians was supported by Pyrrhos, called upon for help by Syracuse in 278 B.C. Unpopular with the very Greeks who had asked his help, and preoccupied by what was happening in Italy, in 275 B.C. Pyrrhos left the island and, after a defeat at the hands of the Romans at Maleventum, returned to Macedonia.

In the same year, the Syracusan general Hieron, who had fought alongside Pyrrhos, managed to get himself nominated first *strategos* and then king. His very long and unchallenged reign over the city lasted until 215 B.C., the year of his death, and coincided with a period of great prosperity for the city, owing to its close alliance with Rome, which guaranteed it the control of many cities in eastern Sicily.

The death of Hieron coincided with the end of the freedom of Syracuse which, having gone over to the Carthaginian side with Hieronymos, successor of Hieron II, in 212 B.C., was conquered and sacked by the Roman army led by the consul Marcellus.

The General Topographical Picture

The peninsula of Ortygia was the heart of the Greek city, as it continued to be in medieval times and is still today. It covered about 99 acres (40 hectares), and its road network partly retraces, as we shall see, that of the Greek city. This network, as early as the Late Archaic period, extended beyond the island into the Acradina quarter. The superimposition of medieval and modern structures upon the ancient ones, while it helps the reading of the urban network—as occurred also in the case of Naples—does, however, make archaeological excavation more difficult.

Information about the city has been derived from various ancient sources, especially those from the Roman period, but undoubtedly the most vivid description is that of Cicero, whose position as quaestor of Sicily allowed him to spend time there. In that historian's opinion, Syracuse was the most beautiful and, above all, the largest Greek city, to the extent that it seemed like four cities in one. The "four cities" he was referring to were the great

urban nuclei of Ortygia, Acradina, Tyche, and Neapolis. Ortygia, the long, narrow island, was quite a popular landing place, as were those of Augusta, Thapsos, and Ognina, on the same Sicilian coastline. In ancient times, as now, its position offered two ports, a small one, open on the side of the sea, and a large one to the east of Ortygia. The physical aspect of the area is considerably different today, modified by the two conflicting influences of the advancing coastline, caused by the accumulation of the material washed up by the current into the Porto Grande, and the concurrent advance of the sea on the east side of the peninsula, which has resulted in the total disappearance of Lakkios, the ancient Porto Piccolo.

The perimeter of the latter, bounded on the north and south by two promontories, has been completely submerged, while the inner area of the present Porto Piccolo was formerly part of the old

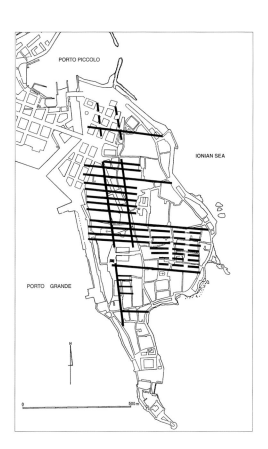

Plan of Temple of Apollo

On opposite page: Temple of Apollo, first quarter of the sixth century B.C.

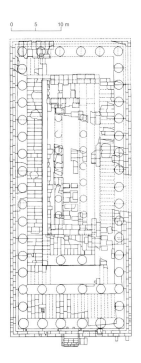

0   5   10 m

Porto Grande. On this ancient isthmus, which can now only be represented graphically, since it bears no resemblance to the present one, was what Cicero called the "Narrow Bridge"—the prolongation toward the north of the main road that bordered the sanctuaries of Ortygia to the west and linked the island to the mainland. The crossing from the isthmus in the Archaic period was by a jetty built of stone blocks, according to what we can gather from the poet Ibycus, who lived in the middle of the sixth century B.C. The other port, protected to the north by Ortygia and to the south by the promontory of Plemmyrion, was much larger.

Immediately beyond the isthmus was the vast plateau occupied by the city in the course of the great urban development in the fifth and fourth centuries B.C. The inhabited area on the mainland was bounded, and closed off to the north, by the Epipole plateau, a vast limestone terrace, more or less triangular in shape, at whose point, on the eastern slope, was the locality known as Euryalos (in Greek: large nail). It was a fairly weak point in the defense of the city because a narrow passage in this sector gave an enemy access to the plateau from where a siege could be directed. Dionysios, as we shall see, used an extraordinary means in an attempt to solve this problem.

Many caves, the *latomie*, excavated into the southern slope of the plateau in the course of quarrying activities and subsequently abandoned, were used from the end of the fifth century B.C. as prisons. The most notorious of these—known as the "Ear of Dionysios" because it resembled an enormous ear—was noted for its extraordinary acoustics and was used by the tyrant Dionysios to listen in on the conversations of the prisoners locked inside it. Equally interesting are the *latomie* of Paradiso, Intagliata, Santa Venera, and Cordari. Further to the east, but still on the same axis, we find the *latomie* of Casale and Broggi, while, still further to the east, are those of Cappuccini.

Between Epipole and Acradina were the other two quarters mentioned by Cicero: Tyche, which was on the eastern side, and Neapolis, the new city built on the western slope. In this latter urban nucleus were the theater, the Altar of Hieron, and the amphitheater from the Roman period, now inside the Archaeological Park. Not far from there is the Regional Archaeological Museum, dedicated to the memory of the great archaeologist Paolo Orsi, to whom we owe the major archaeological discoveries in Southern Italy in the years straddling the nineteenth and twentieth centuries. In Neapolis was the Temenite hill, which took its name from the sanctuary (*temenos*) of Apollo, located on the summit. The southern slope of the hill also constituted the northern boundary of the Fusco quarter, where the oldest and most important of Syracuse's *necropoleis* was found. This was situated on the eastern edge of the city, in the Lisimeleia marsh which extended south to Anopo and the Ciane River, parts of which are now a nature reserve; papyrus plants grow at the river's mouth, where it discharges into the Porto Grande.

The acropolis was crossed by one of the roads that ran from the interior to the south coast. The limits of the Archaic city were marked by three burial grounds in addition to the necropolis of Fusco: one located in the present Via Paolo Orsi, in the region of the civil hospital, formerly the Spanish Garden; one near Piazza Vittoria, in the area between Via Biansizza and Via Enna; and, last, the one in Via Ragusa. These burial areas that ring the city from the north and the west were partly destroyed by the subsequent development of the city, and especially by the building of Neapolis.

Ortygia

The earliest evidence of the city has been found on the Ortygia peninsula, even though, as we have already said, there was no lack of groups of housing in the Acradina area. The new Greek settlement swept away the earlier Sicel dwellings, of which a few remains of huts and tombs have been found.

The earliest phases of the Greek city were made up of square dwellings measuring about 4 × 4 m, like those seen at Naxos and Megara Hyblaia, with stone foundations and mudbrick walls, and wells to supply their water. The houses opened to the south and, as at Megara, in the course of time they were enlarged by the addition of further rooms. Visible traces of these structures, dating from the end of the eighth century B.C., have been uncovered in the Palazzo della Prefettura area.

Even though the medieval city was built over the whole of the peninsula, an image of the plan of the Greek city, put into place in the first decades of the colony, can still be partially discerned. It consisted of at least two main, north–south roads and narrow streets at right angles running east–west, 2.5–3 m wide, which delineated blocks 23–25 m wide.

This nuclear settlement, in the Archaic period, presumably had its own political and religious spaces, in a central area of the peninsula, where the cathedral now stands, giving on to the Piazza Duomo. The very latest excavations, carried out beneath the pavement of the square, have brought to light a small shrine dating from around the time of the foundation of the city. The building was a small temple, probably dedicated to Artemis, and was replaced a short while afterward by a larger building. Dating from the middle decades of the sixth century B.C. was another small temple, excavated by Paolo Orsi, and located a little to the east of the present Via Minerva, in the area that later became the site of the great Ionic temple and of the *Athenaion*. The temple dedicated to Athena, of which some architectural parts can still be seen in the cathedral, was of the Doric order and was presumably built by Gelon to celebrate the great victory at Himera in 480 B.C., as was the case of the temple of Victory at Himera and the *Olympieion* at Akragas (Agrigento). The temple had a colonnade (*peristasis*) of six by fourteen columns, a *pronaos* (entrance porch) with two columns, a *cella*, and an *opisthodomos*—the chamber symmetrical with the *pronaos*, which had no communication with the *cella*. On the façade was a statue of Athena, whose gilded shield, sparkling in the sun's rays, was a landmark for navigators. From the account by Cicero, we know that the temple was still richly decorated in the first century B.C., before the arrival of the Roman governor Verres, who plundered the decorations and ornaments, among them some painted tablets kept in the *cella*. The transformation of the temple into a church required a few modifications of the structure not dissimilar to those carried out in the Temple of the Concordia at Agrigento. From the sacred area came a splendid painted terracotta panel from the mid-

dle of the sixth century B.C., depicting a running gorgon with knees bent.

Beside the Temple of Athena, in the area now occupied by the Palazzo Vermexio, was a large Ionic temple, with six by sixteen columns. Dating from the end of the sixth century B.C. and never finished, it was inspired by the great contemporary buildings of Asia Minor. From the area around the temple came an extraordinary fragment of painted terracotta resembling a sphinx.

In the northern part of the peninsula, along the road that crosses Ortygia in the direction of the northern quarter of the city, a little to the east of the present Umbertino bridge, are the remains of a third temple, of Apollo, of which a part of the wall is clearly visible. The temple, which had one of the earliest stone colonnades of six by seventeen around its *cella*, dates from the first quarter of the sixth century B.C. Built in sandstone, it had a double colonnade at the front and monolithic columns almost 8 m high. The *cella* had three aisles, separated by two rows of columns. On the steps of the west side ran the inscription that recorded the name of the architect: "Kleomedes, son of Knidieidas, built the temple of Apollo, and raised the columns, a fine work."

The island was given its own fortification by Dionysios I, who transformed Ortygia into a real personal fortress. He transferred his entire court there, together with the mercenaries, obliging them to build a palace with a ditch and a drawbridge. This last was destroyed by Timoleon and reconstructed by Agathokles, who saw himself as the equal of the great Hellenistic kings of his time. Two square towers which flanked a gate, located in Via XX Settembre and dating from between the fifth and the fourth centuries B.C., probably belonged to the island's system of fortifications.

Acradina and Urban Development in the Classical and Hellenistic Periods

The layout of the oldest *necropoleis* that were spread between the Fusco quarter and Piazza Vittoria demonstrate the expansion of the city which, in the Archaic period—as we have already mentioned—extended onto the mainland. This is shown by materials, and even structures, dating

Terracotta face of a sphinx, 560–550 B.C., from the area of the Ionic temple at Ortygia (The "Paolo Orsi" Regional Archaeological Museum, Syracuse)

On opposite page: columns of the *peristasis* of the Temple of Athena, assimilated into the wall of the Duomo sull'Ortygia (Syracuse)

View of the theater at
Syracuse

On opposite page: view of
the *cavea* of the theater at
Syracuse

from the eighth and sixth centuries B.C., and discovered in several places (the area of Via Somali and Corso Umberto I, the central part of the Corso Gelone). The layout of the Archaic houses, but also of later structures, like the Altar of Hieron II, helps us to reconstruct the orientation of the whole quarter, which was in the northeast–southwest direction. This orientation, so prevalent that it was even applied to the siting of the more recent Roman amphitheater, was certainly determined by the main road that crossed the whole city. This northwest–southeast road, a good 13 m wide at the corner of Piazza Marconi where it has been uncovered, climbed up to Acradina and carried on toward the *Hexapylon* and the territory of Megara Hyblaia, passing between the *latomie* of Paradiso and those of Santa Venera.

In the northern part of the quarter, in the area that is now Piazza Vittoria, excavation uncovered a sanctuary dedicated to Demeter and Kore, with a temple of which only the foundations and the altar have survived. A little farther to the east was a fountain consisting of a rectangular reservoir

and a basin of roughly the same size. The fountain dates from the fifth century B.C., but was reconstructed in the third century B.C.

To the south of the quarter, near Piazza Marconi, the point where the aforementioned road running north crosses another road, oriented east–west, which carried on to the Lakkios, was Cicero's *forum amplissimum*. This corresponded to the great square of the Greek city, which perhaps had been located in that area since the Archaic period. We know that in this *agora*, later the Roman Forum, was the *Timoleonteion* (the gymnasium constructed around the tomb of Timoleon), the great sundial ordered by Dionysios the Elder, a temple to Zeus Olympios constructed by Hieron II, the *prytaneion*, and the *bouleuterion*—all buildings that have not yet been located. To the east of the *agora*, at the end of Via dell'Arsenale, are traces of docks for the storage of ships pulled up on dry land and repaired under sheds. These installations, close to the present Porto Piccolo, related, as previously explained, to the Porto Grande.

To the fifth and fourth centuries B.C., a period that corresponds to a notable amount of urban development, is owed the construction of Neapolis, in the area north of Acradina. Pivotal to the quarter was the east–west road, barely 5 m wide, located between the amphitheater and Piazza Vittoria, which joined the streets coming from the south, even the oblique ones from Acradina. This road, probably dating from the Archaic period, joined at right angles with the 3 m wide streets from the north that marked out blocks 38 m long in the area between Via Cadorna and the northern stretch of the Corso Gelone. The new quarter occupied the area beginning from the *necropoleis* of the Archaic city and extending as far as the *latomie* situated on the southern slopes of Epipole. The theater and the Altar of Hieron II were built in this new quarter.

The oldest phase of the theater dates from the fifth century B.C. It was built by the architect Damokopos, known as Myrillas. The part of the structure that is visible was the result of a radical refurbishment in the time of Hieron II. The grandiose *cavea*, 168 m in diameter, was surrounded by 67 tiers of seating divided into nine segments,

each one dedicated to a deity or a member of the royal family. Of the theater today there remains only the lower part of the *cavea*, which was carved out of the rock, and little or nothing of the orchestra and the stage.

Great buildings were also erected on the Teenite hill, to the west of the theater, where there was a sacred area dedicated to Apollo; the deity was represented by a colossus. The sanctuary, of which the first phase dates from the seventh century B.C., was rebuilt a number of times, as a result of work needed to extend the *cavea* of the theater, and also when the hill was cut into in order to construct an artificial terrace. On this terrace were two porticoes, bordering the western side of the *cavea*, which contained the *Museion*, the seat of the corporation of actors. To the southwest of the hill one can see more tiers of seating, linear ones in this case, which belonged to the same sanctuary and could hold a thousand people.

A little way south of the theater was the Altar of Hieron II, a structure of which the very long base cut into the rock is visible. The west-facing building, located in a large square with large porticoes on three sides, was oriented according to the ancient street plan rather than that of Neapolis. According to Diodoros, this immense altar was built for the sacrifice of 450 bulls on the occasion of the *Eleutherie*, the annual feast in honor of Zeus Eleuterios, instituted after the victory at Himera, in 480 B.C.

Epipole and the System of Fortifications

The northern part of the city was bordered by Epipole, a limestone terrace fortified by Dionysios the Elder between the end of the fifth and the beginning of the fourth century B.C., on the eve of a new encounter with the Carthaginians. The work of fortifying the plateau was necessary because it constituted an optimum point from which the enemy could control and command a siege of the city, which is precisely what had happened during the war with the Athenians. The account detailing the work, carried out in a very short space of time, at least as regards the northern sector, which covered more than 30 stadiums (that is, over 3.1 miles [5 km]), was furnished by Diodoros Siculos. The

historian describes the fortifications as the longest perimeter wall of any Greek city.

The system of fortifications was almost certainly finished several years later, definitely after the war with Himilcon's Carthaginians, who, in 396 B.C., arrived to sack the sanctuary of Demeter and Kore. When the work was finished, the fortifications ran for a total length of 180 stadiums (almost 20 miles [32 km]). Firmly rooted on the rocky crag of the plateau, it deviated at a point on the southern slope to take in the necropolis of Fusco and join the wall of Acradina. Forming part of this imposing fortification work was a castle, subsequently rebuilt several times, built on the most vulnerable part of the terrace, in the locality known as Euryalos, where a kind of isthmus permitted access to the plateau. The castle, of which the principal phase dates to the time of Agathokles, was a complex fortified system made up of three ditches, walls, and galleries. The main nucleus consisted of a trapezoidal keep and five towers.

A little to the north of the castle, a gate in the wall was a set within a big trapezoidal recess with three entrances, then lessening to two, hidden by two false walls followed by very strong wall. This incredible fortification was an addition to the one already present on the island of Ortygia.

The *Necropoleis* and the Territory

The boundaries of the Archaic inhabited areas are suggested by the location of the *necropoleis* which, beginning from the Fusco quarter, extended toward the northeast in the area immediately to the south and east of the Archaeological Park, continuing on to the region of Piazza Vittoria. Between the fourth and third centuries B.C. new burial grounds were moved immediately to the north of the wall. The ancient southern entrance to the city was near the present locality of Scala Greca, where the *Hexapylon*—the six gates—stood. At this point various roads came together, and in particular the main one, which, after crossing Epipole, entered the city and carried on to Acradina and the *agora*. This was the main road that went toward the territory of Megara in the north, giving access to Leontinoi. Immediately outside this entrance,

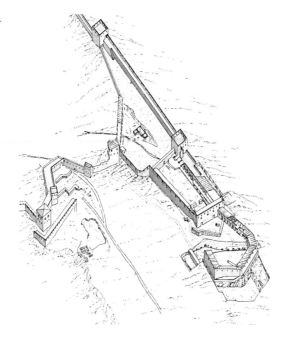

Top: axionometric reconstruction of the Euryalos castle, seen from the west

Below: the gallery in the Euryalos castle

On opposite page: view of the Euryalos castle from the outside

between two grottoes located along the provincial road between Syracuse and Katane, are the remains of a sanctuary to Artemis, which have yielded a number of terracotta votives.

To the west of Syracuse was a large plateau bordered on the north by the Anapo River and in the south by the Telaro, the ancient Eloro. This extends into the interior for several kilometers and constitutes a real link to the indigenous areas and toward the east coast of Sicily. As protection for this fundamental passage, Syracuse, in the course of the seventh century B.C., established two settlements, Acre in 664 B.C. and, twenty years later, Kasmenai.

In the southern territory, bounded in the east by the Porto Grande, numerous incidents occurred, linked to various sieges suffered by the city. One of these was located at the *Olympieion,* the extraurban sanctuary found beyond the Anopo and the Ciane rivers, on the other side of the unhealthy Lisimeleia marshes. Hippokrates of Gela camped near the sanctuary of Zeus Olympios after the victory over Syracuse at Eloro, and later over the Athenians in 414 B.C. According to Thucydides, the sanctuary, which was extremely important since it housed the list of the citizens of Syracuse, was in the middle of a village called Polichne. The temple, built at the beginning of the sixth century B.C., was a long, narrow building with six by seventeen columns (only two from the south side are still standing), and a double colonnade at the front of the *cella*—this latter consisting of a *pronaos* and perhaps an *adyton,* the inaccessible chamber to the rear of the *cella.*

At the source of the Ciane was a small sanctuary, of which a few ruins remain, which was mentioned by the historian Diodoros. It was near this source that the nymph Kyane tried to bar Hades' way; he turned her into a spring and immersed himself, together with Persephone, in the waters in order to descend to the underworld.

The city's control over the territory extended, probably from the beginning, to the mouth of the river Tellaro, site of the settlement of Eloro, which was considered one of the major outposts of the Corinthian city.

Eloro, Acre, and Kasmenai

Unlike the other cities we have dealt with, Eloro, Acre, and Kasmenai are special settlements. They are not, in fact, real cities, with their own territory, an *ekistes* (founder of the colony), a mint, and all the other aspects common to every *polis*, but rather centers constructed for the particular purpose of guaranteeing the control of one city's territory—in this case Syracuse—against threats either from other Greek cities or from the native population.

These centers differ, for example, from Kamarina, a Syracusan settlement of 598 B.C., which was a colony founded in the customary way

on the southwest coast of Sicily, perhaps to check the expansion of Gela, but still with all the characteristics of an independent city, the equal of Syracuse in its dealings with the mother city, Corinth. Throughout the description of the three settlements, we will point out the peculiarities of each site, bearing in mind that they fit into a system of territorial control put in place by Syracuse for reasons of defense, and do not constitute advance posts of territorial expansion aimed at the anachronistic aim of creating an empire.

The occupation of the small hill at the mouth of the river Tellaro, the old Eloro, toward the south side of the island was of an early date. Acre and Kasmenai, however, were settlements that were established on the vast plateau behind Syracuse, at a point of strategic importance for passage to the southwest coast of Sicily and toward the interior; these two settlements were thus closer to Syracuse both physically and chronologically.

ELORO

Facing the Ionian Sea to the left of the mouth of the Eloro River, now the Tellaro, about 5 miles (8 km) southeast of Noto, the inhabited area occupied a rise hardly more than 20 m above sea level. The city is mentioned in the sources because it was close to the site of a famous battle in which the army of Hippokrates of Gela defeated the Syracusans in 493 B.C. The sources also tell us about a road called

Walls and gate at Eloro

the Via Elorina that linked the city with Syracuse. To these small bits of information gleaned from the literary sources can be added what is contributed by archaeologists, which confirms an increasing Greek presence here from the end of the eighth century B.C. onward.

We know nothing of the history of this center in the earlier centuries. From 263 B.C. the settlement was a part of the dominion of Syracuse, as is confirmed in the pact of alliance between Hieron II and the Romans. In 214 B.C., Eloro surrendered to the Romans, ahead of Syracuse. Many of the works of art present there at the start of the first century were taken by Verres when he was quaestor of Sicily.

The inhabited area, which covered barely 25 acres (10 hectares), was encircled by a fortified wall, .87 of a mile (1.4 km) long, of which the earliest part, preserved near the city gate on the north side, dates from the sixth century B.C. This oldest phase consisted of a double line of masonry, 2.8 m wide, with an internal filling (*emplekton*), and a gate on the west side that was blocked following reconstruction work in the fourth century B.C. To this later phase also belong the square towers jutting out from the walls that have survived along this stretch of the fortification. Two gates have been identified: one, in the direction of Syracuse, and one to the south, near the Stampaci tower, toward the mouth of the Tellaro. The Via Elorina ran between these two gates; built on a base of natural rock, in which it is still possible to see the ruts made by chariot wheels, it followed a sinuous route dictated by the morphology of the terrain.

The north–south road constituted the main axis of the living area and was crossed by streets running east–west, such as the two that have been identified more or less at the center of the plateau on the east side. These streets outlined rather irregular blocks, one of which measured 100 × 28 m. To the north of that was a small, trapezoidal area measuring 25 × 15 m, bordered by a road to the north and by two buildings with porticoes (*stoas*) to east and west. This space has been identified as the site of the *agora*.

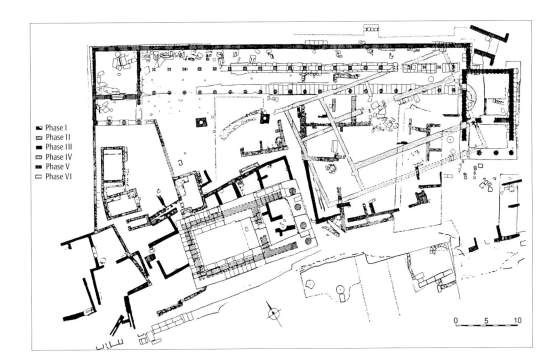

Southeast of the hill, in an area that has been extensively explored, three more roads have been identified; unlike the main axis road, they ran northwest–southeast. Other items to have come to light in this area include some square houses with walls of limestone slabs, dating from the eighth century B.C., similar in floor plan to those found in Syracuse and Megara Hyblaia, and some more recent dwellings from as late as the fourth century B.C.

Also dating from that period is a complex consisting of a small temple and some buildings, possibly used for reception purposes, one of which it was hoped might be an *Asklepieion*, and a sanctuary with a large prostyle-tetrastyle temple (a temple with a porch supported by four columns both ends) dedicated to Demeter. We know this from an inscription on a small terracotta altar, and as we may deduce from some pieces of figured terracottas representing a deity with a torch. At the start of the second century B.C., the sanctuary was enclosed on the north side by an imposing portico of the type known as a *paraskene*, that is, with two structures jutting out at either end. The portico, 68 m long overall, had Doric columns along the front, while inside it was divided into two aisles by rectangular pilasters. The sanctuary area was destroyed by fire in the sixth century A.D., and a Byzantine basilica was subsequently built there. In this area of the hill, but just outside the wall, was the theater, dating from the fourth century B.C. The *cavea* had as many as seventeen tiers of seats, separated by six flights of steps into five wedge-shaped areas.

Outside the city walls on the north side, near the beach, about 100 m from the walls, was another sanctuary, in use between the sixth and third centuries B.C. Within were structures made up of chambers with benches around the walls, upon which were found numerous votive offerings; these indicate that the sanctuary was a *Koreion*—a sanctuary dedicated, like the urban one, to Demeter and Kore. Ovid, in his *Fasti*, places Demeter's search for her daughter Persephone in the valley of the Eloro. Persephone (Kore) had been carried off by the god Hades, who took her with him to the Underworld.

Above: plan of the sanctuary of Demeter

Below: the superstructure and section of the burial chamber at La Pizzuta at Eloro

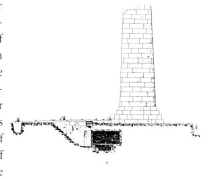

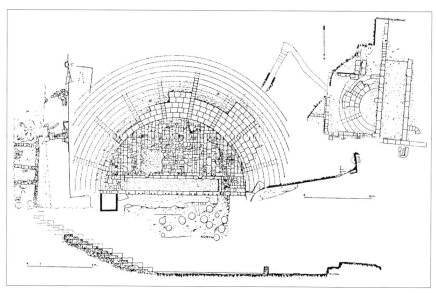

Outside the walls, as always, were the burial grounds, located to the north, west, and south. The graves date from between the sixth and third centuries B.C. A funerary monument from the Hellenistic period, known as La Pizzuta, stands on the hill to the north of Eloro. Within an enclosure, a few fragments of which remain, made up of a limestone wall with a small Doric colonnade, was a column constructed of unmortared limestone blocks, which still stands to a height of 10.5 m. The diameter at the base is 3.8 m. The structure stands on a platform of leveled rock which also houses, in an underground chamber, the tomb of an eminent person.

ACRE

The inhabited area of Acre, which was not far from the present Palazzio Acreide, was located on a hill, known as the Serra del Palazzo, with steep slopes on all sides, except to the east toward the plateau of Syracuse, 770 m above sea level. The site, already on a natural defensive position, was protected by a fortified wall that encircled the plateau, enclosing an area of 86.5 acres (35 hectares). Little is left of the walls, but on the eastern side we can place the Porta Selinunte, mentioned in an inscription. Thucydides says that Acre was founded seventy years after Syracuse, and archaeological research would appear to confirm this.

The Greek-inhabited area occupied a site that had been frequented during the Late Paleolithic Age and became a settlement in the Late Bronze Age; cave tombs found at the southern foot of the Pinita hill date to this period. The settlement's dependence on Syracuse never waned, even after the encounter with the Roman army at the end of the third century B.C. The *strategos* Hippokrates took refuge at Acre after he was defeated by Marcellus. Their fierce opposition to the Romans cost them dearly; after the conquest, the Romans imposed a status of *civitas stipendiaria* on the settlement. With this standing, the city minted bronze coins carrying the images of Persephone and Demeter.

It is known that the acropolis was on the southern hill, where excavations have uncovered an Archaic temple from the sixth century B.C., perhaps that of Aphrodite recorded in an inscription which also mentions an *Artemision*. Other inscriptions mention the existence of sanctuaries dedicated to Zeus Akraios and to Kore, and also to a cult

of the nymphs. Of the sanctuary of Aphrodite, dating from the second half of the sixth century B.C., nothing has survived except the foundation level and a few other remains which hint at the existence of a double colonnade at the front, the rear wall in the *cella*, and decoration for the entablature in architectural terracotta.

The inhabited area was crossed from east to west by a main road, 4 m wide and paved with igneous rock; about 250 m of it has been uncovered. The unpaved streets, 3 m wide, running north–south 27 m apart, converged from the north and from the south at an oblique angle on this main *plateia*. They did not cut straight across it but joined it at staggered intervals, on the same principle as that applied at Herakleia. To the east, the road led to the front of the theater, running parallel with it at a distance of twenty meters or so.

The theater, carved out of the side of the hill, dates from the third century B.C. The *cavea*, which opened toward the valley of the Anopo and Mount Etna, was divided into nine wedge-shaped sectors separated by eight curved flights of steps; the orchestra was perfectly circular. Of the tiered seating, like the stage, very little remains, since the theater was quarried for stone for use in the construction of the Palazzuolo.

Still on the same hill, on the western slopes, is the *bouleuterion*, the seat of the council. Inside a square chamber 8.65 × 8.15 m in size was a *cavea*, with six tiers of seating divided into three wedge-shaped sectors by two flights of steps. The entrance was at the front, where there was an abbreviated portico. The space immediately behind this building must have been the area of the *agora*.

To the east of the theater are two *latomiai*, stone caves similar to those of Syracuse, one called the Intagliata and the other, smaller, one the Intagliatella. Between the fourth and third centuries B.C., these *latomiai*, when they were no longer quarried, were used as sites for a hero cult; in Christian times they served as burial chambers. A large number of rectangular cavities were found in the Intagliatella *latomiai*, which were used as receptacles for votives sculpted in relief, made from stone or wood, or even painted directly on to the rock, or carved into it, in honor of the dead. The largest of these relief sculptures is one on the west side of the Intagliatella: 80 centimeters high by 2.13 m wide, it represented a sacrifice being celebrated on an altar by a group of three people, in honor of a warrior who, since he is much larger in size, must certainly have been the defunct hero who was being honored. To the right of it is a banqueting scene. To the east of the hill on which Acre stands, is another *latomiai* and a sculpted rock wall. Dating from the same period, between the fourth and third centuries B.C., they were both used as cult sites. The *latomiai* known as the Grotto of the Funeral Temples, consisting of two large, rectangular rooms cut into the rock, was found to contain square niches for relief sculptures and inscriptions with dedications to dead heroes.

At the foot of the same hill is the sculpted rockface known as the Santoni, which is characterized by a series of aligned rupestral sculptures connected with the cult of Cybele, the *Magna Mater* (Great Mother of the Gods). They were executed, in the majority of examples, according to a recognized iconography in which the goddess, wearing a tall headdress, is seated, surrounded by various alternating figures (young girls, cult attendants, Attis, etc.). The largest and most complex of these reliefs is one sculpted inside one of the niches, measuring 3.1 × 2.15 m, at the center of which is the goddess, standing between two lions, with one foot on a smaller lion; her hands are placed on the heads of two smaller figure, Hermes and Attis, while at her back is a woman with the Dioskouroi, figures strictly reserved for the cult of Cybele.

KASMENAI

Barely 7.5 miles (12 km) to the west of Acre and established twenty years later are the foundations of Kasmenai, discovered in the settlement at Monte Casale, an isolated plateau with craggy, inaccessible slopes, 830 m above sea level. The west side, cut in half by a narrow valley that tends to disappear toward the east, corresponds to the highest part, the acropolis. We have no information about the history of the site, but we do know that it was the place of exile for the *Gamoroi* of Syracuse, wealthy landowners expelled in 491 B.C. following internal strife. It was from here that Gelon took them back to their own city when he transferred his command from Gela to Syracuse.

The plateau of Monte Casale, which extended over a length of 0.85 mile (1370 m) by 0.28 mile (450 m) wide, was enclosed in a megalithic boundary wall, made from large irregular blocks of igneous rock; the wall is 2.1 miles (3.4k m) long and 3 m thick, with external rectangular towers. In the fourth century B.C., a wall was erected at the western edge of the acropolis, backing on to the fortifications, oriented north–south and made up of a double line of masonry with three jutting towers.

Of the urban plan, 38 streets have been traced, all 3.5 m wide and running parallel to each other in a northwest–southeast direction, marking out very long blocks 25 m wide, each divided in half by a low wall or a narrow passage 0.5 m wide. The arrangement of the blocks appears to have been much the same as those in Megara Hyblaia, and even without precise information about the date we can be reasonably sure of placing the settlement at the time of foundation. Within the blocks were lots 25 m square, each containing four houses about 12.5 m square, built of igneous rock or, on rare occasions, limestone, in polygonal masonry. With very few exceptions, the houses had an entry facing the street and were built around a courtyard (sometimes no more than a corridor). Around the north side of each house, with a southern exposure, were three "residential" chambers, while those on the other three sides were smaller, perhaps simply service rooms. In the absence of transverse streets, passage between one street and the next was made via informal paths through the blocks.

Life in the settlement does not appear to have gone on beyond the fourth century. Identified on the acropolis were the very long foundations, 27 × 7.5 m, of an Archaic temple, with the same orientation as the urban center, of which only a few pieces of architectural terracottas have survived.

In Kasmenai, we undoubtedly find ourselves faced with an Archaic settlement of a military nature, quite different from those of the Classical period with which we have been mostly concerned. The characteristic features of the urban network

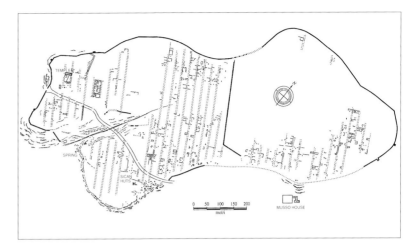

appear to be similar to those of Megara Hyblaia, however its defensive function is very much in evidence. Of particular significance is the absence of main longitudinal arteries, forcing the use of simple and irregular intermediate paths between the houses. The military nature of the settlement also seems to be confirmed by the votive offerings in the sanctuary of the acropolis, offerings which consist of thousands of arrowheads and other arms.

Gela

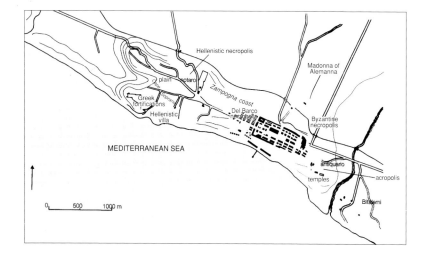

The foundation of the city did not come about in a peaceful manner, but only at the end of a series of encounters with the native population. The literary sources also record internal struggles between the different factions during the Archaic phase; this information helps us understand the events leading up to the foundation of Agrigento at the start of the sixth century B.C.

At the end of that century Kleandros, son of the Olympic champion Pantaris, seized power with the help of mercenaries. In 498 B.C. Kleandros succeeded the tyrant Hippokrates, who was responsible for the conquest and subsequent "refoundation" of Kamarina. At his death, power passed to Gelon, member of the Rhodian Deinomenides family, victor in the Olympic games of 488 B.C., and supporter of the tyrant Theron of Agrigento. After a short while, Gelon succeeded in conquering Syracuse, where he proclaimed himself tyrant of that city and moved in part of the population of Gela. The city of Gela then passed into the hands of Gelon's brother, Hieron, and subsequently into those of Thrasybulos, whose tyranny ended in 466 B.C.

In 480 B.C. Gela, with its cavalry, made an important contribution to the victory at Himera against the Carthaginians. In 405 B.C. the encounter between Dionysios of Syracuse and the Carthaginians led by Hamilcar resulted in the destruction of the city, which was razed to the ground after the defeat of Syracuse. Gela was only revived in the

Plan of Gela

On opposite page: acroterion decoration in terracotta, first half of the fifth century B.C., from Gela (Regional Archaeological Museum, Gela)

History

From the literary sources we know that Gela was founded forty-five years after Syracuse—that is, in 689 B.C.—by Rhodians led by Antiphemos and Cretans led by Antimos. The foundation came shortly after an earlier Rhodian settlement called Lindioi, for Lindos, a city on the island of Rhodes from which the new inhabitants originated. The Greeks established themselves on the east side of the hill and later moved progressively onto the west side until, by the fourth century B.C., they occupied the promontory of Cape Soprano.

second half of the fourth century B.C., thanks to Timoleon, who refounded the city with a contingent of new settlers from Ceos. Occupied by Agathokles in 311–310 B.C., it was totally destroyed in 280 B.C. by Phintias, tyrant of Agrigento, who transferred the inhabitants to the new city of Phintias, near present-day Licata.

The General Topographical Picture

The Greek city stood on a long, narrow ridge parallel to the coast, barely 54 m above sea level. The inhabited area developed over the course of the centuries between the two ends of a spine of land running between Molino a Vento and Cape Soprano—a length of about 2.5 miles (4 km).

Immediately to the interior was the vast and fertile plain bordered by mountain ranges that constituted the territory of the city between the river Dirillo (the Acate in ancient times) and the river Salso to the west. Closer to the city, immediately east of the acropolis, was the river Gela, at the mouth of which we can assume there was a port.

The Inhabited Area, Sanctuaries, and Territory at the End of the Fifth Century B.C.

The east end of the ridge, immediately above the mouth of the river Gela, in the area now occupied by the castle built during the reign of Frederick II, was the site of the acropolis. Built in this area in the seventh century B.C. was the first small temple dedicated to Athena, divine protector of the Rhodians; this was subsequently assimilated into the *Athenaion,* built in the fourth century B.C. Foundations from this temple measuring 34.22 × 17.75 m have been uncovered, leading one to suppose that it was a peripteral temple of the Doric order, probably with six columns along the front.

Excavations within the temple have revealed hundreds of fragments of painted architectural terracottas, made to decorate the façade of this and other shrines in the sanctuary. Some of the fragments are from an ornamental frieze, but there are also large figures, or groups of figures, now housed in the Regional Archaeological Museum at Syracuse. Typical are long, tubular spouts that were fixed to the lateral strips of the *cyma*—the part of the frieze that ran beneath the cornice (the *geison*).

Some remains of another temple, dating from the middle of the sixth century B.C., are visible below the Molino di Pietro (stone mill), while to the southeast of the Temple of Athena are the foundations of a large Doric temple built in 480 B.C. Of this one, which replaced the earlier *Athenaion*, there remains only a single column, which was reerected in its original position in 1951.

The Archaic settlement extended immediately to the west of the acropolis and was split into various nuclei, within an urban network consisting of several regular main roads. From the beginning, the buildings on the acropolis were arranged to follow the orientation of the ridge; this was crossed by the principal road axis, from which the narrower streets led off at right angles.

Another sanctuary, dedicated to Hera, was built in the seventh century B.C. in the area now occupied by the town hall, on a shelf of land close to the sea; it continued in use until the middle of the fourth century B.C.

Of the Archaic fortifications a few expanses remain north of the acropolis. Their date can be fixed around the end of the sixth century B.C., but there are also signs of rebuilding in the fifth century B.C. Other sectors have been located in the modern city between the Calvario and Vallone Pasquarello areas.

The inhabited area, from the first generation onward, was bounded by a series of sanctuaries. The most famous without doubt was the Bitalemi, named for the little church of the Madonna of Bethlehem. This overlooks the small hill facing the acropolis, on the east bank of the Gela River. In the sanctuary, which dates from the time of the first generation of colonists, are the remains of small buildings from the middle of the sixth century B.C.; the abundant series of votive deposits that were discovered there—some of which are now kept in the museum—comprise some of the most important finds in all the Greek cities of Magna Graecia and Sicily. Among the many votive offerings was an Attic vase from the fifth century B.C. bearing a dedication to *Thesmophoros*. It was the first epigraphic evidence documenting the ritual of the *Thesmosphoroi*, the feast that was celebrated in honor of Demeter Thesmophoros.

Dating from around the same period is the sanctuary of Prendio Sola, also dedicated to Demeter, on the southern slope of the hill, where another sacred area has also been found recently. And two sanctuaries were discovered to the north, near Via Fiume, in the Corrubazza quarter. At the northwest end of the hill, in the locality of Madonna dell'Alemanna, there is a sanctuary dedicated to Hera.

The territory of Gela is among the best known of all those in Sicily, thanks to research activities conducted in the 1950s by Dinu Adamesteanu and Piero Orlando. The plain, very fertile before the arrival of the Greeks, was controlled by native groups that occupied the northern hill. With the foundation of Gela and the destruction of the indigenous habitat, the new territorial arrangement was put under divine protection by the establishment of rural sanctuaries, evidently linked to the agricultural activities carried out not only in the immediate vicinity of the city, as we have seen in a previous chapter, but also in the Dirillo valley.

The *necropoleis* were spread over the western slopes of the city. The Archaic ones, whose rituals included cremation in urns and burial in earth graves or in sarcophagi, were closer to the city, in the Borgo quarter.

The City of Timoleon

At the end of the fifth century B.C., Gela was completely destroyed. The reconstruction, following its refoundation, was carried out by Timoleon in a project that involved a clean break with the social and urban order of the earlier city. The inhabited area was extended to the west, while houses were built on part of the sanctuary area. The slope of the acropolis was terraced in order to accommodate new houses, which were abandoned a decade later following the conquest by Agathokles. Several roads belonging to the previous network were eliminated, and others were adapted or lengthened. The acropolis underwent a major transformation, becoming the new artisan quarter. A significant change that underscores the great urban transformations that overtook the city of Timoleon was the demolition of the

Left: clay antefix of a Silen head, 470–460 B.C., from Gela (Regional Archaeological Museum, Gela)

Right: the walls and postern gate of the fortifications at Cape Soprano, Gela

sixth-century B.C. *Athenaion* and the extension of the roads over the site. However, a different fate awaited the other cult areas, at the eastern end, which were rebuilt.

With the enlargement of the inhabited area, the city walls were extended as far as the promontory of Cape Soprano. Today, preserved by the silting-up process, splendid and outstanding sections from the fourth century B.C. have survived. The lower part of the walls was built of isodomic blocks of stone, with mud brick above. In some places the surviving parts of this wall reach a height of 13 m.

The burial grounds of the refounded city were laid out in the area near the promontory, Cape Soprano.

Kamarina

History

Kamarina was founded by Syracuse in 599–598 B.C.; there were two *ekistes* (founders of the colony), Daskon and Menekolos. Only a few decades later, Kamarina's failure to respect the boundaries controlled by Syracuse led to a confrontation with the mother city, which subjugated it in 553 B.C. Rebuilt in 492–491 B.C. by Hippokrates, the tyrant of Gela who conquered Syracuse in the battle on the river Eloro, the city was again destroyed in 484 B.C. by Gelon of Syracuse, who transferred some of the inhabitants to Syracuse. The reconstruction and repopulation in 461 B.C. was again the work of Gelon. In the course of this third refoundation, the land was redistributed, by a process of lots drawn by a mixed civic body, which included some former citizens of Kamarina who had been brought back from Syracuse and reintegrated.

Kamarina's political situation was notably reinforced following the Congress of Gela, in 424 B.C., which concluded the war in which the Athenians supported Kamarina and Leontinoi against rival Syracuse. After that Kamarina, with the aid of a monetary settlement, managed to gain control of Morgantina, whose fertile territory was particularly suited to the growing of grains. In events relating to Sicily and the Peloponnesian War, Kamarina assumed an equivocal attitude, its support vacillating between the Athenians and

Syracuse until, at a crucial moment in the war, it found itself on the side of Syracuse. A few years later, the conflict between the Sicilians and the Carthaginians ended with a victory for the latter and the conquest of Kamarina. This time the city walls were demolished and the inhabitants forced to take refuge at Leontinoi, from which they returned only in 396 B.C. as tributaries of Carthage.

In the second half of the fourth century B.C., the city went through a period of prosperity following its reconstruction by the Corinthian general Timoleon. However, having taken the side of the Carthaginians against Syracuse in 311 B.C., it was duly sacked in 309 B.C. by Agathokles' army. The city was not spared the violence of the Mamertines in 279 B.C. either, nor that of the Roman army in 258 B.C. After the Roman destruction, the city continued to be inhabited until the Augustan age, as is shown by the reoccupation and partial reconstruction of the western areas, and signs of a reorganization of the urban area, indicated by a realignment of the housing blocks on the main axis (*plateia* B), which scarcely differed from that of the Classical period.

The General Topographic Picture and the First Signs of Human Occupation

The land on which the Greeks chose to establish their city was a promontory, the Cammarana hill, which, at 60 m above sea level, offered a level sum-

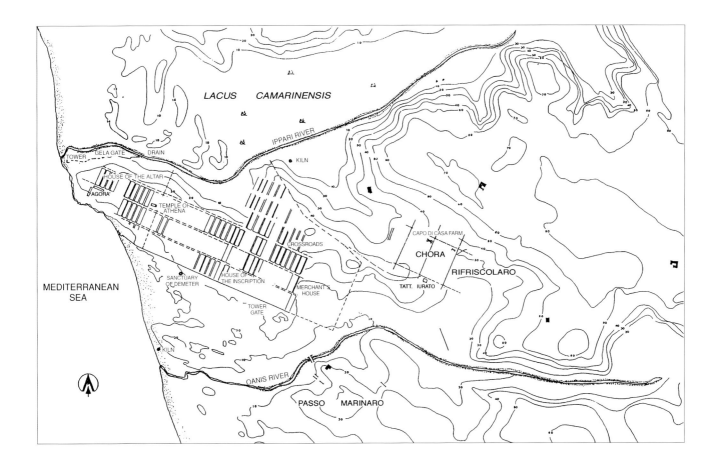

mit and slopes that descended in the south toward Oanis (now Rinfrescolaro) and north to the Ippari River, which in ancient times fed the marsh known as the *lacus camarinensis* and also provided an excellent landing place. On the west side, the promontory overhung the sea, while to the east it was bounded by two low hills known as Eracle and Casa Lauretta.

The first signs of human occupation, dating from the Early Bronze Age, have been found in the area that was to become the site of the Temple of Athena. This habitation fits into the well-known framework of prehistoric settlements in this coastal area.

The City's First Settlement
At the time of the colonial foundation the hill appears to have been uninhabited. The new arrivals most probably occupied only the eastern part of the promontory along the ridge, between the future site of the sanctuary of Athena and the sea.

The fortifications, dating from the middle of the sixth century and built of very small stones encased in plaster, covered a distance of about 4.45 miles (7 km) and enclosed an area of about 370 acres (150 hectares); this area was never completely urbanized. We know that the wall, which was restored in the fifth and fourth centuries B.C., had three gates—one each on the east, west, and south.

In the course of the first phase, the inhabited area was probably arranged around the main road that ran along the crest of the hill and linked the sanctuary of Athena with the public square, the *agora*.

The *Necropoleis* of the Archaic Period

Outside the city walls on the eastern side, near Rinfrescolaro, along the road that leads inland, just 1.25 miles (2 km) from the sanctuary of Athena, were the *necropoleis* used by the inhabitants of the area occupied in the Archaic period; these contained more than two thousand tombs. Another burial area relating to this period was found to the north of the city, in the area of Scoglitti. The *necropoleis* continued to be used right through the fifth century B.C. Other little burial groups have come to light below the Iurato farm, dating from the Classical period. Clearly there was already a permanent presence in the territory during the Archaic period.

From the Third Geloan Refoundation to the Destruction by the Carthaginians

A very recent discovery has given us extra information about the years immediately following third Geloan refoundation, that is, the period around the middle of the fifth century B.C. Near the Temple of Athena were found about 150 small, folded strips of lead (many more had already been removed) which must originally have been stored in a wooden case, though only the nails of this were left. Each of these lead strips bore the name of a citizen, his patronymic, and his relevant affiliation to a civic group that corresponded to a unit of territory (the term *phratry* appears on some of the lead strips). The wooden case, kept near the temple, contained therefore the archive of those citizens who had the right to participate in political life (to draw lots for elective posts, assemblies, etc.).

The second half of the fifth century saw a period of economic development in the city, which started to mint money again after a brief pause in 492–491 B.C. The middle of the fifth century B.C. also saw the establishment of an urban network in line with the earliest orientation, the construction of the roads, and the building of the Temple of Athena and the monuments in the *agora*.

The principal road axis of the network covering the inhabited area was *plateia* B, which ran the whole length of the crest of the hill, dominated at the center by the sanctuary dedicated to Athena—

cited by Pindar in his ode exalting Psaumide's victory at Olympia in the contest for chariots drawn by mules. The remains of the temple, transformed into a church during the Byzantine era and then systematically destroyed for its stone, are now on display in the Archaeological Museum and have furnished enough information to permit the reconstruction of the edifice as a small temple, lacking a *peristasis* but with a tripartite *cella* 39.75 × 15 m in size.

Plateia B continued west along the edge of the large space reserved for the *agora*—where excavations began in 1980—which is not far from the port, to which it was linked by a road joining it at right angles, and near the mouth of the Ippari River.

In the course of the Carthaginian attack at the end of the fifth century B.C., immediately east of the Temple of Athena, a fortified wall was built inside the city to create a north–south link between the northern and southern arms of the fortifications. The completion of this defensive work failed to save the city from destruction.

From the fifth century B.C. onward, new areas were put to use as *necropoleis*, to the east in the Piombo area and to the south in the Passo Marinaro, Cozzo Campisi, and Randello localities. These remained in continuous use until the end of the third century B.C.

The redistribution of the land—an unavoidable consequence of the Geloan refoundation—engendered a great deal of activity in the territory too. Together with the development of an extensive road network, we have documented a redivision of land in which properties were enclosed in low walls and assigned to farm managers. In the case of these farms, we know a certain amount about the buildings and related burial areas that have been located and partially excavated near Oanis. For example, the house on the Capodicaso property was built on a rectangular floor plan with courtyard and rooms to the east, south, and west, while another, only 250 m away, on the Iurato property, was square and very large: in fact more than 748 square yards (625 square meters) in area. The recent discovery of a third farm (Kastalia) has, by virtue of its distance from the other two agricultural settlements, enabled us to calculate the size of the uniform lots of ground as 67,813 square yards (56,700 square meters).

The City Refounded by Timoleon

One consequence of Timoleon's activities was the enlargement of the inhabited area, which now extended onto the adjacent hills, Eracle and Casa Lauretta, which had not been part of the earlier urban network. The city of Timoleon was divided by five main arteries (*plateia*) running east–west and a series of narrower north–south streets (*stenopoi*), creating blocks of 34.5 × 135–138 m, some of them on very uneven ground.

Typical of these blocks was the one excavated on the slopes of the Casa Lauretta hill. Measuring 34.5 × 135 m, it was divided along its length by a narrow alley (*ambitus*) barely 1 m wide; there were ten houses on either side of this alley. The houses, whose floor plan and construction technique are by now familiar, were built with three or four rooms, aligned on the north, opening onto a courtyard that occupied the whole of the south side.

Timoleon's refoundation, including the redistribution of land, seems also to have been reflected in the territory. In fact, a farm uncovered a good 4.45 miles (7k m) from the city in the Mente quarter would appear to date from this phase.

Also to be attributed to the Timoleon phase are most of the buildings in the *agora*, the essentially civic public space that occupied at least two blocks. The square was bordered on the west, north, and south by *stoas*—long, colonnaded buildings. The *stoa* to the north consisted of a row of 17 rooms facing onto a deep portico with of 34 columns, among which were placed a number of bases for statues. The western side was occupied by a long, narrow building, perhaps with no portico, with entrances to the east and west; at the north end were several rooms containing baths and benches. Most extraordinary was the discovery in the southern part of this structure of a deposit of about 800 commercial amphoras, of the Italo-Greek type, dating from the third century B.C. and now exhibited in the Archaeological Museum.

Parallel with the *stoa* on the north side, but shorter, perhaps to avoid encroaching on a previ-

ous sacred building, was a third *stoa*. On the east wall of this portico was an imposing, double L-shaped addition with six columns on its east side; the building ran along the rocky crest of the plain and opened toward the south onto another open space situated on a lower level: a kind of low *agora* that contained only a few unidentifiable structures connected in some way with water. The upper square, enclosed on three sides, opened toward the west, where there were four altars and three small shrines facing east and oriented along a north–south axis, similar to the layout at Morgantina.

It is assumed that an area to the east of the west *stoa*, commonly called the *Agora* of Ponente, also had some kind of public function; other monuments recognized in this area were a large open enclosure with no constructions and, further to the north, a monumental fountain.

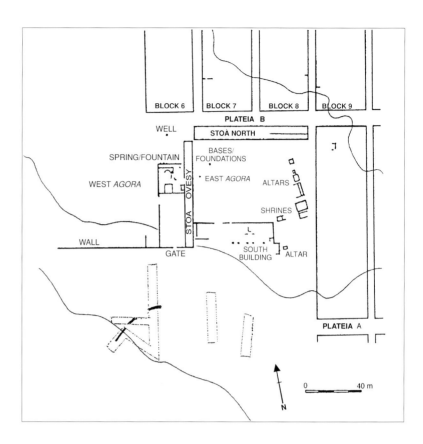

Plan of the *agora* area of Kamarina after recent excavations

Morgantina

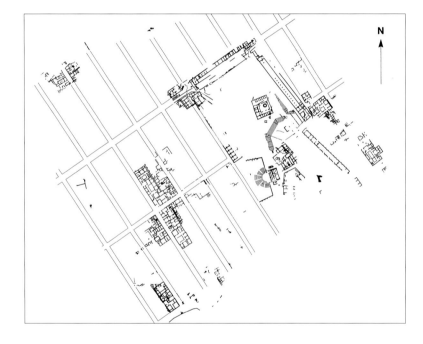

Central area of the settlement at Morgantina in the Hellenistic phase

On opposite page: the terracing and steps of the *agora* at Morgantina

History

The site of Morgantina was permanently occupied from the sixth century B.C. onward, but there is evidence that the acropolis, at least, had been in use since the Early Bronze Age. The presence of Apennine pottery and the remains of huts indicate the arrival there in the Late Bronze Age of people from the Italian peninsula, whom ancient tradition refers to as the Morgetes, the people who inhabited this part of central Sicily. According to the literary sources, the city was in fact founded by Sicels, led by Morges, forced to invade this region after they were expelled from Calabria by the Oinotrians. Situated not far from Gela and Kamarina, in very fertile territory, the native settlement must have quickly come into contact with the Greek population on the coast, which would have had enormous repercussions on the cultural and economic development of the center.

In the sixth century B.C., small temples decorated with architectural terracottas and modest houses with courtyards appeared on the acropolis. A small sanctuary from the Archaic period, with associated separate buildings, in a terraced area was located in the San Francesco quarter.

The settlement was destroyed for the first time at the end of the sixth century B.C. In the middle of the fifth century, Morgantina was conquered by Ducezio, the indigenous king who managed to unite the Sicels in a confederation. Ducezio was credited with the creation of the settlement running at right angles to the earlier one, which extended over the whole plain. The native king's venture did not last long; defeated by armies from Agrigento and Syracuse in 451 B.C., Ducezio was forced to abandon the island and leave Morgantina in the hands of Syracuse. After the peace of Gela, Syracuse ceded the city to Kamarina.

In 396 B.C. Morgantina was conquered by Dionysios I of Syracuse, but less than four years later, in 392 B.C., the city allied itself with the Carthaginian general Magon to fight against Syracuse.

In the course of the Second Punic War, Morgantina was occupied by Romans but rebelled against them a short while afterward. Conquered once again, it was given over to a group of Iberian soldiers. During this phase, the size of the city was reduced and many quarters were completely abandoned. The public buildings were obliterated, as was a small enclosure with an altar in the *agora*. This cult area was turned into a covered market, the *macellum*, with the result that a house of the Roman era was built over the sanctuary of Demeter and Kore, located on a hill 300 m from the *agora*.

The General Topographical Picture
Located in the heart of Sicily on the northern border of the territory controlled by Syracuse, the area where the city was established corresponds to the present locality of Serra Orlando, 3.8 miles (6 km) northeast of Aidone, on an isolated plateau extending for 1.7 miles (2.8 km) and ending on the Cittadella, a high hill, 535 m above sea level, which became the acropolis of the city.

The plateau of Morgantina comprises a continuing succession of hills and depressions—physical features that influenced the route taken by the city walls. The city was protected by a system of fortifications consisting of two encircling walls. The acropolis had its own fortifications, built at the end of the sixth century B.C. or the beginning of the fifth century B.C., independent of those of the inhabited area. The walls that enclosed the plateau—an area of 185 acres (75 hectares), much greater than that enclosed by the settlement wall, with its circumference of about 4.45 miles (7 km)—were constructed in the second half of the fourth century B.C. These walls, built in the form of a double line of masonry with an internal filling, had four gates, laid out roughly at the four cardinal points, and various bastions.

There were three known areas dedicated to *necropoleis:* in one to the north, on the slopes of the acropolis, evidence has been found of both burials and cremation, dating from the middle of the sixth to the beginning of the fifth centuries B.C.

The Urban Settlement
The settlement, set at right angles to the earlier one and still quite visible, dates from the second quarter of the fifth century B.C. and was aligned southwest–northeast. The urban network was divided by a main artery (*plateia*), the surface of which has been partly uncovered, and by a series of narrower streets (*stenopoi*) delineating blocks that were of equal width (37.5 m) but varying length, from 110 to 130 m.

Exploration to the northeast has brought to light expanses of the Hellenistic city. Included in the urban plan was a large public area which occupied a central and dramatic position on two different levels.

The *Agora*
The perfect setting of the *agora* in the urban grid allows us to date the planning of this public space to the beginning of the fifth century B.C., even though the associated buildings, both around its perimeter and inside it, were only built later. The square, roughly rectangular in shape, occupied a depression with an undulating surface that required two different levels to be created before it could be developed. On the upper terrace, in a slightly trapezoidal shape, three long *stoas* enclosed the square to the northwest, northeast, and southwest. Along the margins of this open area buildings of a political nature were added over the years, including the *bouleterion,* the meeting place of the *Boule*—the restricted assembly for citizens only. The square building, dating from 240–230 B.C., contained a meeting room that was entered through a narrow portico. The central part of the *agora* square was occupied by a series of little sanctuaries with small temples and altars—these, too, were vital to the functioning of the political life of the city. One of these, as mentioned above, was obliterated in the Roman era by the *macellum*, a large, square building that acted as a covered market and consisted of a large courtyard within which

was a roofed circular structure (*tholos*) with porticoes and shops, similar to those at Pompeii or Pozzuoli.

In the second half of the third century B.C., in the northwest corner of the *agora,* a monumental fountain was built with a wooden portico and two basins for water; the wall that separated the two basins supported an *aedicula* of the Doric order with four columns on the side, which no longer exists.

The two levels of the *agora* were linked by a structure dating from the end of the fourth and the beginning of the third centuries B.C.: a monumental staircase made from hard local limestone. The structure may have also functioned as a sort of *ekklesiasterion* for meetings of the citizens' assembly, occasions which, at that period, normally took place in theaters.

The proximity of the sanctuary of the chthonic deities, just below, means that it, too, could have taken a part in religious meetings. The structure consisted of a series of steps divided into three sections, in a way that formed a tiered

scenic background to the area below, extending to a total width of 52 m. The western section had 15 steps, that in the center 12, and the section to the east 13. The steps led down to an open space known as the "lower *agora*," where in the course of the fourth century B.C., a theater was carved out of the slope of the hill that bordered the lower part of the square on the eastern side, and where a sanctuary was built dedicated to Ge, Hermes, and the chthonic deities.

This last sanctuary was made up of a small, trapezoidal space surrounded by a wall; in the center was a courtyard containing a circular enclosure with an altar. The space between the wall and the altar was found to be filled with lamps, vases, and other votive objects, including small lead strips bearing curses, which made it possible to identify the deities venerated in the sanctuary. The two exedrae and a small temple with an altar belonged to this sanctuary.

Not far away, in the center of the lower square, two granaries were built at a later date, also various shops, one of them for the sale of pottery.

The southern boundary of the lower terrace in the course of the fourth century B.C. was indicated by the walls, which followed a somewhat irregular route along this stretch.

The Residential Quarters

To the east and west of the *agora* several residential quarters have come to light that, to judge from their lavishness, must have belonged to the local aristocracy. Near the *stoa* to the east investigators found an imposing dwelling, now known as "House with the Doric capital," while a little further south is "The House of Ganymede," so named because of the figure represented on the elaborate mosaic paving.

To the west of the *agora* a large quarter has come to light with houses that in some cases occupy as much as half a block—an indication of the emergence of a dominant group and the associated concentration of property in its hands. Some of these houses, which date from the original phase in the middle of the third century B.C., continued to be inhabited even after the violent encounter with the Romans in 211 B.C.

Agrigento (Akragas)

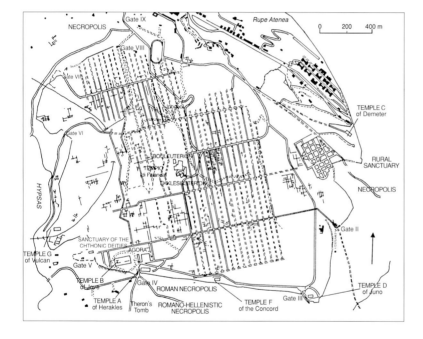

Plan of Agrigento

On opposite page: the
recontructed columns of
Temple I, the "Temple of the
Dioskouroi"

History

Akragas (Agrigento) was founded in 582 B.C. by a
contingent from Gela that was led by Aristonoos
and Pistilos. Scarcely ten years after its foundation
the city suffered under the tyranny of Phalaris, a
man of noble family whose successful political
career allowed him to seize power. After the fall of
Phalaris, around 554 B.C., he was succeeded by two
tyrants, Alkamenes and Alkandros. Next to become
tyrant, in 488 B.C., was Theron, who belonged to
the Emmenide family of Rhodes, the mother city
of Gela, with which he forged a solid alliance
though his marriage to the daughter of Gelon, at
that time tyrant of Gela. Theron was responsible
for the conquest of Himera and the exile of its
tyrant, Therillos, who was then replaced by
Trasydios, son of Theron and noted in the ancient
sources for his cruelty.

Later, in 480 B.C., the year of the Battle of
Salamis, at which the Greeks defeated the Persians,
the armies of Theron and Gelon, now tyrant of
Syracuse, defeated the Carthaginians at Himera.
This was a period of particular importance for
Akragas, whose political influence was also
demonstrated by victories in the Panhellenic
games at Olympia, which were lauded by the poet
Pindar, who, together with Simonides, was a frequent visitor to court of Theron. The great wealth
that came into the city after the victory over the
Carthaginians, and the slave labor provided by the
numerous prisoners, allowed the city to embark on
an extraordinary building program which, in the
eyes of Pindar, made Agrigento seem the most
beautiful of mortal cities.

Of the various works undertaken by the tyrant,
the ones that stood out were undoubtedly the
colossal temple to Zeus Olympios, built to honor
the victory over the Carthaginians, and the system
of subterranean aqueducts designed by Pheas.

These discharged into a pool containing fish and swans, the *Kolymbetra,* which some claim to have discovered in the valley immediately to the west of the rocky spur that houses the sanctuary of the chthonic deities.

In 472 B.C. Theron died and Agrigento, which had heaped heroic honors on its tyrant, was obliged to endure the cruelty of his successor Thrasydios, who, scarcely a year after being installed, clashed with Syracuse and Himera in a war in which he was defeated and thereby obliged to flee. The city, having thus freed itself of the tyranny of the Emmenide, installed a new regime consisting of a government that Diodoros characterized as democratic, with a council of one thousand citizens. For a short intervening period the philosopher and politician Empedokles set up a different government, but at the end of this experiment, lasting only three years, he was sent into exile. In this period the city became enormously wealthy. Empedokles famously declared that his fellow citizens dedicated themselves to luxury as if they were about to die tomorrow and, at the same time, to building as if they were destined to live forever.

In 466 B.C. Akragas was involved in the war against Ducezio, the indigenous commander who had succeeded in uniting the Sicels into a kingdom and was turning his hunger for conquest toward Akragas. Allied with Syracuse, Akragas defeated Ducezio, who was subsequently exiled to Corinth. Syracuse's excessive indulgence toward Ducezio was the cause of a new clash between Akragas and that city, a war which ended in Syracusan victory in 446 B.C., near the river Salso.

The period that followed was influenced primarily by the city's good relations with Carthage, which guaranteed it a certain prosperity. In the war between Athens and Syracuse, however, Akragas chose to stay neutral, which did not save the city from the advance of the Carthaginians, led by Hannibal, nephew of the general Hamilcar who was defeated in the Battle of Himera. In 406 B.C. Hannibal's troops entered the abandoned city and sacked it.

Following the peace between Carthage and Syracuse, the people returned to their city, although as a tributary to Carthage. With the

On page 244: the "Oratorio of
Phalaris" and part of the
ekklesiasterion

On page 245: the sanctuary of
the chthonic deities. In the
foreground, the circular altar
with a *bothros* in the center;
at the back, Temple I, the
"Temple of the Dioskouroi"

Top left: plan of Temple D, the
"Temple of Juno"

Top right: plan of Temple F,
the "Temple of the Concordia"

Below: columns of Temple D,
the "Temple of Juno"

On opposite page: view of
Temple D, the "Temple of
Juno"

On pages 248–49: western
façade of Temple F, the
"Temple of the Concordia"

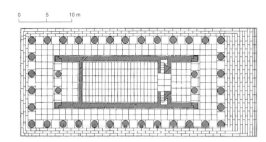

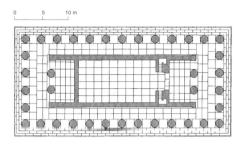

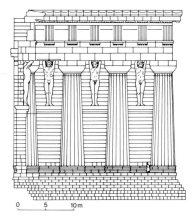

Above: a telamon from Temple B, the "Temple of Zeus Olympios"

Below: the side of Temple B with entablature, first half of the fifth century B.C., with detail

treaty of 383 B.C., Akragas lost partial control of its eastern territory, a situation that lasted until 344 B.C., year of the victory of Timoleon, the Corinthian commander who a few years later refounded the city with a new contingent sent from Elea, led by Megillos and Pheristos. The start of the third century B.C. saw a new tyranny: that of Phintias, who held power between 289 and 280 B.C. In the following years control passed into the hands of the pro-Punic party and Akragas became an important operational base for the Carthaginians in the war against Rome. The city, however, was forced surrender to the Romans in 262 B.C. Occupied by Carthaginian troops since 255 B.C., following the victorious conclusion of the First Punic War, Akragas allied itself with Rome.

Retaken by the Carthaginians in the course of the Second Punic War, it was finally destroyed and sacked by the Romans led by the consul Marcellus Valerius Levinus.

The General Topographical Picture

A little more than 1.9 miles (3 km) from the sea, the city ranged over two hills, the Girgenti hill to the west and the Rupe Atenea to the east, linked by a narrow passage and a low area of plain ending, on the south side, in a sharp rise dominated by temples. The highest part of the area covered by the city was the Rupe Atenea, at 351 m above sea level; however, investigations have located the acropolis on the Girgenti hill, where the medieval settlement was later built. The high plateau on which the city developed was bounded by the river Hypsas, now the Sant'Anna stream; to the north and west, in the valley immediately north of the two hills, flowed the Akragas, now the San Biagio. The two rivers combined a little further south to form a watercourse, now named the San Leone. At the mouth of this river, at Montelusa, 3.8 miles (6 km) south of the city, was the commercial port, which Polybios described as "so important that the city enjoys all the advantages of a marine city."

The wealth of the city came, nevertheless, from its fertile lands, which stretched to the east toward Gela and to the west toward Platani, the ancient Halykos, near which Selinunte, probably in order to check the expansion of Akragas, founded Herakleia Minoa which passed into the control of Akragas in the fourth century B.C.

The Inhabited Area and the Fortifications

The inhabited area extended over a vast plain which included the Girgenti and the Rupe Atenea hills to the north and the Collina dei Templi (Temple Hills) to the south, taking in some 1,170 acres (450 hectares). This vast area, already protected by natural defenses, was surrounded by a fortified wall from the middle of the sixth century B.C. onward. The wall enclosed the Rupe Atenea and the perimeter of the Temple Hills, then continued along the bank of the Hypsas to the Girgenti hill. The wall had nine gates, which were placed, as was customary, to coincide with the roads going outside the city, rather than in line with the city grid itself. Two of these gates were on the east side, three on the south, two on the west, and two more on the northwest. Of particular interest is gate 1, located on the southern slope of the Rupe Atenea, at one of the weakest points of the wall; this entrance was designed as a "pincer" bulwark, consisting of two sections of wall that met at an acute angle.

The Urban Settlement

Dating from the earliest years of the foundation, the urban settlement was arranged around six main east–west roads (*plateiai*) 7 m wide (except for II and IV, which were much wider) and a web of smaller roads (*stenopoi*) meeting them. In the layout of these roads, two key elements from the Archaic urban network have been recognized: the southernmost east–west *plateia* of the Romano-Hellenistic settlement, which linked the eastern part of the city with the sacred zone on the hill, and the *stenopos* in the San Nicola quarter that connected the central part of the valley to the *plateia* described above. The network thus produced marked out blocks 35 m wide and varying in length from around 300 m, occupied by individual dwellings. The urban grid consisted of two slightly divergent sectors, one northwest and the other center-south. Where the two sectors met, at the center of the inhabited area 125 m above sea level, was the public area, the *agora* of the Greek city.

Occupied in the Archaic period by sanctuaries, this area contained two important public administrative buildings, the *bouleuterion*, the meeting place for the council, and the *ekklesiasterion,* the building where the citizens assembled. These two political monuments are today separated by the Norman/Cistercian complex of San Nicola, which houses the Museum. A second public area has been found in the quarter immediately to the east of the of the Temple of Zeus Olympios. This area was split into two terraces, separated by the south *plateia*. To the north of the road are the remains of a Hellenistic portico; in front of this are two lines of steps with an inscription which allows the complex, obviously a school, to be dated in the first century B.C.

The Public Administrative Buildings

The *ekklesiasterion* consisted of a *cavea* cut out of the rocky bank that sloped gently down to the foot of the Hellenistic sanctuary, the so-called Oratorio of Phalaris, and covered an area of 1,945 square yards (1,250 square meters). The *cavea* was made up of a series of concentric cuts in the rocky bank, forming tiers of seating, slightly shaped for comfort, which were capable of accommodating 3,000

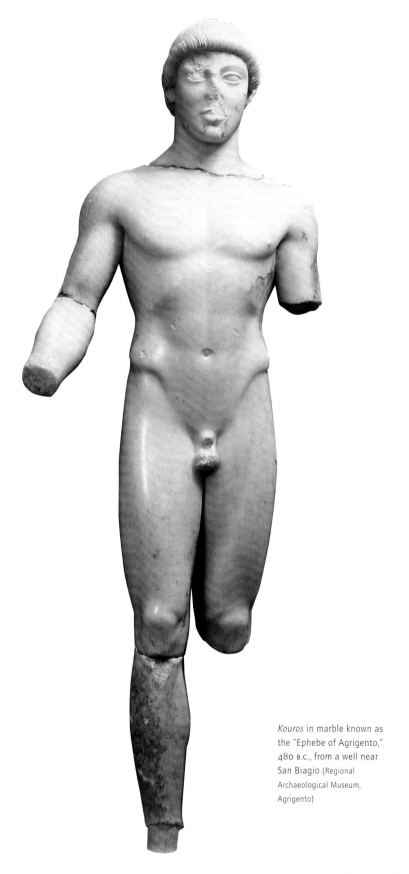

Kouros in marble known as the "Ephebe of Agrigento," 480 B.C., from a well near San Biagio (Regional Archaeological Museum, Agrigento)

On opposite page: colonnade
on south side of Temple A,
the "Temple of Herakles"

citizens. Comparison with similar monuments in Metapontion and Poseidonia indicates that the *ekklesiasterion* of Akragas dates from the fifth century B.C., rather than the third, which has also been suggested.

In the course of the second century B.C., the building was abandoned and completely covered over. Built in the new square were a prostyle temple (the so-called Oratorio of Phalaris), a square altar, and a semicircular exedra. At the foot of the San Nicola hill, to the north of the *ekklesiasterion* and the *bouleterion,* was a square building constructed at the end of the fourth century B.C., on an artificial terrace consisting of a series of tiers with six rows of stone seating. The *cavea,* which faced east (like the building itself) and opened on to a large colonnaded area, was traversed by four short, radial flights of steps, with an ambulatory around the orchestra, giving a total of 300 places. Of the external structure, a few sections of wall have survived. In the late Hellenistic period the area was partially abandoned, as was demonstrated by the layer of well-trodden earth that covered some of the monumental features of the building.

During the Imperial Roman period the urban layout of the area underwent changes consisting of a raising of the pavement levels and, in the fourth century A.D., the transformation of the *bouleterion* into a covered theater, the *odeion.*

The Dwelling Houses

Of the inhabited areas, we are most familiar with the Romano-Hellenistic quarter at the heart of the valley, just to the east of the Church of San Nicola. This quarter followed the roads and blocks of the earlier city. The blocks maintained their original longitudinal divisions using *ambitus*—narrow alleys subsequently put out of use by the extension of some of the houses, like the "House of Aphrodite" or the "House of the Rhombus Mosaic." The design of the houses, even during the Roman period, was in the Hellenistic form, with rooms set around a central peristyle, and probably with a second floor which served as a *gynaeceum*—an area reserved for women. The men's area—the *andron,* occupied the rooms around the peristyle, on the ground floor.

The Sanctuaries

The sanctuaries that have come to light so far were arranged in a circle inside the walls of the city, dominated by the Rupe Atenae and the Girgenti hill. This was originally the site of a Doric temple of which the earliest remains date from 480 to 460 B.C. and are now incorporated into the Church of Santa Maria dei Greci. Part of the structure of the temple, a *peripteros* of six by thirteen columns, and a *cella* with *pronaos* and *opisthodomos,* is still visible in the atrium of the church.

The little medieval church of San Biagio, on the Rupe Atenea, also includes a small Doric temple dedicated to Demeter and Kore, with which two circular altars were associated. Not far from the temple, but outside the city walls, was the so-called rural sanctuary, in reality a fountain. Finds of clay busts and Archaic ceramics indicated that it was a sacred place, a common occurrence in places where water was available in ancient times. The complex consisted of springs issuing from natural grottoes which had been adapted to channel the water to a fountain made up of two cisterns set on different levels, and interlinked basins.

The southern boundary of the upland plain where the city was built was a rocky crest on which stood a series of temples, albeit almost all anonymous and known only by nicknames given to them by the local people. The exception was the *Olympieion,* the colossal temple to Zeus Olympios, built to honor the victory of 480 B.C. against the Carthaginians. The temples that were built on the height, along the line of the fortifications, were all very similar in size, with the same design and stylistic features. The floor plan had a colonnade (*peristasis*), which enclosed the *cella* consisting of an entrance (*pronaos*) and symmetrical rear chamber (*opisthodomos*), both with columns in front.

At the southwest corner is Temple D, known as the Temple of Juno Lacinia, a Doric building from 450 B.C., with six columns at the front and thirteen on the sides; all the columns on the south side have been partially restored to their original elevation.

On toward the west, the next is Temple F, the Temple of Concord (440–430 B.C.), which consists of a platform with four steps on which stands an exterior colonnade of six by thirteen columns. It is one of the best preserved temples of the ancient

world, a stroke of good fortune owing to its transformation into a Christian basilica at the end of the sixth century A.D. The change of use involved a reversal of the orientation, with the entrance moved to the rear of the Greek temple and the consequent demolition of the rear wall of the *cella*.

Similar in design to the previous temples is Temple A, called the Temple of Herakles, which, with its elongated *cella* and a *peristasis* of six by fifteen columns, stands on a rocky spur overlooking gate IV. According to a recent theory, the temple would have had a marble façade, something very exceptional in Southern Italy. The statue of a fallen warrior, now in the Regional Archaeological Museum at Agrigento, came from the façade of this temple, although another view holds that such a piece of sculpture belonged, more likely, to the nearby temple to Zeus.

Beyond gate V, known as the Porta Aurea, is the area of plain dominated by the immense and incredible ruin of the Temple of Zeus Olympios, the *Olympieion*. The majestic temple, measuring 112.5 × 56.3 m, was equaled in size only by Temple G in Selinunte; built on a magnificent base, it has some very special characteristics. Like Temple F in Selinunte, and Temple B in Metapontion, the colonnade that encircled the *cella* was replaced by a solid enclosure. The walls surrounding this inaccessible *peristasis,* were set with half-columns; between these and set-half way up the structure from the top of the five steps on which it was built, were pedestals supporting telamons, monumental figures 7.75 m tall, with arms held high behind their heads to hold up the superstructure the building. The roof covered only the *peristasis,* while the *cella* appears to have been open to the sky. Over the centuries the temple has unfortunately been plundered by stone masons and so little of the architectural features remain.

Between the Temple of Zeus and gate V was another small sacred area within which were two small temples, bordered on the north and east sides by a colonnaded structure in the form of an L. This area was not used after the fourth century B.C., when the space it occupied was partly taken up by a circular building. From a well immediately to the north of the sanctuary came the splendid head of a warrior in terracotta, identified by some as Athena, which must have been part of a group, perhaps one that decorated one of the temples in the area.

Beyond gate V is a large paved square that formed the entrance to the sanctuary of the chthonic deities, a sacred complex dating, in its initial phase, from the sixth century B.C. The best preserved of the buildings in this sacred area is Temple I, also called the Temple of the Dioskouroi, dating from 480–460 B.C. Following work carried out in the nineteenth century, which restored them to a standing position, today one can see four columns of the southeast corner, together with their related entablature. At the western end of the Collina dei Templi, beyond gate V, there is a rocky spur dominated by the temple known as the Temple of Vulcan which, like most of the other temples, has a *peristasis* with six columns on the short sides and thirteen on the long ones. Hardly anything remains of the structure other than a few broken pieces of architectural material: a building of the Doric order, dating from 430 B.C., it enclosed an earlier shrine built between 570 and 560 B.C.

Outside the walls, on the plain of San Gregorio, to the south of gate IV, inside a sanctuary in which other temples have been identified, stood Temple H, known as the Temple of Asklepios. It is a small temple without colonnade or *cella,* with a false *opisthodomos,* dating from the end of the fifth century B.C.

The *Necropoleis*

The earliest necropolis, used by the first generation of colonists, was located to the west, not far from gate VII, while those from the fifth and fourth centuries B.C. extended immediately to the south of the preceding burial area, and to the northeast, near gate IX. Among the items found in these *necropoleis* are the Attic red-figured vases that are exhibited in the Archaeological Museum. Between the fourth and third centuries B.C., the people of Akragas used an area at the foot of Rupe Atenea, to the northeast of the city, as a necropolis. In the Hellenistic period, the burial area used was that found to the north, between Rupe Atenea and the Girgenti hill.

The Romano-Hellenistic necropolis, which contained, among others, the monumental tomb known as the "Tomb of Theron," is to the south of the Collina dei Templi, not far from gate IV. Farther away from the city are the *necropoleis* in the Montelusa area, near the sea, along the road from Akragas to Gela.

Selinunte

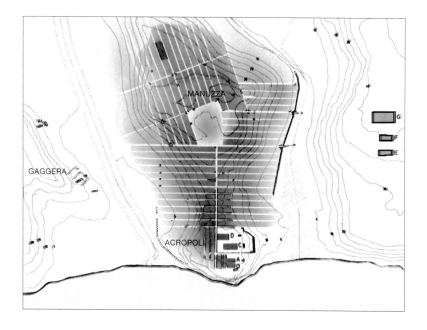

History

The most western of the Sicilian colonies, Selinunte was founded by Megara Hyblaia together with a group of colonists sent from its own metropolis, Megara Nisea, under the leadership of the *ekistes* (founder of the colony) Pammilos. According to Thucydides the foundation took place one hundred years after the founding of the

mother city, which puts it at 628–627 B.C., but nowadays the date of 651–650 B.C., suggested by Diodoros, seems to be more in line with the available archaeological data.

The city's history was molded by its frontier position on the south coast of the island, in the heart of the territory of the Sicans and the Elymians and in close contact with the Phoenician and Carthaginian territories. Its relationship with the indigenous community, particularly with the Elymians, whose capital was Segesta, frequently degenerated into conflict, but it must also have involved more friendly contacts and exchanges, as is demonstrated by a treaty of *epigamia* which authorized intermarriage between the inhabitants of the two cities.

Its dealings with Carthage, however, were very different. In the course of the sixth century B.C. the Carthaginians extended their control over the ancient Phoenician colonies in western Sicily (Palermo, Solunto, Mozia, and, later, Lilybaion), but Selinunte enjoyed a privileged relationship with them from the beginning, based on their considerable mutual economic interests. The Greek colony was able to profit from the Mediterranean trade network operated by the Phoenicians and the Carthaginians, offering in exchange the surplus cereal production of its vast and fertile territory. While not without its moments of conflict, the economic alliance between Selinunte and Carthage

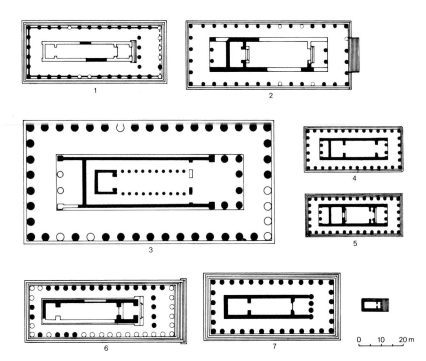

Top: plans of the temples

1. Temple F   5. Temple A
2. Temple E   6. Temple C
3. Temple G   7. Temple D
4. Temple O

Above: view of the temples on the eastern hill

On opposite page: Temple E

enjoyed with its powerful Punic and Phoenician neighbors, and the favorable position of the site, with its vast agricultural hinterland. This led to its expansion along the coastal strip and to the border with the territory of Segesta in the interior. To the west, the physical advance of Selinunte probably stopped at Mazara del Vallo, while to the east the foundation of the subcolony of Herakleia Minoa (about 570 B.C.), along the line of the Platani River, established its border with the territory of Agrigento.

This was the era of the tyrannies; ancient sources quote the names of Pythagoras and his successor Euryleon, who governed Selinunte in the second half of the sixth century B.C., and whose pursuit of prestige was responsible for the great architectural projects that filled the city with fine monuments.

When the government of Euryleon was violently deposed, the regime that followed it—probably drawn from among the city's aristocrats—seems to have made no changes. It maintained the same policies toward the Phoenicians and Carthaginians, to the point where Greek Selinunte even remained neutral throughout the Punic War that ended with the Battle of Himera (480 B.C.).

We know little about the history of Selinunte in the fifth century B.C.; the great "Tablet of Selinunte," the monumental inscription preserved in Temple G on the hill to the east, records a victory won by Selinunte with the blessing of the gods but makes no mention of the identity of the enemy it vanquished. Certainly the city was involved in repeated encounters with Segesta, one of which, triggered in 416 B.C. by a boundary dispute, furnished Athens with a pretext for intervening in Sicily; the Elymian city turned to Athens, with whom it had established a pact of alliance sometime before, when the other Siciliote forces failed to respond to its call for assistance.

The Athenian expedition ended in a resounding defeat, and a few years later in 410 B.C., again under attack by Selinunte, Segesta sought the help of Carthage. A series of Carthaginian victories in Africa, which opened a new agrarian market, and the rise to prominence of the pro-Syracusan

remained substantially intact until the end of the fifth century B.C., when profound changes in the international political picture brought about the encounter in which the Carthaginians decimated their former ally.

The city's rapid economic and demographic development in the course of the sixth century B.C. was largely due to the good diplomatic relations

Top: metope with a couple on
a chariot drawn by two mules,
with rampant horses to the
sides, 575 B.C., from Temple C
on the acropolis at Selinunte
(The "A. Salinas" Regional
Archaeological Museum, Palermo)

Below: metope depicting Zeus
and Hera, 470–460 B.C., from
Temple E at Selinunte (The "A.
Salinas" Regional Archaeological
Museum, Palermo)

democratic party in Selinunte created a new situation in Sicily, and changed the balance of the
internal politics and economics of the two cities.
This was probably at the root of Carthage's oppor-
tunistic attack on its former ally in 409 B.C.
Selinunte, besieged by the Carthaginian army,
capitulated at the end of nine days of strenuous
resistance. A few years later the city saw an attempt
by Hermokrates—the Syracusan commander who
had fought against the Athenians—to rally the
Siciliote forces and oppose the new and persistent
Carthaginian interference in the affairs of Sicily,

but the operation failed and, from that time on, Selinunte remained in Carthaginian hands.

This state of affairs continued until the end of the First Punic War (250 B.C.), when the population of Selinunte was transferred to Lilybaion; the site has remained unoccupied from that time to the present day, apart from sporadic occasions during the Byzantine period.

The Settlement

The colony developed on the southwest coast of the island, occupying three low, limestone terraces

Top: metope with *quadriga* of Apollo, 575–550 B.C., from the acropolis at Selinunte (The "A. Salinas" Regional Archaeological Museum, Palermo)

Below: Actaeon changed into a stag and attacked by his own hounds, urged on by Artemis, 470–460 B.C., from Temple E at Selinunte (The "A. Salinas" Regional Archaeological Museum, Palermo)

On pages 262–63: Temple E at Selinunte

Marble head of a female, 470–460 B.C., from Temple E at Selinunte (The "A. Salinas" Regional Archaeological Museum, Palermo)

separated by the river Modione (formerly the Selinos) to the west and to the east by the river Cotone, at the mouth of which were two large bays that served as ports.

The inhabited area was built on the central height, divided into two sectors by natural features of the terrain: the promontory of the acropolis, sheer above the sea and, connected to it by a saddle, the less steep, internal part of the plateau, the Manuzza hill. The sanctuary areas that ringed the city like a sort of "sacred crown" were installed on the Marinella hill to the east and the Gaggera hill to the west.

Toward the interior and along the coastal strip, the hills sloped down to a vast plain which was the *chora* (territory) of Selinunte; the areas used as burial grounds were located on the spurs of the hills toward the interior, on the edges of the territory. When the colonists first arrived, the site was occupied by native people, as the presence of a Sican village on the upland plain of the Manuzza hill shows; there is not yet enough evidence available, however, to establish whether there was a period of peaceful coexistence between the two groups or if, as is more probable, the *apoikia* exploited the area to the detriment of the indigenous element.

The Urban Settlement and the Fortifications

No particular planning seems to have gone into the arrangement of the available space during the earliest phase of the settlement, in the seventh century B.C. The houses, built along the paths that had developed naturally between the two hills, occupied large open spaces spread over the sectors of both the acropolis and the Manuzza hill, which had a necropolis at its center.

In the first quarter of the sixth century B.C., the urban settlement underwent a radical reconstruction which involved a grandiose project of unification implemented gradually over the years, probably fuelled by the powerful oligarchic—perhaps even already tyrannical—forces emerging in the government of the city. The new urban plan, which provided for the division of the available space into modules, was arranged in two distinct sectors, and took account of the structure of the terrain around the hills.

The layout of the acropolis was centered on a large north–south *plateia* running the length of the plateau, intersected at right angles by minor streets. The road network established in the Manuzza area, however, diverged from this by 23°, with arteries running northwest–southeast, crossing main roads at right angles to them; the central *plateia* constituted the main axis of the network. In the center, where the two sectors came together, a large area, roughly trapezoidal in shape and left completely free of buildings, was probably the site of the *agora*.

At the same time as the road network was being put into place, a system of fortifications was built around the city; recent excavations brought to light a stretch of wall—a double line of masonry with *emplekton* (filling)—on the eastern slopes of the inhabited area along the valley of the Cotone.

After the destruction of the city by the Carthaginians, the new Graeco-Punic residential area was concentrated in the acropolis region, certainly the easiest to defend. A new city wall, surrounding just this area, was built at the end of the fifth century B.C., probably during the brief occupation by Hermokrates, and was subsequently reconstructed several times. One of these phases, dating from around the end of the fourth century B.C., included the addition of the "North Gate," a complex defensive structure with three floors, furnished with semicircular keeps, designed according to the most advanced fortification-building techniques available at the time.

The Acropolis *Temenos*

The southeast sector of the acropolis was destined, probably from the start, to house the main urban sanctuary. At the beginning of the sixth century B.C. the entire sacred area was integrated into the urban network when a *peribolos* (surrounding wall) was built parallel to the main arterial roads and a terrace created to extend the eastern sector. Inside the *temenos* the earliest buildings were simple, elongated shrines; the restructuring of the sanctuary, and the addition of the imposing buildings which gave it its monumental form, only occurred after the middle of the sixth century B.C.

At the center of the sacred area, on the site of the old *megaron*, was Temple C—known only by a letter of the alphabet because, like many of the temples at Selinunte, there is no confirmation of the deity to whom it was attributed. It was the largest building on the acropolis, a monumental *peripteral* temple of the Doric order, with six by seventeen columns and a *cella* with *pronaos* and *adyton*. Leading up to the temple, which was oriented toward the east, was an imposing flight of steps which enhanced its monumental effect. The dramatic effect of the entrance was also reflected in the building itself. The eastern façade was decorated with metopes sculpted with mythological subjects—Herakles and the Cercopi, Perseus and the Gorgon, and the *quadriga* of Apollo—treated in a bold, formal manner to great effect.

Concurrently with the building of the temple, the entire eastern side of the *temenos* was newly terraced with an enormous embankment supported by an imposing, stepped retaining wall that constituted a kind of grandiose, scenic entrance to the sanctuary. Sometime later, around the last quarter of the sixth century B.C., another majestic temple building, Temple D—a Doric peripteral with *peristasis* of six by thirteen columns and *cella* with *pronaos* and *adyton*—was constructed beside Temple C. It is uncertain to which deities these temples were dedicated; the recovery of some inscriptions among the ruins of the temples and a comparison made with the natural features of the sacred areas at Megara Nisea (the metropolis of Megara Hyblaia, and in turn the metropolis of Selinunte), which also had two separate acropolises, lead one to suppose that Temple C may have been attributed to Apollo and Temple D to Athena, but this is still only theory.

This same uncertainty in the reconstruction of the cultural areas reoccurs in the southern sector of the *temenos*, to which parallel temple buildings, Temple A and Temple O, were added in the course of the first half of the fifth century B.C.; these additional buildings were of the Doric order, but designed according to a new architectural model in the Severe style.

The sanctuary, clearly one of the principal public sacred areas in the colony, was radically transformed during the fourth century B.C. The modest houses in the Carthaginian residential quarter spilled over into the entire area and a sanctuary was installed in the *pronaos* of Temple A, identifiable by the mark of Tanit present on the pavement.

The Eastern Hill

Outside the urban area, with close links to the port at the mouth of the Cotone River, the Marinella hill was home to a vast and imposing sacred area where only the ruins now remain of the three large temple buildings formerly standing there. Nothing is known about the boundaries of the *temenos* or of those buildings connected to the cults that were associated with it (altars, service areas, and so forth). The position of the temples, parallel to each other and aligned on the same east–west orientation as the road network of the acropolis, indicates that the arrangement of the sacred area formed part of the same grand urbanization project that reorganized the residential area.

Stepped wall on the east side of the *temenos* on the acropolis at Selinunte

Herm of Zeus Meilichios, fifth century B.C., from the sanctuary of the *Malophoros,* Selinunte (The "A. Salinas" Regional Archaeological Museum, Palermo)

The most northerly of the three buildings, the colossal Temple G—one of the most impressive architectural feats in the Greek West—was never finished. Built in the Doric order, its features—pseudodipteral floor plan (that is, with the *peristasis* some distance from the *cella*), large *cella* open to the sky with a small shrine (*naiskos*) to the rear—are very similar to those of the great temple of Apollo at Didyma in Asia Minor. While it is quite possible that it may have been an *Apollonion,* it may, however, equally well have venerated Zeus, as seems to be indicated by the "Tablet of Selinunte," the great stone inscription found in the ruins of the same Temple G. The epigraph expresses the thanks of Selinunte to the gods for a military victory and the particular stress laid on the name of Zeus—the only god it mentions twice and to whom it gives special thanks—would seem to indicate that the cult could well have been attributed to the father of the gods.

Immediately to the south was another, smaller temple building: Temple F. This was a Doric peripteral temple, containing a long *cella* with *pronaos* and *adyton,* and a *peristasis* of six by fourteen columns partially enclosed by partition walls—an unusual feature, surely indicative of a type of cult that involved a preliminary initiation-type ritual. The mysterious nature of the cult has been linked to

Dionysos, a deity who is sure to have been represented in the *pantheon* of Selinunte and was venerated on the Carian acropolis at Megara Nisea with the name Nykteilos. The eastern slopes of Selinunte would therefore have been a perfect reproduction of the acropolis at Megara Nisea. Reasoning along those lines, the southernmost of the three buildings, Temple E, already in existence in the first half of the sixth century B.C., and rebuilt several times, could rationally be attributed to Aphrodite.

The building that is currently visible—the only one to have undergone a restoration process which reconstructed the fallen items in their original, upright position—was built between 470 and 460 B.C. in the form of a Doric *peripteros,* having a long *cella* with raised *adyton, opisthodomos,* and *pronaos,* the latter decorated with metopes bearing mythical subjects (Herakles and Antiope, Artemis and Encelado, Zeus and Hera) sculpted in a formal manner that wavers between Late Archaic and the Severe style.

The presence of Hera on one of the metopes, together with the extraurban location of the sanctuary, within striking distance of the port below, has convinced some scholars that the queen of the gods, the deity traditionally linked with areas outside the city and to commercial and trade activities, is a more likely candidate than Aphrodite.

The Gaggera Hill

Outside the city walls, overlooking the valley of the Modione and the port area, the Gaggera hill was the site of a succession of sacred areas, the most important being the one dedicated to Demeter Malophoros, a divine figure with markedly chthonic and infernal features but who is also linked to reproduction and the renewal of the growing cycle. The connection with death is underlined by the fact that the sanctuary is located only a short distance from one of the city's largest *necropoleis.*

The use of the sanctuary seems to date from the end of the seventh century B.C., when the earliest cult building was constructed; this was a simple *megaron* facing east, preceded by a kind of porch whose function has not been determined. In the

course of the sixth century B.C. the sanctuary was monumentalized; the primitive *megaron* was replaced by a temple with *pronaos* and *adyton* and, to the east, an imposing altar with a cavity, which, when found, was filled with votive offerings and the ashes from sacrifices. The *temenos* was surrounded by a wall, which followed an irregular path dictated by the undulation of the terrain and the presence of a little watercourse that crossed the sacred area. During the fifth century B.C. the entrance to the sanctuary was monumentalized with the construction of a *propylon*. Evidence of the importance of the cult of the *Malophoros* at the center of the religious life of the colony is provided by the high quality of the votives found in the sanctuary, made up predominantly of ceramic materials and clay offerings (masks, busts, and statuettes). The sanctuary, at the height of its importance in the Archaic period, nevertheless remained active throughout the Punic phase, since the cult of the goddess was recognized and officially accepted by the Carthaginians.

At the southeast corner of the *peribolos* of the sanctuary stood a small *temenos*—a simple shrine surrounded by its own enclosure—dedicated to Hekate, the three-formed deity with a dual nature, infernal and lunar, who guided and protected all symbolic and physical passings. The

deliberate placing of the encircling wall beside the *propylon* evoked the goddess's role of guardian of the doorway.

To the north of the *temenos* of the *Malophoros* was another independent cult area—that is, not devoted to a principal deity (as is that of Hekate)—dedicated to Zeus Meilichios (sweet as honey), another divine figure linked to the world beyond the tomb. The *temenos* consisted of a colonnaded enclosure with a small distyle temple at its center. To the west, a vast area outside the enclosure was used for the dedication of a particular type of offering: stelai, either aniconic or embellished with anthropomorphic figures. These were often inscribed, and the presence of large number of them demonstrates the popularity of the cult in the Greek period and especially in the Punic phase. The field containing the stelai was dominated by an altar topped by three large slabs set edgeways, probably connected with the three *betili* of the Phoenician/Punic religion.

The sequence of sacred areas continued to the south, with another *temenos*, consisting of a temple surrounded by a *peribolos,* that was probably built at the beginning of the sixth century B.C. A fragment of an inscription found with it, and the type of votive offerings it contained, indicate that it formed part of the cult of Hera.

Votive lamp in marble, 625–600 B.C., from the sanctuary of the *Malophoros*, Selinunte (The "A. Salinas" Regional Archaeological Museum, Palermo)

Herakleia Minoa

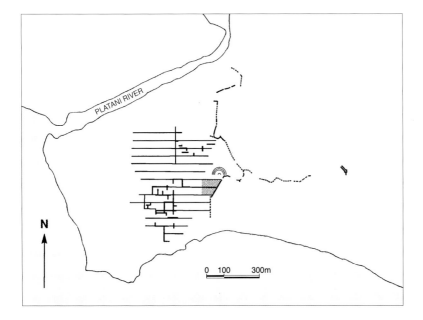

Plan of Herakleia Minoa

History

The colony of Herakleia Minoa was founded by Selinunte in the course of the sixth century B.C. to protect the eastern limit of its territory where it bordered the *chora* (territory) of Agrigento. According to Herodotos, the expedition that was responsible for the foundation of the *apoikia* was led by Euryleon, a friend of Dorieus, the Spartan commander who had attempted to colonize the area of Eryx and was subsequently killed in a battle with the coalition forces of the Elymians and the Phoenicians.

From numismatic evidence it seems that the original name of the city was Minoa, and that only later, in the course of the fourth century B.C., was it given the name Herakleia. One legend has it that Diodoros gave it the name Minoa from Minos, the Cretan king who came to Sicily in search of Daidalos and was killed by the Sicel king, Kokalos. This tradition could have originated from an earlier occupation of the site in the Mycenaean era, but for the moment archaeological data does not appear to substantiate this theory.

The city was quickly absorbed into Agrigento's sphere of influence, remaining its westernmost outpost until 409 B.C., when the Carthaginians' great expedition against the Siciliote *poleis* forced its submission. From then on, because of its strategic position, it was a constant source of contention between the Carthaginians and the Greeks. Conquered and refounded during the time of Timoleon, it was subsequently retaken by the Carthaginians, who used it as a base until the Second Punic War, when it was definitively conquered by the Romans.

The Settlement

The colony developed on the southern coast of the island, on the left bank of the Platani River (the old Halikos), on a natural progression of terraces descending to the sea.

We know virtually nothing of the Archaic settlement, to the point that it has even been postulated that the city was founded on the opposite bank of the river, in the region of Borgo Bonsignore, where materials dating from the first half of the sixth century B.C. have been found.

We are more familiar, however, with the physical appearance of the city that was established according to a regular urban plan in the time of Timoleon, during the fourth to the third century B.C. The settlement was arranged on a network of roads running east–west, marking out blocks about 35 m wide, within which were dwellings divided into a number of rooms, set around a central courtyard. In a later era (from the second to the first century B.C.), the lots were filled with smaller houses, also with several rooms but arranged in a much more haphazard way.

The theater was inserted into the urban network in the second half of the fourth century B.C. The *cavea*, 33 m wide, was built on an artificial mound supported by a wall (*analemma*). The stage was probably constructed from some kind of perishable material and has not survived.

On the higher part of the hill, which overlooked the theater and the houses and probably served as the acropolis, was a sacred area, as indicated by the ruins of a shrine and a temple building.

The inhabited area was encircled by a fortified wall that followed the curves of the terrain; various phases of its construction, dating from the end of the sixth to the end of the fourth century, can be seen in a well-preserved section in the area to the northwest.

Clay *arula* with a lion and a gazelle, second half of the sixth century B.C., from Herakleia Minoa (Antiquarium near the excavations at Herakleia Minoa)

Pages 270–71: the theater at Herakleia Minoa

Segesta

urbanization, the result of its close contacts with the Greek element in the neighboring colonies, put it on a different level from that of the other indigenous centers in Sicily. Only later, and in a different historical context, were these other centers able to assimilate the essential elements of the Greek urban experience. The city's strong links with the colony at Selinunte are illustrated in the sources, which record the existence of a treaty of *epigamia* authorizing intermarriage between citizens of the two communities.

Nevertheless, relations between the two cities of Segesta and Selinunte often degenerated into conflict, as is shown by repeated confrontations. One of these arose from a territorial dispute and furnished the Athenians with a pretext for intervening in the political affairs of Sicily. Called upon for help by Segesta, Athens undertook a military expedition to Sicily, which resulted, as has been noted, in its resounding defeat.

It was Segesta that was later responsible for the destruction of Selinunte. At the end of a whole series of attacks, it appealed to its traditional ally, Carthage, who in 409 B.C. came to its aid with a powerful expedition that overthrew many of the Siciliote cities. The Elymian city maintained a firm alliance with Carthage over the years, interrupted only by the brief periods when it was conquered first by Dionysios of Syracuse and then by Agathokles.

In 260 B.C. it transferred its allegiance to the Romans.

History

Segesta was not numbered among the Greek colonies of Sicily but was in fact one of the principal centers of the Elymians, the indigenous inhabitants of the western part of the island. Other Elymian centers included Eryx, Entella, and Iaitai (Monte Iato). However, the "Hellenization" of Segesta, which happened very early and had a profound effect on its people, meant that its rapid

The Settlement

The city was established in northwest Sicily, not far from the coast, on a plateau on the slope of Mount Barbaro. Most of what is known about the urban settlement is provided by aerial photography, which shows that it seems to have been fairly standard, built on terraces to compensate for the different levels of the terrain and surrounded by a fortified wall.

The only building of note within the urban area was the theater, which occupied a prominent position to the north of the city, overlooking the beautiful panorama of the Segestan *chora* (territory). Probably before the middle of the fourth century B.C., it was partially carved out of the side of the hill and partly erected on an artificial embankment supported by a containing wall (*analemma*). At the center of the *cavea*—of which twenty of the tiers have been preserved—was a horseshoe-shaped orchestra at the back of which was the large building containing the stage, with lateral proscenium decorated with figures of Pan.

Two extraurban sacred areas were found outside the walls, but it is not yet known to whom they were dedicated. The earliest one was located in the Mango quarter, on the southern slopes of the city, and was already in use in the eighth century B.C. The sanctuary consisted of a large *temenos* surrounded by a wall built of large stone blocks, inside of which was a peripteral temple that was probably built by workmen from Selinunte.

Selinuntan workmanship is exemplified also by the other sacred building, the famous Temple of Segesta that stands on the hill to the west of the city. A monumental peripteral building of the Doric order, it was built in the second half of the fifth century B.C., around 430–420 B.C., when the city was at the height of its power. The temple was meant to be a symbol of the city's desire for a leading role on the Sicilian political scene. This ambitious monument, however, was never finished, as is shown by the absence of a *cella* and various other components, and the lack of the customary fluting on the columns.

Bibliography

This bibliography gives references to the major works that cover the essential facts; the citations are intended to be used as basic sources for those who wish to delve more deeply into the problems touched on in the introductory pages and in the chapters on the individual cities.

On the Greek cities, there is a recent volume by E. Greco, *La città greca antica: Istituzione, società, forme urbane,* published by Donzelli, Rome 1999, which examines the various aspects of the *polis;* it is fundamentally based on E. Greco and M. Torelli's *Storia dell'urbanistica: Il mondo greco,* published by Laterza, Rome-Bari, 1983.

Another basic history of Magna Graecia is the study by E. Ciaceri, *Storia della Magna Grecia* I–III, a reprint of the 1928 edition, Arte Tipographica, Naples 1976. For Sicily there are always A. Holm's *Geschichte Siciliens im Altertum,* 3 volumes, Leipzig 1870–1898 (Italian translation *Storia della Sicilia nell'antichità,* a reprint in 3 volumes, Bologna 1965) and M. I. Finley's *A History of Sicily: Ancient Sicily to the Arab Conquest,* London 1968 (Italian translation *Storia della Sicilia antica,* Laterza, Rome-Bari 1985).

Summaries and problems of a general kind are admirably dealt with in the manual by E. Greco, *Archeologia della Magna Grecia,* Laterza, Rome-Bari 1992, with critical analysis and bibliography. More recent is the manual by E. De Juliis, *Magna Grecia,* Edipuglia, Bari 1998. Still valid in many ways is the volume by J. Bérard, *La Magna Grecia,* Einaudi, Turin, 1963. An up-to-date synthesis of the history of the territories of the Greek cities along the Ionian coastal strip can be found in the book by M. Osanna, *Chorai coloniali da Taranto a Locri: Documentazione archeologica e ricostruzione storica,* Rome 1992.

On the Strait of Messina, in addition to the basic work by G. Vallet, *Rhégion et Zancle: Histoire, commerce et civilisation des cités chalcidiennes du détroit de Messine,* Paris 1958, there is also a recent volume by M. Gras, E. Greco, and P. G. Guzzo, *Nel cuore del Mediterraneo antico: Reggio, Messina e le colonie calcidesi dello Stretto,* Meridiana Libri, Corigliano Calabro 2000, which includes a series of contributions both on general themes (trade, economic and

political history, monetization, artistic and craft production, cults) and on individual cities such as Zankle-Messina, Metauro, Mylai-Naxos, and the Kalchedian cities which gravitated to the Gulf of Naples.

On the concept of colonial cities there is the contribution by B. Greco, *Sulle città coloniali dell'occidente greco antico,* in *Les grecs et l'Occident,* Actes du colloque de la Villa "Kerylos" 1991, Rome 1995, pp. 83–93.

Dealing with the subject of colonies and colonization is the work by B. Lepore and M. I. Finley, *Colonie degli antichi e dei moderni* (with a preface by E. Greco and introduction by M. Lombardo), Fondazione Paestum—published by Donzelli, Paestum-Rome 2000, and also a collection in one volume of the acts of a convention in memory of Georges Vallet, *La colonization grecque en Méditerranée occidentale,* Rome 1999. On the subject of Achaian colonization in particular, now in preparation for the third volume in the Tekmeria series of the Paestum Foundation are the acts of the international convention *Gli Achei e l'identità etnica degli Achei in Occidente,* Paestum, 23–25 February 2001, Pandemos, Paestum (in press).

Some aspects of the *agorai* of Greek cities are dealt with in E. Greco's contribution, "Agora eumeghetes: l'espace public dans l'Occident," in *Public et privé en Grèce ancienne: Lieux, conduites, pratique,* found in *Ktema* 23, 1998, pp. 153–58.

On the religious aspects of the colonial world there is now I. Malkin's *Religion and Colonization in Ancient Greece,* E. J. Brill, Leiden 1987.

The following are excellent as points of reference for general aspects and for bibliography: the essays contained in the volumes published by Garzanti (Milan) in the "Antica Madre" series: *Megale Hellas* (1983), *Sikanie* (1985), *Italia Omnia Terrarum Alumna* (1988), *Italia Omnia Terrarum Parens* (1989); the four volumes from Electa (Milan), *Magna Grecia* (1985–1991); also *Storia della Calabria antica* (in 2 volumes), Cangemi, Reggio Calabria-Rome 1987 and *Storia del Mezzogiorno* (only the first part in two volumes), published by del Sole, Naples 1991; *La Sicilia antica* (2 works in 5 volumes), published by Stonia of Naples, Southern Italy, and Sicily, Naples, 1980.

A few years ago an exhibition, dedicated to the Greeks in the West, was mounted in Venice (Palazzo Grassi) with a catalogue which, apart from listing the items on display, produced a series of contributions by major authorities on the subject: *I Greci in Occidente,* Bompiani, Milan 1996. Along with this exhibition were other so-called peripheral events, organized concurrently in Naples, Paestum, Policoro, Reggio Calabria, Vibo Valentia, Sybaris, and Taranto, dealing with individual problems and with respective catalogues published by Electa (Naples): *Poseidonia e i Lucani* (Paestum), *Le collezioni della Magna Grecia al Museo Archeologico Nazionale di Napoli* (Naples), *Greci, Enotri e Lucani nella Basilicata* (Policoro), *I santuari della Calabria* (Reggio Calabria, Vibo Valentia, Sybaris), *Arte e Artigianato in Magna Grecia* (Taranto).

Various aspects and problems of the individual cities of Magna Graecia are dealt with in the annual International Conventions on the Study of Magna Graecia, which this year produces its forty-second edition, which also contains preliminary information on the excavations and finds. The Sicilian equivalent of the Tarantan Conventions are the International Conventions, Ancient Sicily, published in the journal *Kokalos.*

Regarding the individual cities dealt with in this volume, a good point of reference is the *Bibliografia grafica delle Colonie Greche e delle Isole Tirreniche* (BTGCI), a work begun by G. Nenci and G. Vallet in 1981 and nearing completion. Also useful are the entries in the *Enciclopedia dell'Arte Classica, Antica ed Orientale* from Treccani, which has recently published a second supplement (1971–1994) in 5 volumes.

Still very useful are the three archaeological guides from Laterza (Rome-Bari): E. Greco, *Magna Grecia* (1981); S. De Caro and A. Greco (Pontrandolfo), *Campania* (1981); F. Coarelli and M. Torch, *Sicilia* (1984).

And finally, there is the series: *Guide archeologiche Preistoria e Protostoria,* published in 1995 at Forlí on the occasion of the XIII International Congress of Prehistoric and Protohistoric Sciences: G. F. La Torre, ed., *La fascia tirrenica da Napoli a Reggio Calabria,* vol. 9; R. Griffoni Cremonesi and F. Radina, eds., *Puglia e Basilicata,* vol. 11; and A. M. Bietti Sestieri, M. C. Lentini, and G. Voza, eds. *Sicilia orientale ed Isole Eolie,* vol. 12. Apart from the treatment of specific aspects of prehistory, these lavishly illustrated volumes contain interesting catalogues of museums and archaeological parks.

For the individual cities, apart from the sources already mentioned, there are the following bibliographical references.

Ischia/Pithekoussai and Cumae: L. Jannelli, "Ischia e Cuma," in E. Greco, ed., *La città greca antica,* Rome 1999, pp. 303–27 (with bibliography); L. Jannelli, "La frequentazione dell'acropoli di Cuma in Età Pre-Protostorica: I dati dello scavo Buchner," in *Annali dell'Istituto Universitario Orientale di Napoli* n.s. 6, 1999, pp. 73–90; G. Gasparri, "Gli scavi dell'Università degli Studi di Napoli Federico II nel Foro di Cuma," in *Notiziario dell'Università degli Studi Federico II,* 1997, pp. 273–82; S. Adamo Muscettola, "La triade del Capitolium di Cuma," in *I Culti della Campania Antica,* Rome 1998, pp. 219–30; "Cuma: Il Progetto Kyme. Gli scavi dell'Università di Napoli 'Federico II' (1994 e 1996)," in *Nova Antiqua Phlegraea: Nuovi tesori archeologici dai Campi Flegrei,* Napoli 2000, pp. 94–100; B. d'Agostino and A. D'Andrea, eds., "Cuma: Nuove forme di intervento per lo studio del sito antico," in *Quaderni dell'Istituto Universitario Orientale* 2000 (in press); M. Catucci, L. Jannelli, and L. Sanesi Mastrocinque, *II deposito votivo dall'acropoli di Cuma (Corpus delle stipi votive in Italia),* Rome 2000 (in press).

Partenope and Naples: S. De Caro, "La necropoli di Piazza Falcone a Napoli," in *Rendiconti dell'Accademia di Napoli* 48, 1974, pp. 37–64; E. Greco, "Forum duplex: Appunti per lo studio delle agorai di Neapolis in Campania," in *Annali dell'Istituto Universitario Orientale di Napoli* 3, 1981, pp. 139–57; A. M. D'Onofrio and B. d'Agostino, "Ricerche archeologiche a Napoli: Lo scavo in largo S. Aniello (1982–1983)," in *Quaderni dell'Istituto Universitario Orientale* 4, 1987; F. Zevi, *Neapolis,* Naples 1994; D. Giampaola, F. Fratta, and C. Scarpati, "Neapolis: Le mura e la città indagini a San Domenico Maggiore e a San Marcellino," in *Annali dell'Istituto Universitario Orientale di Napoli* n.s. 3, 1996, pp. 115–38; D. Giampaola and others, *Tracce: Sotto le strade di Napoli,* Napoli 1997; B. d'Agostino and D. Giampaola, "Osservazioni storiche e archeologiche sulla fondazione di Neapolis," in *Storia antica e Archeologia dell'Italia preroma e romana: Testimonianze e modelli,* Atti Convegno, Capri 2000 (in press).

Poseidonia/Paestum: E. Greco and D. Theodorescu, *Poseidonia/Paestum,* vols. I (1980), II (1983), III (1987), IV (1999); *Paestum: La città e il territorio,* Rome 1990; M. Cipriani, "II ruolo di Hera nel santuario meridionale di Poseidonia," in *Hera: Images, espaces, cultes* (Cahiers du Centre Jean Bérard 15), 1997, pp. 211–25; M. Torelli, *Paestum Romana,* Rome 1999; F. Longo, "Poseidonia," in *La città greca antica,* Rome 1999, pp. 365–84 (with bibliography); E. Greco and F. Longo, *Paestum: Scavi, studi, ricerche. Bilancio di un decennio (1988–1998)* (Tekmeria 1), Paestum 2000; G. Greco, *L'Heraion alla foce del Sele,* Rome 2001; E. Greco and F. Longo, *Paestum: La visita della città,* Rome 2002; M. Cipriani, in *Gli Achei e l'identità etnica degli Achei in Occidente* (Tekmeria 1), Paestum (in press).

Velia: "Velia e i Focei in Occidente," *Parola del Passato* 108–10, Naples 1966; "Nuovi Studi su Velia," *Parola del Passato* 130–33, Naples 1970; F. Krinzinger and G. Greco, eds., *Velia: Studi e Ricerche,* Modena 1994; "Il culto di Hera ad Elea," G. Tocco Sciarelli, in *Hera: Images, espaces, cultes* (Cahiers du Centre Jean Bérard 15), 1997, pp. 231–34; E. De Magistris, "Appunti per una lettura della Porta Rosa di Velia," in *Tra Lazio e Campania: Ricerche di Storia e di Topografia antica* (Quaderni del Dipartimento di Scienze dell'Antichità 16), Naples 1995, pp. 87–94; F. Krinzinger and G. Tocco, eds., *Neue Forschungen in Velia,* (Velia-Studien 1), Vienna 1999; L. Cicala, "L'edilizia domestica di Elea in età tardo-arcaica: Problemi di analisi e definizione," in F. Krinzinger, *Die Agäis und das westliche Mittelmeer,* Vienna 2000, pp. 55–65.

Lokroi: M. Barra Bagnasco, ed., *Locri Epizefiri* I (1977), II (1989), III (1989), IV (1992); L. Costamagna and C. Sabbione, *Una città in Magna Grecia: Locri Epizefiri*, Reggio Calabria 1990; F. Costabile, *Polis e Olympeion Locri Epizefiri*, Soveria Mannelli 1992.

Kroton: *Crotone e là sua storia tra IV e III sec. A.C.*, Naples 1993; R. Spadea, *Il tesoro di Hera: Scoperte nel santuario di Hera Lacinia a Capo Colonna di Crotone*, exhibition catalogue, Milan 1996; also R. Spadea, "Santuari di Hera a Crotone," in *Hera: Images, espaces, cultes* (Cahiers du Centre Jean Bérard 15), 1997, pp. 235–59; R. Spadea in *Gli Achei e l'identità etnica degli Achei in Occidente* (Tekmeria 3), Paestum (in press).

Sybaris-Thurii: E. Greco, "Turi," in E. Greco, ed., *La città greca antica*, Roma 1999, pp. 413–30; E. Greco and S. Luppino, "Ricerche sulla topografia e sull'urbanistica di Sibari-Thuri-Copiae," in *Annali dell'Istituto Universitario Orientale di Napoli* n.s. 6, 1999, pp. 115–64; E. Carando, "Sibari-Thuri: note per una revisione dei dati," *ibidem*, pp. 165–76; and L. Tomay, in *Gli Achei e l'identità etnica degli Achei in Occidente* (Tekmeria 3), Paestum (in press).

Metapontion: D. Mertens, "Metaponto: Il teatro-ekklesiasterion," in *Bollettino d'Arte* 57, series VI, 16, 1982, pp. 1–18: E. Greco, ed., *Siritide e Metapontino: Storia di due territori coloniali*, Paestum-Naples 1998; J. C. Carter, *The Chora of Metaponto: The Necropoleis*, Austin 1998; A. De Siena, "La colonizzazione achea del metapontino," in *Storia della Basilicata* 1: *L'Antichità*, D. Adamesteanu, ed., Rome-Bari 1999, pp. 211–45; D. Mertens, "Metaponto: L'evoluzione del centro urbano," *ibidem*, pp. 247–294; L. Giardino and A. De Siena, "Metaponto," in E. Greco ed., *La città greca antica*, Rome 1999, pp. 329–363; J. C. Carter, "The Chora and the Polis of Metaponto," in E. Krinzinger, *Die Agäis und das westliche Mittelmeer*, Vienna 2000, pp. 81–94; F. De Juliis, *Metaponto*, Bari 2001; and A. De Siena, in *Gli Achei e l'identità etnica degli Achei in Occidente* (Tekmeria 3), Paestum (in press).

Siris and Herakleia: *Ricerche archeologiche all'Incoronata di Metaponto* 1 (1991), 2 (1992), 3 (1995), 4 (2000), 5 (1997); A. Pelosi, "Qualche considerazione sull'Incoronata di Metaponto," in *Annali dell'Istituto Universitario Orientale di Napoli* 15, 1992, pp. 35–44; E. Greco, ed., *Siritide e Metapontino: Storia di due territori coloniali*, Paestum-Naples 1998; P. Orlandini, "La colonizzazione ionica della Siritide," in *Storia della Basilicata* 1: *L'Antichità*, D. Adamesteanu, ed., Rome-Bari 1999, pp. 197–210; "Herakleia e la sua chora," L. Giardino and G. Pianu, in *Da Leukania a Lukania: La Lucania centro-orientale fra Pirro e i Giulio-Claudii*, Rome 1992, pp. 136–42; B. Otto, ed., *Herakleian in Lukania und das Quellheiligtum der Demeter*, Innsbruck 1996; L. Giardino, "Herakleia: Città e territorio," in *Storia della Basilicata* 1: *L'Antichità*, D. Adamesteanu, ed., Rome-Bari 1999, pp. 295–337; D. Adamesteanu, "Le poleis della costa nel V sec. a.C.," *ibidem*, pp. 339–57.

Taranto: E. Greco, "Dal territorio alla città: Lo sviluppo urbano di Taranto," in *Annali dell'Istituto Universitario Orientale di Napoli* 3, 1981, pp. 139–57; E. Lippolis, "La città e la storia, in AA.VV., *Tappeti di pietra: I mosaici di Taranto Romana,* Fasano 1989, pp. 15–25; also E. Lippolis, "Taranto, la necropoli: aspetti e problemi della documentazione archeologica dal VII al I sec. a.C.," in *Catalogo del Museo Archeologico Nazionale di Taranto* III, 1, Taranto 1994, pp. 41–68; E. Lippolis, S. Garraffo, and M. Nafissi, *Culti greci in Occidente* I: *Taranto*, Taranto 1995.

Naxos: M. C. Lentini, "Nuove esplorazionia Naxos (scavi 1989–1994)," in *Kokalos* 39–40, 1993–1994, pp. 1001ff.; M. C. Lentini, *Naxos a quarant'anni dall'inizio degli scavi*, Archaeological Museum of Naxos, 1998, with history of the studies and collection of all previous bibliography.

Taormina: M. Santangelo, *Taormina e dintorni*, Rome 1955; G. M. Bacci, "Ricerche a Taormina negli anni 1977–1980," in *Kokalos* 26–27, 1980–1981, pp. 737ff.; also G. M. Bacci, "Due antefisse arcaiche dal centro di Taormina," in *Damarato: Studi di antichità classica offerti a P. Pelagatti*, Naples 2000, pp. 50–57.

Leontinoi and Katana: G. Rizza, "Leontini e Katane nell'VIII e nel VII secolo a.C.," in *Annuario della Scuola Archeologica Italiana di Athene* 59 (n.s. 43), 1981, pp. 313–317; M. Frasca, "Leontini, Necropoli di Piscitello: Campagna di scavi 1977–78," in *Cronache di Archeologia* 21, 1982, pp. 37–66; G. Rizza, "Stipe votiva di un santuario di Demetra a Catania," in *Bollettino d'Arte* 45, 1960, pp. 247–62; *Catania antica. Atti del Convegno della Società Italiana per lo studio dell'antichità classica* (Catania 1992), Pisa 1996; M. Frasca, "Sull'urbanistica di Catania in età greca," in *Damarato: Studi di antichità classica offerti a P. Pelagatti*, Naples 2000, pp. 119–25.

Zankle/Messina and Mylai: G. Vallet, *Rhégion et Zankle*, Paris 1958; G. M. Bacci and G. Tigano, eds., *Da Zancle a Messina*, Palermo 1999; G. M. Bacci, "Topografia archeologica di Zancle-Messina," in M. Gras, E. Greco, and P. G. Guzzo, eds., *Nel cuore del Mediterraneo antico: Reggio, Messina e le colonie calcidesi dell'area dello Stretto*, Roma 2000, pp. 237–49; C. Tigano, "Milazzo," *ibidem*, pp. 135–44; G. M. Bacci and G. Tigano, *Da Zancle a Messina: Un percorso archeologico attraverso gli scavi*, Messina 2001; L. Bernabò Brea and M. Cavalier, *Mylai*, Novara 1959.

Lipari: L. Bernabò Brea and M. Cavalier, *Il Castello di Lipari e il Museo Archeologico Eoliano*, Palermo 1958 (and successive editions); by the same authors, *Mélichunis Lipàra* I (1960), II (1965), III (1968), IV (1980), V (1991), VI (1991); L. Bernabò Brea, *Menandro e il teatro greco nelle terrecotte liparesi*, Genova 1981; L. Bernabò Brea, "Gli Eoli e l'inizio dell'età del Bronzo nelle isole Eolie e nell'Italia meridionale," *Quaderni dell'Istituto Universitario Orientale di Napoli* 2, Naples 1985; L. Bernabò Brea and M. Cavalier, *La ceramica policroma liparese di età ellenistica*, Milan 1986; L. Bernabò Brea and U. Spigo, *Da Eschilo a Menandro: Due secoli di teatro greco attraverso i reperti archeologi Liparesi*, exhibition catalogue (Lipari 1987), Milazzo 1987; L. Bernabò Brea, M. Cavalier, and U. Spigo, *Lipari, Museo eoliano*, Palermo 1994; U. Spigo, "Lipari fra lo Stretto di Messina e il mondo italiota: Approccio ai dati archeologici," in M. Gras, E. Greco, and P. G. Guzzo, eds., *Nel cuore del*

Mediterraneo antico: Reggio, Messina e le colonie calcidesi dell'area dello Stretto, Rome 2000, pp. 161–85.

Tindari: R. Ross Holloway, "Tindari: The Latest Colony of the Sicilian Greeks," in *Archaeology* 12, 1960, pp. 116ff.; L. Bernabò Brea, "Due secoli di studi, scavi e restauri del teatro greco di Tindari," in *Rivista Istituto di Archeologia e storia dell'arte* 13–14, 1964–1965, pp. 99ff.; L. Bernabò Brea and M. Cavalier, "Tindari, Area urbana": L'insula IV e le strade che la circondano," in *Bollettino d'Arte* 1965, pp. 205ff.

Himera: AA.VV., *Himera* I (1970) and II (1976), Palermo; AA.VV., *Quaderno Imerese* I (1972) and II (1982); D. Palermo and N. Allegro, "Himera," in E. Greco, ed., *La città greca antica,* Rome 1999, pp. 269–301.

Megara Hyblaia: G. Vallet, F. Villard, and P. Auberson, *Mégara Hyblaea* I: *Le quartier de l'Agora archaïque,* Rome 1976; also G. Vallet, F. Villard, and P. Auberson, *Megara Iblea: Guida degli scavi,* Rome 1983; M. Gras and H. Treziny, "Megara Hyblaea," in E. Greco, ed., *La città greca antica,* Rome 1999, pp. 251–67; F. Villard, "Le cas de Mégara Hyblaea: Est-il exemplare," in *La colonization grecque en Méditerranée occidentale,* Rome 1999, pp. 133–40; H. Tréziny, "Lots et Ilots à Mégara Hyblaea: Questions de métrologie," *ibidem,* pp. 141–83; F. De Polignac, "L'installation des dieux et la genèse des cités en Grèce d'occident: Une question résolue?" *ibidem,* pp. 209–29; H. Treziny, "Mégara Hyblaea: Retours sur l'agora," in E. Greco, ed., *Architettura, Urbanistica, Società nel mondo antico* (Tekmeria 2), Paestum 2001, pp. 51–63.

Syracuse: H. P. Drögenmuller, *Syrakus,* Heidelberg 1969; G. Voza, "Bilancio degli scavi a Siracusa sulla terraferma," in *Greci Italia e Sicilia nell VIII e VII sec. a.C.* (Annuario della Scuola Archeologica Italiana di Atene 60), 1982, pp. 165–67; G. Voza, *Siracusa 1999: Lo scavo di Piazza Duomo,* Palermo-Syracuse 1999; by the same author, "Primi risultati dello scavo di Piazza Duomo a Siracusa," in *Un ponte fra l'Italia e la Grecia,* Padova 2000, pp. 131–38.

Eloro: G. Voza, "Eloro," in *Kokalos* 26–27, 1980–1981, pp. 685–88.

Acre and Kasmenai: L. Bernabò Brea, *Akrai,* Catania 1956; A. Di Vita, "Un contributo all'urbanistica greca di Sicilia: Casmene," in *ACIACl* VII, II, Rome 1961, pp. 68–77; G. Voza, in *Archeologia della Sicilia Sud-Orientale,* exhibition catalogue, Naples 1973, pp. 127–32; L. Bernabò Brea, *Il tempio di Afrodite di Akrai,* Naples 1986. On the Syracusan expansion in eastern Sicily, see E. Greco's entry in a book by E. Greco and M. Torelli, *Storia dell'urbanistica: II mondo antico,* Rome-Bari 1993, pp. 180ff.

Gela: P. Orlandini and D. Adamesteanu, "Gela: Nuovi scavi," in *Notizie Scavi* 1960, pp. 67–246; G. Fiorentini, *Gela: La città antica e il territorio,* Palermo 1985.

Kamarina: G. Di Stefano, *Camarina: Guide alla città antica,* Ragusa 1993; G. Di Stefano, *Misurare nell'antichità: Rinvenimenti subaquei a Camarina,* Ragusa 1994; R. Macaluso, "Camarina in età ellenistico-romana," in *Kokalos* 41, 1995, pp. 29–270; P. Pelagatti, "Camarina nel VI e V sec.: Problemi di cronologia alla luce della documentazione archeologica," in *Un ponte fra l'Italia e la Grecia,* Padua 2000, pp. 173–90; F. Cordano, "Camarina fra il 461 e il 405 a.C.: Un caso esemplare," *ibidem,* pp. 191–93; G. Di Stefano, "I recenti scavi di Camarina," *ibidem,* pp. 194–212.

Morgantina: F. Kolb, "Agora un Theater in Morgantina," in *Kokalos* 21, 1975, pp. 226–30; "Urbanism in Archaic Morgantina," in *Urbanization in the Mediterranean,* Copenhagen 1997, pp. 167–93; M. Bell III, "Centro e periferia nel regno siracusano di Hierone II," in *La colonization grecque en Méditerranée occidentale,* Rome 1999, pp. 257–77; M. Bell III, "Morgantina e Camarina al Congresso di Gela," *ibidem,* pp. 291–97.

Akragas: J. De Waele, *Akragas graeca,* Roma 1971; G. Fiorentini, ed., *Gli edifici pubblici di Agrigento antica,* Agrigento 1990; L. Braccesi and E. De Miro, eds., *Agrigento e la Sicilia greca,* Rome 1992; "Da Akragas ad Agrigentum: Le recentissimi scoperte archeologiche nel quadro della storia amministrativa e culturale della città," *Kokalos* 42, 1996; E. De Miro, *Agrigento I.1: I santuari urbani: L'area sacra tra il tempio di Zeus e Porta V,* Rome 2000.

Selinunte: F. Gabrici, "Il santuario della Malophoros a Selinunte," *Monumenti Antichi dei Lincei* 32, 1927; G. Vallet and F. Villard, "La date de fondation de Sélinonte: Les données archéologiques," in *Bulletin de Correspondance Héllenique* 1958, pp. 16ff.; A. Di Vita, "Selinunte fra il 650 ed il 490: Un modello di città coloniale," in *Annuario della Scuola Archeologica Italiana di Atene* 62 (n.s. 46), 1984, pp. 7–68; A. Di Vita, "Le fortificazioni di Selinunte classica," *ibidem,* pp. 69–79; C. Parisi Presicce, "La funzione delle aree sacre nell'organizzazione urbanistica delle colonie grece alla luce della scoperta di un nuovo santuario periferico di Selinunte," in *Archeologia Classica* 36, 1984, pp. 19–132; D. Mertens, "Die Mauern von Selinunt," in *Römische Mitteilungen* 96, 1989, pp. 87–154; H. I. Isler, "Les necropoles de Selinonte," in *Necropoles et sociétés antiques* (Cahiers du Centre J. Bérard 18), Naples 1994, pp. 165–68; C. Marconi, *Le metope dell'Heraion di Selinunte,* Modena 1994.

Herakleia Minoa: E. De Miro, *L'Antiquarium e la zona archeologica di Eraclea Minoa,* Rome 1965; E. De Miro, "Il teatro di Heraclea Minoa," in *Rendiconti Accademia dei Lincei* 1966, pp. 151ff.; R. J. A. Wilson, "Eraclea Minoa: Ricerche sul territorio," in *Kokalos* 16–17, 1981–1981, pp. 656–67; R. J. A. Wilson, "Eraclea Minoa: Gli scavi eseguiti nel territorio negli anni 1980–1983," in *Kokalos* 30–31, 1984–1985, pp. 489–500.

Segesta: V. Tusa, "Il santuario arcaico di Segesta," in *Atti VII Congresso Internazionale di Archeologia classica,* Rome 1961, II, pp. 31ff.; D. Mertens, *Der Tempel von Segesta und die Dorische Tempelbaukunst des griechischen Westerns in Klassischer Zeit,* Mainz 1984; J. de La Genière, "Ségeste et l'hellenisme," in *Mélange de l'École Française de Rome, Antiquité* 90, 1978, pp. 33–49.

Glossary

Types of Greek Vases
1. bell-krater
2. calyx krater
3. column krater
4. volute krater
5, 6, 7. nestorides
8. Panathenaic amphora
9. neck amphora
10. amphora with handle over neck
11. *loutrophoros*
12, 13. *pelike*
14. *dinos*
15. *hydria*
16. *lekythos*
17, 18, 19. *oinochoe*
20. *olpe*
21. *epichysis*
22. *lebes gamikos*
23. *situla*
24. *kantharos*
25. *skyphos-pyxis*
26. *askos*
27. *phiale*
28. *skyphos*
29. goblet on low base
30. *lekanis*
31. *alabastron*
32. *bottle*
33. *rhyton*

acrolith: statue of which the visible parts are sculpted in marble or ivory while the other parts, often covered by rich vestments, are of wood.

acropolis: the highest point of the city (from *acro*, "summit," and *polis*, "city"). Not all Greek cities necessarily had an acropolis.

acroterion (pl. acroteria): floral ornament placed at the summit or corners of the façades, or on the cornices of a temple or a funeral stele.

adyton (pl. *adyta*): a chamber at the rear of the *cella* of a temple, which cannot be reached from the *cella*.

agora (pl. *agorai*): Greek term originally meaning assembly and subsequently used to indicate the square where public meetings took place. It contained the important public buildings connected with the political life of the city, but also small sacred buildings and commercial structures.

antefix: decorative element in stone or terracotta completing the outermost edge of the tiles, along the line of the eaves.

arula: small altar.

Athenaion (pl. *Athenaia*): temple dedicated to the goddess Athena.

basilica: public building of the Roman period used for the administration of justice and for commerce. The name is Greek in origin, deriving from *basileos*, "king," and indicated the place where the king or the king-archon dispensed justice. From the fourth century A.D., it was used to designate those buildings, constructed to the design of the Roman basilicas, intended for Christian liturgical meetings. At Poseidonia, due to a misunderstanding that is now embedded in the scholarly literature, it was applied to the urban Temple of Hera.

black-figure: technique of decorating pottery consisting of filling sketches of figures with black glaze and leaving the background the natural color of the clay; the figures were later retouched with purple-red or white, and details were incised.

bothros (pl. *bothroi*): pit containing votive offerings or sacrificial remains.

bouleuterion (pl. *bouleuteria*): meeting place of the *boule*, the city council.

capital: the upper part of a column between the shaft and the architrave.

cavea: area reserved for the audience in the tiers of a theater, an amphitheater, or a Roman circus (see also *theater*).

cella: the enclosed part of the temple surrounded by the *peristasis* and within which was kept the cult statue.

cenotaph: literally an "empty tomb"; a monument erected to the memory of a person whose remains are elsewhere. An example is the "Hypogeal Shrine" at Poseidonia.

cyma: molding crowning the long sides or eaves of the façade, generally in the form of simple molding decorated with leaves or flower motifs. On the long sides are spouts to discharge rainwater from the roof.

dinos (pl. *dinoi*): large-bellied vase with a wide mouth, used for the same purpose as the krater.

diphros: folding stool.

dromos (pl. *dromoi*): literally a "corridor"; used to refer to a running track and also to the long corridor leading to the burial chamber of a tomb.

echinus: cushion-shaped upper part of the capital of a Doric column.

ekistes: the leader of a group that founded a new settlement. In the colonies, the founder was given a hero's burial in the *agora*.

ekklesiasterion (pl. *ekklesiasteriai*): meeting place of the *ekklesia,* the popular assembly. From the fourth century B.C. onward, political meetings were often held in the theater.

entablature: the combination of architrave, frieze, and cornice.

herm: a pillar surmounted by a sculpted male head representing Hermes, protector of wayfarers and property. Herms were generally located along roads, particularly at crossroads, or to mark boundaries. Other deities, such as Dionysos, were also depicted on herms.

fibula: pin used to fasten garments.

frieze: part of the entablature of the building between the architrave and the cornice, which covers the ends of the joists and is often decorated. Characteristic of those of the Doric order are metopes (smooth, painted, or sculpted) and triglyphs; those of the Ionic order are continuous sculpted bands surmounted by rows of dentils.

geison (pl. *geisa*): the cornice, the final framework of the entablature.

gorgoneion (pl. gorgoneia): decorative element depicting the head of a gorgon, a winged monster with snakes for hair and large teeth.

Heraion: temple dedicated to Hera, wife of Zeus.

heroon (pl. *heroa*): building or place consecrated to a hero.

hestiatorion (pl. *hestiatoria*): building where communal meals were taken.

hoplite: soldier armed with helmet, breastplate, holster belt, shield, greaves, lance, and sword (the whole array covered by the term "panoply").

hydria (pl. *hydriai*): vessel with three handles used by women to carry water from a spring.

incuse: a coin on which the imprint of the die on the reverse appears in relief on the obverse.

insula: literally "island"; here a plot of land with its associated buildings, bounded by roads. A Latin term used incorrectly by the Greek world.

hypogeum: subterranean chamber, generally used for mystery cults or for burials.

kore (pl. *korai*): literally a "maiden"; name given to standing statues of clothed young women representing a goddess or offerant. Kore is also the name given to Persephone, one of the goddesses of the Underworld; daughter of Zeus and Demeter and wife of Hades, who abducted her.

kouros (pl. *kouroi*): literally a "youth"; name given to statues of naked, standing young men representing a god or an offerant.

krater: large vessel used for mixing wine and water.

lebes: bronze or clay vase with pedestal, used to heat or store liquids; also used for ritual ablutions.

lekanis (pl. *lekanides*): low, wide vessel with lid and two horizontal handles.

lekythos (pl. *lekythoi*): vase with a bell-shaped mouth and a long, narrow neck.

macellum (pl. *macella*): more or less complex structure used by the Romans as a covered marketplace; generally square or rectangular, with rooms opening onto a peristyle and other small annexes.

metope: in Doric architecture, an element of the entablature consisting of smooth panels, decorated or painted and set between two triglyphs.

naos: literally the "temple"; the term generally refers to the *cella.*

naiskos (pl. *naiskoi*): *aedicula* or small temple.

necropolis: literally "city of the dead"; the area set aside for burials, known to Christians a cemetery (place of sleep). *Necropoleis* in Greek and Roman cities were always outside the walls and generally alongside the roads leading out to the countryside.

nike (pl. *nikai*): goddess of victory represented by a winged young woman carrying a palm frond.

odeion (pl. *odeia*): covered theater used for musical spectacles.

opisthodomos: chamber to the rear of the *cella* in a Doric temple in symmetrical opposition to the *pronaos* and without passage to the *naos* or the *adyton.*

opus incertum: literally "irregular work"; indicating a concrete wall studded with irregular-shaped pieces of stone dressed only on the outside.

opus reticulatum: "reticulated work"; that is, truncated pyramid-shaped stone blocks set diagonally in rows into a concrete wall to form a network pattern.

orchestra: the circular area reserved for the chorus of dancers (*orchesis*) around the altar of Dionysos (in the theater).

pelike (pl. *pelikai*): type of amphora with differing kinds of wide neck and bulbous lower part.

peribolos: perimeter wall of a sanctuary.

peripteral: type of temple with colonnade along all four sides of the *cella.*

peristasis: colonnade around the *cella* of a temple.

peristyle: courtyard surrounded by porticoes typical of Greek and Roman houses.

pinax (pl. *pinakes*): painted wood or terracotta tablet.

pyxis: cylindrical box made of wood, clay, metal, or bone, used to hold small objects such as cosmetics.

pithos (pl. *pithoi*): a jar, a large vessel used to store liquid or victuals.

3   4

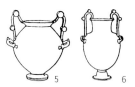
5   6

7   8

9   10

11   12

13   14

15   16

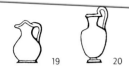

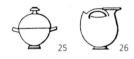

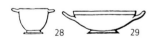

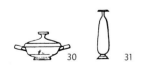

plateia (pl. *plateiai*): term used for the large roads that constitute part of the urban grid of a city.

potters' quarter (*kerameikos*): area where pottery and ceramics were made.

prytaneion: building that held the sacred flame of the city. Not to be confused with *prytanikon,* the seat of the *prytaneis,* the senior magistrates of the city, although sometimes the functions of the two were carried on in the same building. The *prytanikon* was where illustrious guests or meritorious citizens were entertained at public expense and where public sacrifices and banquets were held.

pronaos: porch area in front of the *cella* of the temple.

propylaion: monumental entrance, with or without colonnade, generally found at the entrance to a sanctuary or, more generally, as part of the surrounding wall.

proscenium: in the theater, the front part of the stage area set in front of the stage itself, above the level of the orchestra.

prostyle: describes a temple or other building with columns at the front.

red-figure: technique of decorating pottery consisting of lightly tracing the outlines of figures then glazing the surrounding parts of the vase in black. The figures were then retouched in black or also white.

sacellum: small sacred area around an altar; used to designate aediculae, shrines, columns, statues, tables for offerings, fountains, trees sacred to a deity, and also a private or public sanctuary that is of less consequence than a temple.

sarcophagus: rectangular box in wood, terracotta, stone, or marble with a flat cover or sometimes with a pitched roof, intended to hold the body of the deceased.

stele, or **boundary stone:** (Greek *horos* and Latin *terminus*) a rectangular or cylindrical stone, often inscribed or sculpted, set in the ground to mark a boundary or indicate a sacred or consecrated area.

stenopos (pl. *stenopoi*): term used for the small roads running between or meeting the *plateiai,* the main roads of a city.

stipe: offerings that had been dedicated in sanctuaries and collected in pits, special repositories, or wells, or even thrown into sacred fountains.

stoa (pl. *stoas*): colonnaded building with one or two porticoes, sometimes with two stories, located within a public area (within a sanctuary, in the *agora,* or along main roads). They could be used as seats of the magistracy, to house shops, or simply as shelters for the worshipers inside sanctuaries.

theater: word derived from the Greek verb *theaomai,* meaning "to contemplate, to observe." *Theatron* was thus the tiers of seating, known to the Romans as the *cavea,* used by the audience. The tiers were divided radially by staircases called *kerkydes* and by horizontal terraces called *diazomata.* In most cases the theater was carved out of the hillside or—rarely in the case of Greek theaters but almost characteristically in the case of Roman ones—supported by walls. The central space, generally circular, was the orchestra. When, in Greek theater, the actors began to stand out from the chorus, they were made to perform on a stage with relevant *proscenium,* built in part of the space destined for the orchestra, which was duly reduced in size. Between the *cavea* and the stage were the lateral entrances for the chorus and the actors known as *paradoi.*

telamon: male figure corresponding to the female caryatid employed in architecture to support the entablature or cornice.

temenos (pl. *temene*): literally "space set aside"; the area of the sanctuary consecrated to the deity.

thermal baths: often grandiose buildings, surrounded by gardens and containing meeting room, gymnasium, and library in addition to hot and cold baths. The areas given over to bathing were the *apodyterium* (changing room), the *frigidarium* (cold baths, consisting of one or more pools), the *tepidarium,* the heated area which preceded the *calidarium* (the hot bath, consisting of one or more pools) and the *laconicum* (the steam bath). Water heated by a large furnace was piped to the appropriate pools, while the areas were warmed by the air circulating beneath the floors and though perforated bricks behind the walls.

thesauros (pl. *thesauroi*): building dedicated to a deity as a votive offering; it was not dedicated to the cult but housed valuable objects—offerings and possessions of the sanctuary.

triglyph: vertical element of a Doric frieze, consisting of slabs carved with three slots; the triglyphs alternate with the rectangular metopes.

Reconstruction of a temple

Detail of the corner of a temple

Plan of a *peripteral* temple

The Doric order

The Ionic order

The Corinthian order

Reconstruction of a temple
1. façade
2. entablature
3. intercolumniation (space between the axes of columns)
4. colonnade, or *peristasis*
5. pediment

Detail of the corner of a temple
6. antefix
7. triglyph
8. regulae
9. metope

Plan of a peripteral temple
1. *cella*
2. *opisthodomos*
3. *naos*, here divided into three parts
4. *pronoas distyle in antis* (porch with two columns between the end walls)
5. *peristasis*, or colonnade

Architectural Orders

The Doric order
1. stylobate
2. column shaft
3. capital
4. entablature
5. pediment
   a. echinus
   b. abacus
   c. architrave
   d. frieze
   e. cornice
   f. triglyph
   g. metope

The Ionic order
1. stylobate
2. column base
3. column shaft
4. capital
5. entablature
6. pediment
   a. volute
   b. ovolo
   c. abacus
   d. torus
   e. trochylos/scotia (concave base molding)

The Corinthian order
1. stylobate
2. column base
3. column shaft
4. capital
5. entablature
6. pediment
7. plinth
   a. acanthus leaves
   b. acanthus stalks
   c. abacus

Index

Note: Page numbers in *italics* indicate illustrations.